The Dilemma of
Arnulf of Lisieux

The Dilemma of Arnulf of Lisieux

New Ideas versus Old Ideals

Carolyn Poling Schriber

INDIANA UNIVERSITY PRESS

Bloomington and Indianapolis

The paper used in this publication meets the minimum requirements of American National Standard for Information Sciences—Permanence of Paper for Printed Library Materials, ANSI Z39.48–1984.

Manufactured in the United States of America

Library of Congress Cataloging-in-Publication Data
Schriber, Carolyn Poling.
The dilemma of Arnulf of Lisieux : new ideas versus old ideals /
Carolyn Poling Schriber
p. cm.
Includes bibliographical references.
ISBN 0–253–35097–2 (alk. paper)
1. Arnulf, of Lisieux, d. 1184 2. Europe—Church history—
Middle Ages, 600–1500. I. Title.
BX4705.A742S27 1990

282′.092—dc20
[B]   89–46003
                       CIP
1 2 3 4 5 94 93 92 91 90

Contents

Acknowledgments

I first met Arnulf of Lisieux during a graduate seminar at the University of Colorado, Colorado Springs, when my advisor, Dr. Richard M. Wunderli, suggested an exercise in translating medieval Latin. My interest in Arnulf's letters was spurred by Dr. Wunderli's constant question: "Who is this man and how do you know he is important?" The answer to that question gradually developed into a doctoral dissertation at the University of Colorado, Boulder. My colleagues in the field of Anglo-Norman studies suggested that the topic of Arnulf's contributions to the world of the twelfth century deserved fuller development—hence, this book.

Many people have assisted me in the production of this work. Advice and encouragement in the early stages of research came from Mary G. Cheney (Lucy Cavendish College, Cambridge); Giles Constable (Institute for Advanced Studies, School of Historical Studies, Princeton); Susan Reynolds (Lady Margaret Hall, Oxford); and R. Allen Brown (King's College, London). David S. Spear (Furman University), Stanley Chodorow (University of California, San Diego), and William W. Clark (Queens College, New York) willingly shared their unpublished research. Frank Barlow not only encouraged this work but also produced the raw material on which it is based. Without his authoritative edition of the Arnulf correspondence, further analysis of Arnulf's life would have been impossible.

Genevieve Ramos Acker (Directeur Adjoint, Commission Franco-Américaine d'Échanges Universitaires et Culturels, Paris) and Anne Collins (Cultural Attaché, United States Embassy, London) expedited my use of European archives. Mlle. Lamarque (Les Archives Départmentales du Calvados, Caen), Claire Fons (Bibliothèque Municipale, Rouen), Philippe Castaing (Les Archives Seine-Maritime, Rouen), and the staffs of the Bibliothèque Nationale (Paris), Bibliothèque Municipale (Lisieux), The Bodleian Library (Oxford), and Norlin Library (University of Colorado, Boulder) generously assisted in locating manuscripts and obscure reference materials.

The Graduate School Foundation Fund, University of Colorado, Boulder, helped to finance one of my trips to Normandy, and the Department of History provided a fellowship that allowed concentrated work on this project. Faculty members and colleagues gave unstintingly of their advice and support. Most important, my husband and son traveled with me to trace Arnulf's steps, took most of the photographs included here, and showed extraordinary patience in sharing their house and lives with a twelfth-century bishop. To all of them, I owe an enormous debt of gratitude.

Introduction

Arnulf, bishop of Lisieux from 1141 to 1181, is one of the neglected and misunderstood figures of medieval history. The only historical study of Arnulf in this century has been included in a Latin edition of his correspondence.[1] English historians have almost unanimously dismissed him as an unreliable witness—scheming, wily, and unscrupulous; American historians have simply followed the lead of their British colleagues.[2] The historical evidence, however, does not completely support these judgments. Twelfth-century popes, clerics, and kings spoke of him with affection and admiration. The discrepancy between Arnulf's contemporary and modern reputations, which originally suggested this study, reflects a broader disunity within twelfth-century Norman society.

Arnulf was a well-educated and widely traveled churchman. His early activities as archdeacon of Sées earned him the friendship of reforming abbots such as Bernard of Clairvaux and Peter the Venerable. On the Second Crusade, he accompanied Louis VII of France as legate in charge of the Norman contingent. Abbot Suger employed him as an ambassador between the court of France and the court of Geoffrey of Anjou. Arnulf lent his support to Henry, Duke of Normandy, in his attempts to consolidate his continental holdings in Normandy and accompanied him across the channel to witness his coronation as King Henry II of England. He returned to Normandy to serve as Henry's chief justiciar and traveled several times to the papal court in Henry's interests. During his career as bishop, he maintained a vigorous correspondence with the leading ecclesiastical figures of France and England. Arnulf made his opinions known during the Becket controversy, striving to find a settlement that would placate all sides. Within his own diocese, he encouraged the efforts of Cistercians and canons regular to reform the practices of monastic life. He thus played an important role in many of the crucial developments of the twelfth century.

The changing world of the twelfth century presented Arnulf with a series of difficult choices. In the papal schisms of 1130 and 1159 he was forced to choose between rival claimants to the see of Rome, a task further complicated by the fact that his ecclesiastical superiors and his monarchs did not always agree about which candidate deserved their support. In the civil war that wracked the Anglo-Norman kingdom from 1135 to 1154, as well as in the 1173 rebellion of the Young King against Henry II, Arnulf had to select a side, knowing that possession of his diocese hinged upon the outcomes. His land holdings, both as a bishop and as an Anglo-Norman baron, required him to maintain a precarious balance between his clerical duties and his secular responsibilities. The attempts of the papacy and of the English monarchy to

extend their legal jurisdictions cast Arnulf in the alternating roles of royal
justiciar and papal judge-delegate. Within his diocese he was challenged by
efforts to reform monastic life—efforts that in some cases threatened to disrupt
his own authority. Even when he began the construction of the cathedral of
Lisieux, he had to choose between the traditional Romanesque architecture of
Normandy and the Gothic innovations that were appearing in Paris. Each of
these conflicts required Arnulf to make judgments and tested his ability to
adapt to change.

The Becket controversy forced Arnulf to strike a balance between incompatible responsibilities. As a personal friend of Thomas Becket, he was expected to join with his episcopal colleagues in their support of the archbishop's
position. As a loyal bishop and confidante of the pope, he was obligated to
oppose any threat to the freedom of the church. But as the servant of the king,
he also understood Henry's need to maintain firm control of his widespread
and diverse principalities. The ensuing conflict showed Arnulf at his best and
at his worst. His pleas for a reasonable settlement that would allow both sides
to preserve their honor went unheeded, and each side felt betrayed by the
bishop whose loyalties remained divided.

Arnulf was an ambitious man, and, as ambitious people often are, he was
something of a mental gymnast. For forty years—an extraordinarily long time,
given the turbulent nature of the twelfth century—he maintained a balance
that allowed him to secure his position in both the secular and the ecclesiastical
hierarchies. Eventually he made a wrong move that brought down the entire
posture he had labored so long to preserve. He ended his career in disgrace,
out of favor with the king and attacked by the canons of his own diocese.

Arnulf left behind two monuments to his life, one physical and one literary.
The cathedral that he erected in Lisieux, designed and supervised by him and
financed largely out of his own resources, remains as one of the finest examples of early Gothic architecture in Normandy. It stands today virtually
untouched by the passage of centuries, and it still plays an active part in the
religious life of the city. His writings, however, have suffered from both
neglect and misunderstanding. His literary corpus comprises a collection of
his correspondence, a cluster of poems, several sermons, and one political
pamphlet, most of which have never appeared in English translation.

The earliest sample of his writing is the *Invectiva in Girardum Engolismensem
Episcopum*, written in 1133 while he was still archdeacon of Sées. The text of
the *Invectiva* has been reprinted twice in the *Monumenta Germaniae Historica*.
The *Libelli de lite* version is the more complete, with a long introduction and
elaborate textual notes by Julius Dieterich; a less annotated version appears
in *Scriptores*.[3] The only extant manuscript, according to Dieterich, is Codex
Parisinus no. 14193, a fifteenth-century copy that came from the monastery of
Albi Mantelli in Paris. This vitriolic pamphlet, which attacked one of the
French supporters of the antipope Anacletus, did not appear in any of the
manuscripts of Arnulf's letters, although Migne did include it in his edition
of the bishop's writings.[4]

It would be tempting to assume that, in his later years, Arnulf was somewhat embarrassed by the excesses to which his youthful enthusiasm had led him and that he preferred to forget this particular work. That, however, does not seem to be the case, for in a letter to Pope Alexander III on the occasion of his own schismatic election, Arnulf did not hesitate to remind Alexander of his former activities against a schismatic pope.[5] The omission of the *Invectiva* from his published works seems rather to be a reflection of Arnulf's appreciation of the importance of his bishop's office. Receiving a bishopric involved a major step up from the minor orders of an archdeacon, and it symbolized a definitive break in the life of the bishop. For the modern reader, the *Invectiva* provides a fascinating glimpse into the depth of emotion that surrounded the disputed papal election of 1130. For Arnulf, however, what had been written before his own crucial ordination and consecration could no longer represent his views as a bishop. The sermons the new bishop preached, however, were important as statements of his faith, and several of them were included in the early editions of Arnulf's letters. The best known sermon is the one he preached at the opening of the Council of Tours in May 1163. It was published in 1166 and is accessible in several editions.[6] Just as the *Invectiva* clarifies the problems of 1130, so the sermon at Tours is an important resource for understanding the issues that lay behind the papal schism of 1159.

The evidence to be found in diplomatic documents has contributed immeasurably to this study. During his forty-year tenure, Arnulf was called upon to issue charters within his own diocese, settle court cases, and testify to the acts of his archbishop and his king. As a result of these activities, there are at least 152 twelfth-century documents that contain his name. These sources have never before been collected for the purpose of studying Arnulf's activities, although groups of them have been assembled for other purposes. Printed editions of royal documents have provided the bulk of the collection. *Calendar of Documents Preserved in France*, edited by J. H. Round, contains forty-eight charters, eight of which are mentioned nowhere else.[7] *Regesta Regum Anglo-Normannorum* adds fifteen documents and is particularly useful for the early part of Arnulf's episcopacy.[8] Eyton's *Court, Household, and Itinerary of King Henry II* refers to forty-two royal charters witnessed by Arnulf after Henry became king of England.[9] Twenty-two of these charters are not mentioned elsewhere. The most complete collection appears in *Recueil des actes de Henri II*.[10] A total of ninety charters are to be found here, thirty-six of which do not appear in the other collections.

Most of these editions, however, are badly out of date. Some of the documents mentioned in the various catalogues have been mislaid or lost in the ongoing reorganization of the French departmental archives. Many of the original charters have suffered from haphazard preservation. One such item from the regional archives at Caen had been stored with the seal folded carefully inside; as a result, the acid in the seal has burned a large hole through the middle of the text.[11] Others were lost to fire during World War II. Many documents rescued during the war years are still stored in anonymous cardboard boxes and have been catalogued only in typescript. The documents compiled for this study, therefore, suffer from defects of many types. There is no guarantee that the collection is complete or even representative of Arnulf's activities. Still, the 152 documents discovered have served to supplement the information found in Arnulf's letters.

Dating is a particular problem in this study, for most of the charters of the reign of Henry II give only the day of the month and the place of issuance. Scholars such as Round and Eyton attempted to attach dates to the charters they found, but their efforts were limited by the enormity of the task and the relative lack of information available. Eyton based his dating on identifiable names on the witness lists. By knowing the earliest date at which one signatory had held a title and the death dates of others, he was able, in most cases, to provide a range of probable dates. The Delisle-Berger collection (*Recueil des actes*) followed a similar procedure. Round considered even such efforts unreliable, and his calendar frequently listed a wider possible range.[12] Arnulf's letters, similarly, bear no dates. Barlow's chronological order in his Latin edition has been worked out from internal evidence, but in many cases the letters too can only be assigned a tentative span of years.

In a few cases, a careful comparison of charters with the letters that reveal Arnulf's activities has made it possible to revise the dating. The Delisle-Berger collection, for example, includes a group of charters issued by Henry II and witnessed by Arnulf at Westminster, York, and Lincoln.[13] Delisle gave the date range as 1155 to 1158. Arnulf's itinerary, charters, and several letters written at the end of 1155 show that he had returned to Normandy shortly after the Great Council of Westminster on March 27, 1155, and that he had acted as king's justiciar at Domfront in that year.[14] Furthermore, he traveled to Rome in October 1155 and rejoined the royal court at Rouen on February 2, 1156.[15] A letter to Arnold, abbot of Bonneval, revealed that Arnulf intended to return to his episcopal duties at Lisieux in time to celebrate Easter on April 15, 1156.[16] Several charters show Arnulf acting in his role as chief justiciar of Normandy at the assize held at Caen in January 1157.[17] There is no evidence that he returned to England during that period. Therefore, the five charters listed by Delisle-Berger may safely be dated to the first three months of 1155. Evidence from the charters, combined with information in the letters, clarifies the chronology of Arnulf's movements.

Arnulf's personal correspondence has been preserved in a major compilation of 141 letters. There are nineteen extant manuscripts of Arnulf's correspondence, containing anywhere from 45 to 118 letters. All of these manuscripts date from the twelfth and thirteenth centuries, a fact that indicates the contemporary popularity of the letters. Twelfth-century scholars delighted in trying to rival the style of the ancients and produced collections of their letters for publication. Modern historians, however, have differed over the extent of their usefulness. Charles V. Langlois declared them to be the most valuable source of information on the history of the Middle Ages.[18] William Stubbs, on the other hand, deplored their tendency to contain more sentiment than news or to be nothing more than a formal vehicle to introduce the bearer who brought an oral communication.[19] Some letters can be valuable for their factual content, others for their literary quality or their revelations of attitudes and ideas. There are, of course, many pitfalls awaiting the indiscriminate user of such letters. Giles Constable, in his introduction to the letter collection of Peter the Venerable, suggested several questions that must be considered.[20] Did the sender write the letter personally, dictate it to a scribe, or simply indicate the general context to a secretary? Does the letter tell the whole story or was it meant simply as an introduction for the courier who carried an additional message? Who collected the letters and for what purpose? Were the letters published as originally written or were they edited? Have the details of the letter been distorted by copying errors? Perhaps most important, do the letters contribute to our knowledge of the historical period in which they were written?

There is clear evidence that some events described in Arnulf's letters are fallacious. Arnulf was more concerned with appearances and perceptions than with accuracy. He often had trouble distinguishing between the world as it was and the world as he thought it should be. On occasion he presented a desirable outcome as a fait accompli. And when the situation seemed to warrant it, he did not hesitate to tell an outright lie in support of what he believed to be a good cause. Certain of his writings deliberately deceived his contemporaries, and others have misled modern historians.

In the face of such questionable validity, is it possible to make a case for the usefulness of Arnulf's correspondence? I believe it is. Even a deliberate falsification may have some historical significance. The real key to the question of usefulness lies in discovering the purpose for which the letters were originally assembled. If it is assumed that Arnulf collected and published his letters to portray himself in the best possible light, to enhance his own reputation, or to give a one-sided view of contemporary events, then indeed the letters must be used with extreme caution. But if he published them for some reason unrelated to their factual content, their historical value may be enhanced, albeit unintentionally, by the nature of their arguments.

Arnulf himself described his original collection of letters as a *libellum*—"a little book"—whose value he denigrated because of the "pitiful thinness" of its rhetoric. Yet behind his modest disclaimers lay the assumption that readers would admire the very qualities he professed to lack: "cultured style and skill of expression."[21] There is ample evidence of Arnulf's familiarity with the correct epistolary style that was just coming into popular use in France in the second half of the twelfth century. It is usually assumed that the *ars dictaminis* did not appear in the French schools until the end of the twelfth century, although Haskins believed it was being taught at Chartres as early as the 1150s.[22] Interest in correct epistolary style, however, probably existed for some time before the introduction of formal study. Arnulf had studied in Bologna at the very time when the *ars dictaminis* became an important part of the curriculum. His letters show that he was aware of the rules set out by Hugh of Bologna in his *Rationes dictandi prosaice* for the proper structuring of a formal salutation, so that each indicated "the abilities of the addressee—one for the pope, another for a king, another for a bishop, another for an abbot or monk, another for a soldier, another for a comrade or a beloved friend."[23] Arnulf's letters followed this requirement explicitly. His customary form of address to a pope was "To his most reverent lord and dearest father, Alexander, by the grace of God highest priest of the catholic church, Arnulf, humble servant of the church of Lisieux, sends greetings with all due humility and devotion."[24] He addressed the English king with great pomp: "To his most reverent lord, Henry, by the grace of God the illustrious and glorious king of England, peace, glory, and honor."[25] A letter to a fellow bishop might begin with more restraint: "To his venerable and beloved father and friend, Bartholomew, by the grace of God bishop of Exeter, Arnulf, humble servant of the church of Lisieux, sends greetings."[26] A letter to an underling was noticeable not only by the paucity of adjectives but also by order: "Arnulf, by the grace of God bishop of Lisieux, sends greetings to his beloved brother Herbert, abbot of Grestain."[27]

Similarly, he used the *cursus* being developed by the papal chancery. This was a rhythmical arrangement of syllables that had replaced the more classical emphasis on the quantity of a vowel with one that depended upon accent and syllable counting. Its most common form, the *cursus planus*, required a sentence or a clause to end with a two-syllable word, accented on the first syllable, followed by a three-syllable word accented on the second syllable; for example, *clàmat vocàbat*. A second variation, the *cursus tardus*, added a second unaccented syllable at the end of the clause: *vòces incìpiunt*. Arnulf most frequently employed the third style, the *cursus velox*. This rapid-fire delivery used a three-syllable word accented on the first syllable, followed by a four-syllable word accented on the penultimate syllable: *ùltima elemènta*. A survey of a stratified random sample of the letters included in the first edition of Arnulf's correspondence reveals that over 93 percent of *clausulae* at the ends of his sentences followed the accepted patterns of the *planus, tardus,* or *velox* styles. The content of the letters echoed with classical phrasing and repeated rhetorical figures. Arnulf was at least as concerned with the style of his writing as with its import.

Further, I believe that the original collection of Arnulf's correspondence, like that of Peter of Blois, was published to serve as a "little book" of *exempla* for letter-writers—a formulary compiled from examples of Arnulf's letters that exhibited exceptional literary merit or that had proved to be particularly effective or persuasive.[28] Such didactic collections, according to Constable, can be recognized by the lack of chronological arrangement, the amount of revision from the original text, and a certain stylistically pleasing variety of form and subject matter.[29] The Arnulf correspondence is most accessible to historians today in the 1939 text edited by Frank Barlow. This edition, while admirable in its accuracy and completeness, has imposed upon the collection an artifical arrangement, and the chronological order of the letters has obscured the reasons behind their original publication. To discover the real purpose of the collection—and thus to evaluate its historical contribution—it is necessary to turn to evidence supplied by the manuscript tradition.

Arnulf prepared the first edition of forty-four letters in 1166 and sent it to Giles de la Perche, archdeacon of Rouen. In the accompanying letter, he asked Giles not to make the letters public because he feared that "their obvious imperfections would not permit them to be published" and that potential readers "would be offended by the pitiful thinness of their oratory." He insisted that he had decided not to save copies for the future, "because I was not confident enough of their cultured style or the skill of their expression. Indeed I prefer them to be condemned to the eternal shadows than to be exposed as material for invidious ridicule. . . ."[30]

Such protests, of course, were little more than self-effacing and may be approached with skepticism. Although Arnulf declared that he was only complying with a suggestion to collect his letters out of friendship, his description of his activities indicates that he had expended a great deal of effort to compile his "little book." Modesty dictated that Arnulf not admit that he had kept copies of the letters he had sent; therefore, he insisted that he was forced to retrieve them from their recipients. But some of the letters addressed to popes would have been in the papal archives at Rome and thus in the hands of the antipope, Paschal, at the end of 1166 or early in 1167. It is unlikely that a staunch supporter of Alexander III could have successfully reclaimed them. Further, he said that he was transmitting them exactly as they had been received.[31] One copy of this first edition, Vatican MS Lat. 6024, contains five original and unedited letters. When these are compared with other manuscripts, they reveal that, despite what Arnulf said, he had done some judicious excising of mundane business details before the letters were published.[32]

The first edition is most easily examined in Paris, BN, MS Lat. 15166. This manuscript, in a single hand and dated to the end of the twelfth century, comes from the Abbey of St. Victor in Paris, where Arnulf spent the last several years of his life. The order of the letters reveals no conscious chronology. The subject matter ranges from friendly chatter about his problems with doctors and his need for a new horse to matters of the most serious importance, such as the papal schism of 1159. The letters include decisions in court cases, offers of congratulations and condolences, observations on the duties of the clergy, and even a travelogue and a book review.

Arnulf helped to prepare a second edition of his letters in 1173 at the request of Peter of Pavia, Bishop of Meaux.[33] The introductory letter accompanying them is remarkably similar to the first. Once again, Arnulf disingenuously claimed to be forwarding hastily selected copies, which he had no desire to see published. "Read them," he urged, "and keep them in the secret places of your mind, because, if they should fall into public hands, they would not be assured of your friendly judgment."[34] The letters he chose to add to the collection contain a high proportion of church court cases and the administrative business of his diocese—a reflection, perhaps, of a period in which he was particularly active in church affairs. Still, the letters fall into several categories, and one suspects that the subject matter was selected for its piquancy. The crimes involved in the court cases include a stolen book, a forged seal, and an unpaid bill at the local tavern. The people described include a cantankerous abbess, two drunken fund raisers, a student at the cathedral school, an ungrateful nephew, a greedy abbot who mistreated his tenants, and the disgruntled son of a priest who was trying to succeed to his father's vicarage. Except for minor variations, the second edition reproduced the order of the first and continued the emphasis on variety of subject matter and elegance of language.

This second edition is best exemplified by Paris, BN, MS Lat. 14763, another St. Victor codex that became the parent for most of the continental editions of Arnulf's letters. In 1585, this manuscript was the source for the first printed edition of the Arnulf correspondence. Claude Mignault, who nicknamed himself "Minos," printed Stephen Turnèbu's transcription and sent it to a certain Jacob Gillote, a member of the king's council at Paris. In the accompanying introductory letter, Minos commended only the literary quality of the letters, not their historical accuracy, and suggested to Gillote that they would provide samples of effective rhetoric for his staff of diplomatic letter writers.[35] That may have been the last time Arnulf's letter collection was used for the purpose for which he had designed it.

The three extant Oxford copies of the collection contain several alterations to the manuscripts—changes that ultimately caused historians to lose sight of the rhetorical nature of the collection. The first noticeable difference between the English and the continental manuscripts is that all formal salutations have been omitted from the English versions. In their place, the copyists inserted simple marginal notes recording the intended recipient. In the case of Bodleian, Auctores F.I.8, even these notes appear to have been added in a different and later hand. Arnulf's elaborate scheme of graduated degrees of salutation and commendation disappeared. More important, while the Oxford manuscripts all had a common parent in Paris, BN, MS Lat. 14763, they were expanded to include letters not found in Arnulf's second edition. Both Auctores F.I.8 and Digby 209, which is a clear copy, contain eight additional letters, none of which Arnulf intended to become public. The first is his long letter to Thomas Becket, accurately if somewhat cruelly analyzing the temperament of Henry II and promising secret support to Becket's cause.[36] Three letters contained secret pleas of support for Reginald, bishop-elect of Bath, whose consecration was being delayed by the hostility of the Young King.[37] Others included a rather sniveling complaint to Alexander III about his treatment at the hands of his own canons and a groveling apology to Henry II for having unintentionally angered him.[38]

St. John's College MS 126 contains an additional forty letters, all but one of which dates from the last years of Arnulf's life, when he found himself out of favor with almost everyone. His major, and perhaps only, confidante in those years was Richard of Ilchester, and Barlow speculated that these additions were collected and appended by Richard, or more probably his scribe, Guy of Southwick.[39] The letters themselves provide painful and sometimes embarrassing reading. They are frequently repetitious, often querulous, sometimes even maudlin in their self-pity. Their lack of rhetorical elegance, as well as the almost sing-song quality of a *cursus* restricted to the *velox*, stand them in sharp contrast to the original collection.

When J. A. Giles published his collection of Arnulf's letters as part of the *Patres Ecclesiae Anglicanae* in 1844, he used only two major sources: the printed Minos edition and the newly discovered St. John's College MS 126.[40] Giles then added ten individual letters preserved elsewhere, only four of which proved to belong to the collection. The first two of these were congratulatory letters, one written to Becket when he assumed the title of Archbishop of Canterbury, the other written on the occasion of the birth of Louis VII's son, Philip.[41] The third was a description of Henry's reaction to the news of Becket's death; although Arnulf later tried to suppress its publication, it became his best-known piece of correspondence.[42] The fourth was a recital of grievances sent to the pope when Arnulf resigned his bishopric; it is from this letter that we know the rather sordid details behind his forced retirement.[43]

The Giles edition did several disservices to Arnulf's literary reputation. Giles failed from the first to understand the nature of the early editions of the letters. In his dedication, he praised the historical usefulness of the letters because they added to one's knowledge of famous figures such as Henry II, Thomas Becket, and Gilbert Foliot. He dismissed their rhetoric as "hardly inelegant."[44] He included six misattributed letters, some of which seem to have come from the pen of a certain Ernulf, employed as Becket's secretary.[45] Most of these appear near the beginning of the Giles edition, and their lack of rhetorical skill helps to mask the inherent unity of the collection. More damaging still was Giles's attempt to rearrange the order of the letters. Barlow dismissed Giles's arrangement as merely haphazard, but it was more than that.[46] It was a clumsy but discernible attempt to give the letters some sort of chronological unity. Giles preserved the order of the letters added by Guy of Southwick because they had been collected in the order in which they were received. Then he radically reordered the letters of the Minos second edition so that they reflected the same sort of vague chronological arrangement. He inserted his newly discovered individual letters wherever they best seemed to fit the time-frame. This new organization completed the process of obscuring the rhetorical purpose of the collection. And the error was perpetuated when Migne lifted the Giles edition intact for the *Patrologia Latinae*.

That brings us back to the modern Barlow edition, which increased the collection by an additional seventeen letters discovered in variant manuscripts and other compilations. Barlow once again rearranged the collection to reflect a strict chronological order. His dating of the letters is as precise as it is possible to be when one is working with undated material. The result is a collection that accurately tells the unfolding story of Arnulf's episcopal career. But it is not Arnulf's own collection, nor does it accomplish the purpose for which Arnulf intended it.[47]

The accusations of Arnulf's duplicity and unreliability arise from two sources. During the conflicts of the 1160s, the more ardent supporters of Becket frequently denounced Arnulf as untrustworthy because he appeared to be in the pay of the king. His most outspoken critic was John of Salisbury, a writer whose opinions carried much weight because of his loyalty to Becket. More serious charges arise from the content of the letters themselves. During both the Becket crisis and the rebellion of the king's sons, Arnulf referred to "secret" opinions that he was not at liberty to reveal.[48] Recent studies have shown that Arnulf deliberately distorted the facts in several letters for his own purposes.[49] The overgeneralized conclusion drawn by modern historians has been that his statements are not to be trusted. In some cases, that is obviously true; yet it need not invalidate the entire corpus of his writings. The importance of his writings, as well as his reputation, deserves a more critical examination.

Arnulf's contemporary reputation was badly damaged as a result of a quarrel with John of Salisbury. In 1156, Arnulf raised a question about Salisbury's loyalty to the English crown, and as a result Salisbury found himself out of favor for a time at the English court.[50] Every subsequent reference to Arnulf in the writings of Salisbury is unfavorable. At the time of his disgrace Salisbury wrote to the pope asking him to take revenge on Arnulf for having stirred up such a "storm of indignation" against him that he was afraid to stay in England but unable to leave.[51] A few years later, in a letter to Bartholomew, archdeacon of Exeter, he ridiculed Arnulf's love of rhetoric.[52] In his *Historia Pontificalis,* he described Arnulf's role in the Second Crusade with great malice.[53] Salisbury's animosity was further fueled by the Becket controversy, in which the two men again found themselves in disagreement over the conflict of loyalties to king and church. Salisbury's letters to fellow supporters of Becket, such as the one in which he calls Arnulf "the hammer of injustice for the destruction of the church of God," were full of denunciations of the bishop.[54] John of Salisbury is a perennial favorite among English historians; they tend to accept his judgments without question. Marjorie Chibnall, for example, has credited Salisbury with "impartiality" and "freedom from personal malice," even when he was accusing Arnulf of the worst sorts of avarice, deceit, and incompetence during the Second Crusade.[55] Thus modern assessments of Arnulf echo—and sometimes directly quote— the enmity of Arnulf's most vicious critic.

The question of Arnulf's tendency to handle the truth loosely presents by far the more serious problem. Arnulf was undoubtedly a casuist. His attack on the party of Anacletus during the papal schism of the 1130s included several totally baseless and vile rumors, stories he justified by the need to get rid of an unfit antipope. He was capable of denouncing Empress Matilda as illegitimate at a papal audience in 1139, when he needed to present a favorable case for Stephen's claim to the English throne. Yet at Matilda's death he composed a series of laudatory poems in honor of her as the mother of his sovereign.[56] The exigencies of the moment often overruled literal truth in his mind. He reported the recognition of Alexander III by the court of France as a fait accompli in the hope of persuading the English clergy to help make it happen.

Such faults cannot be denied, but they need not provide insurmountable obstacles to the use of Arnulf's writings as historical evidence. A full understanding of the circumstances under which a lie was told may reveal to the reader more about what was going on than would the literal truth. Even if Arnulf distorted some details, his writings preserve a core of information about the workings of a twelfth-century bishopric that cannot be duplicated in other contemporary literature.[57] Arnulf did not intend to write a chronicle; his letters reflect not so much history as an informed and personal response to the affairs of his own day. Through his comments, the reader gains an appreciation of undercurrents of history that would otherwise remain obscure.

This study of the life and works of Arnulf of Lisieux is an attempt to provide a context in which his writings may be fairly evaluated. It is not a biography per se, for too many facts are irretrievably lost. It is, however, a biographical essay, based on those bits and pieces of his life that Arnulf chose to preserve in his letters and supplemented by the details of his official acts revealed in diplomatic sources. Arnulf played an important role in the affairs of both England and Normandy, and his writings provide vital information about the age in which he lived.

The twelfth century was not only a dynamic period of intellectual advancement and innovation; it was a time in which thoughtful people were confronted with difficult choices. The bishops of Normandy were particularly challenged by conflicting loyalties—between France and England, between their positions as ecclesiastical lords and secular barons, between the rights of church and state, between dual claimants to secular thrones and papal sees. Arnulf was intimately involved in these conflicts. His choices, as well as his explanations of them in his correspondence, reflect a consistent pattern—a paradigm—that determined his reactions.

The concept of paradigms that influence decision making gained popularity in the work of Thomas Kuhn, who used it to explain the history of scientific revolutions. At least one of his definitions of the term has broader applicability. In its sociological sense, he says, a paradigm "stands for the entire constellation of beliefs, values, techniques, and so on shared by the members of a given community."[58] Some social scientists have argued that Kuhn's theories cannot be applied to fields other than normal science because they are based only on experimentation and the nature of scientific discoveries.[59] In the twelfth century, however, scholars would not have recognized the modern distinctions among philosophy, normal science, and political theory. They accepted a concept of the world that united all philosophical, scientific, and legal debates under the single dominant authority of natural law within a Christian commonwealth.[60] Thus, in this sense, the community of twelfth-century thinkers held shared paradigms. The major difference between modern and medieval paradigms is that Kuhn's scientists deal with "what is," while the scholars of the twelfth century were more concerned with "what ought to be."

Arnulf of Lisieux governed his life by a paradigm that he adopted early in his ecclesiastical career. The evolution of this paradigm closely paralleled the stages outlined by Kuhn. It began as a theory that provided workable solutions to a current set of problems concerning the role of the church within society. After a time, it came into conflict with new political developments— anomalies—with which it was ill equipped to deal. A younger generation of theologians proposed new approaches—a paradigm shift—whose conse- quences Arnulf was unwilling to accept. Although he was often fascinated with the new ideas of the twelfth century, he clung to the old ideals that had inspired his episcopal career. Thus he suffered the same fate that befalls Kuhn's older school of scientists, who, when they cling to an outdated paradigm, "are simply read out of the profession, which thereafter ignores their work."[61]

The Dilemma of
Arnulf of Lisieux

I.

The Construction of
a Paradigm

Some people mature slowly, taking years to test the paradigms of their contemporaries, adapting to changing conditions, and then distilling from a lifetime of experience a philosophy that will carry them contentedly into old age. Others crystallize their values at an early age and cling to them throughout their lives, even at the risk of appearing to be out of step with their own generations. Bishop Arnulf of Lisieux followed the latter course. He learned from the exemplars of his youth the values that constituted the building blocks of a paradigm by which he governed his life. Despite the emergence of new ideas and conflicting value systems during the twelfth century, he seldom deviated from the path he defined as a young archdeacon.

Arnulf was born near Sées at the beginning of the twelfth century into a family with a tradition of service to the church. His grandfather was Norman the Dean, a title that suggests his attachment to the cathedral chapter of canons at Sées.[1] His uncle, John of Lisieux, was the most important of the ecclesiastical administrators of Normandy under Henry I.[2] While still an archdeacon of Sées, John had been forced by the enmity of Robert of Bellême to seek sanctuary at the English court of Henry I in 1102.[3] Charter evidence indicates that he accompanied the court of Henry as it moved between Normandy and England, and that almost from the time of his arrival at the Anglo-Norman court, he served as a major witness to the acts of the *curia regis*.[4]

In 1107 Henry appointed John as bishop of Lisieux, and from then on he assumed an even more important role in the government of Normandy. As a trusted advisor of the king, he was often called upon to render judgments in local cases concerning land holdings. Some historians have cited his activities as evidence of a separate exchequer operating in Normandy during the reign of Henry I; John may even have served as that exchequer's first head.[5] He frequently received writs addressed specifically to him, ordering him to see that Henry's wishes in some matter were carried out. John was the most frequent witness among the Norman bishops, attesting to at least sixty-two of Henry's charters, and his name almost invariably preceded those of other ecclesiastical witnesses, with the exception of the archbishop of Rouen. The dates of these documents reveal that John traveled to England in 1107, 1110,

1115, 1122, and 1126. He appears to have been most active in Henry's service in Normandy during the last five years of his reign. John held his diocese until his death in 1141 and, as Orderic observed, "improved the condition of the church and clergy and God's people in many ways."[6]

In 1124, Arnulf's older brother, John, was installed as bishop of Sées. This John was identified by Orderic as "the son of Harduin and nephew of Bishop John of Lisieux."[7] His mother was the sister of John of Lisieux; the identity of the father, Harduin, is unknown, although his family patronymic may have been de Neuville.[8] John of Sées, too, had begun his career at the court of Henry I while he was still an archdeacon.[9] During the reign of Henry I, John of Sées often witnessed royal charters and served as a judge in the secular courts. He traveled to England in 1132 and 1133 and held his diocese until his death in 1144. Orderic indicated that this John was not the equal of his predecessors, either in experience or in education.[10] Arnulf, however, held his brother's accomplishments in high esteem. In a letter addressed to Pope Alexander III, he recalled that John had expended great care on the temporalities of his diocese, returning them with their treasures more embellished and their buildings and possessions better furnished. He also praised his brother's concern with the spiritual state of the diocese and his efforts to install thirty-six Austin canons in the cathedral of Sées. But most important to Arnulf was the balance John demonstrated between his spiritual and secular responsibilities: "However much he resembled a nobleman in his temporal possessions, this magnificent man always strove to show himself more noble in spirit and sanctity, in whom sanctity did not obscure his magnificence nor magnificence disguise his sanctity."[11] This final phrase, *nec sanctitas magnificentiam tolleret, nec magnificentia sanctitatem*, appeared frequently thereafter in Arnulf's writing. He used it to outline for Becket the proper behavior for an archbishop, to describe the virtues of John de Belmeis, bishop of Poitiers, and to evaluate his own performance as a bishop.

Thus Arnulf's early role models were his grandfather, his uncle, and his older brother, all of whom had dedicated their lives to the service of the church. Moreover, both his uncle and his brother had sought preferment at the Anglo-Norman court and had accepted secular positions under the king. For Arnulf the careers of John of Lisieux and John of Sées represented an ideal balance between service to the church and secular responsibility. Arnulf began the construction of his personal paradigm by adopting the career goals exemplified by the older members of his family. Throughout his life, Arnulf would seek to be both a devout servant of the church and a loyal subject of the king.

Arnulf was the third member of his family to begin his studies at Sées, and his education there was directed toward preparing him for clerical life.[12] The progress of his higher education can be traced only indirectly, although there is evidence that he studied at Chartres, Rome or Bologna, and Paris. Certainly he was at Chartres at one time, for he described himself in his *Invectiva in Girardum Engolismensem Episcopum* as the "humble and devoted clerk of

Geoffrey, bishop of Chartres."[13] His personal ties to the monastery of St. Victor, as well as several references to Paris in his correspondence, indicate that he was familiar with the schools of that city. His studies in Italy are more problematic. Noël Deshays stated that Arnulf went to Rome to study Roman law.[14] Julius Dieterich, on the other hand, believed that he went to Bologna for the same purpose.[15] Dieterich's theory may have more validity, for two reasons. Barlow points to Arnulf's vague understanding of Roman affairs during the period from 1130 to 1134 when Rome was in the hands of the antipope, Anacletus, as evidence that he had not witnessed them at first hand.[16] More important, perhaps, is Arnulf's emergence in the following years as one of France's finest and earliest practitioners of the *ars dictaminis*, the art of letterwriting, the study of which flourished at Bologna in the first half of the twelfth century.

Similarly, there is some confusion about the beginning of Arnulf's ecclesiastical career. Deshays passed on the story that Arnulf was for a short time the treasurer of Bayeux before deciding that he was obligated to return to the church in which he had been raised.[17] At some time after 1124 but before 1133, Arnulf became an archdeacon of Sées, and he retained this title until he was elected bishop of Lisieux in 1141 to succeed his uncle. But beyond the indications of the powerful influence his family had upon him, it is difficult to trace the experiences that guided Arnulf's early career and intellectual development. All correspondence before his election as bishop of Lisieux has disappeared. There is little evidence of his activities in the charters of the period before his episcopal nomination, for clergy in minor orders were seldom employed as witnesses to important official documents. And unlike several of his contemporaries whose writings tended to be heavily autobiographical, Arnulf seldom mentioned his early life or personal experiences.

The one notable exception to the obscurity surrounding the early life of Arnulf appears as a vitriolic pamphlet he composed during the papal schism of the 1130s. This schism provided Arnulf with his first introduction to the conflicts inherent in an ecclesiastical career. Arnulf's early education had, perhaps, not been disturbed by the nagging problems of investiture that carried over from the eleventh century, for Normandy was well out of the original dispute and the Anglo-Norman king had been willing to compromise with the pope as early as 1107.[18] But by the time Arnulf arrived in Italy to pursue his legal studies, internal disagreements were once again rocking the church hierarchy with enough strength to affect even the provinces farthest from Rome.

The Concordat of Worms, which closed the Investiture Struggle in 1122, created a split between two developing parties in the papal curia. Essentially this split represented a breakdown of the Gregorian paradigm that assumed a basic conflict between the interests of *regnum* and *sacerdotium*. Kuhn suggests that new paradigms are frequently the creation of members of a young generation who, "being little committed by prior practice to the traditional rules . . ., are particularly likely to see that those rules no longer define a playable game and to conceive another set that can replace them."[19] A similar mechanism was at work within the church hierarchy in the early twelfth century as a new generation of theologians sought to put the artificial divisions of *regnum* and *sacerdotium* behind them.

By 1130, the Roman Curia was deeply divided along ideological lines. The curialists who had shepherded the Investiture Struggle through its worst days were unwilling to grant major concessions to the German emperor, while the newer members of the Curia were anxious to get on with the job of reforming the church as a whole.[20] Within Rome the controlling faction was still the party of the old Gregorians, led by Peter Pierleoni, cardinal-priest of St. Mary in Trastevere. Its most influential members were themselves Romans; at least fifteen of them had held their seats since before the time of Calixtus II.[21] The Pierleoni had been staunch supporters of the Gregorian reforms and were bitterly opposed to the compromises effected by the Concordat of Worms. They remained opposed to all efforts of the emperor to reimpose his influence upon church affairs and sought to protect the gains that had been won in the struggle against lay investiture.

On the other side was the party of Haimeric, the papal chancellor. His supporters, both within the college of cardinals and among the regular clergy, were relatively younger than those of Pierleoni. Many of them were cardinals who had been promoted to the cardinalate between 1123 and 1130 and were still somewhat dependent upon the continued good will of Haimeric.[22] There were geographic differences as well; these prelates were nearly all from northern Italy or France. Among the members of Haimeric's party, the most influential were Lambert of Ostia, who with the military support of the Frangipani became Pope Honorius II in 1124; Bernard of Clairvaux, the great Cistercian mystic who championed monastic reform; Matthew, who was cardinal-bishop of Albano; and Peter the Venerable, who led a new reform effort while he was abbot at Cluny. The party of Haimeric is generally referred to as being "pro-imperial" because its members had favored the terms of the Concordat.[23] The description is unfair. These curialists did not support the claims of the emperor; rather, they regarded the whole controversy as relatively unimportant and were happy to see it settled through compromise. They were much more concerned with the moral welfare of the church and sought to reform the ecclesiastical hierarcy from within. Hans Klewitz characterized the split in terms that Kuhn might have dictated. It was, he said, "the opposition of a strong young minority, to whom the future belonged, against the majority of the elder generation, who could no longer successfully defend a faded ideal."[24]

Arnulf must have recognized in this group of reformers several ideas that fit into his own developing paradigm. Although they were older than Arnulf, they represented a new generation of prelates who were prepared to assume leadership. Their emphasis on spirituality reflected Arnulf's awareness of the need for the moral regeneration of the clergy. Their connections with reformed monastic orders may have reminded Arnulf of the motivation that had inspired his older brother to install canons-regular in the cathedral chapter of Sées. Their studied avoidance of the issues of *regnum* and *sacerdotium* gave tacit approval to the possibility of being both a devout servant of the church and a loyal subject of the king. As Arnulf clarified and refined his own views, his paradigm began to incorporate many of the goals of the party of Haimeric.

The death of Honorius II in 1130 brought the two parties into open conflict. Haimeric, accompanied by several other cardinals, had spirited the dying pope off to the monastery of St. Andrew on the Caelius so that after his death they could be assured of the armed support of the Frangipani. After a hasty burial service for Honorius in the courtyard of the monastery, this group of cardinals elected Gregory, cardinal-deacon of St. Angelus, and immediately invested him as Innocent II. The rest of the cardinals, when informed of the fait accompli, assembled in Rome and chose their own candidate, Peter Pierleoni, as Pope Anacletus II. When the total vote was counted, Innocent had the support of nineteen cardinals, while Anacletus had twenty-one.[25] There was no clear way to determine which candidate had the better claim. Nicholas II's *Decretum de electione papae* of 1059 had not fully dealt with the possibility of a disputed election, although legal interpretations had favored the principle of majority rule.[26] A case can be made for Innocent II because he numbered five cardinal-bishops among his supporters while Anacletus had only two. According to the instructions of 1059, the approval of the cardinal-bishops was essential in any papal election.[27] Anacletus, however, was strongly supported by the cardinal-priests and by the cardinal-deacons. Among contemporary writers, the opinion seems to have been that Anacletus was the duly elected pope because "his electors were not only the majority but were also of greater wisdom and authority."[28]

The schism dragged on for eight years. The party of the Pierleoni had long had the support of the Roman citizenry, so they had no trouble remaining in Rome. Even the Frangipani on whom Haimeric had counted for support came over to the side of Anacletus within a few months. Innocent and his followers were forced to flee to France, where they took refuge at Cluny. There, under the protection of Peter the Venerable and, what was to be more important, with the active campaigning of Bernard of Clairvaux, support for Pope Innocent II began to rally.

Bernard based his arguments for Innocent not on the legal technicalities of the election but rather on grounds of morality. At the Council of Étampes, held in the late summer of 1130, Bernard emphasized "more about the person than about the election."[29] The French king and most of the French clergy declared for Innocent. At the Council of Würzburg in October 1130, the emperor and clergy of Germany followed suit. Henry I of England hesitated longer, but at a meeting at Chartres on January 13, 1131, Bernard was able to convince the Anglo-Norman king to recognize Innocent.[30] In personal appeals as well as public speeches, Bernard hammered home his defense: "Election by the better part, the approval of the majority, and, what is more important, the testimony of his character, commend Innocent to everyone, and confirm him as pope."[31]

The statement was not necessarily true, but it was certainly effective. Among the rulers of Christendom, only Roger of Sicily, David of Scotland, and William of Aquitaine remained unconvinced of the legality of the election of Innocent II.

Young Arnulf, archdeacon of Sées, began to take an active role in the schism in 1133 with the publication of his *Invectiva in Girardum Engolismensem Episcopum*. The date of composition can be determined from internal evidence.[32] In section seven, Arnulf commented that "Innocent's residence in the city [of Rome], his entrance into the city to pass judgment, and his exit from the city were unobstructed."[33] This statement was true only for a short period during the summer of 1133 when Lothar marched an army of some two thousand knights to Rome to defend Innocent's papal rights and to assure his own coronation as German emperor. The coronation took place on June 4, 1133; by September, Lothar had gone home and Innocent had fled to Pisa. In 1133 Arnulf was in Italy pursuing his studies, but he had not forgotten his ties to the French church. It was devotion to his former teacher, Geoffrey of Chartres, as well as his concern for the church, that led him to compose his pamphlet on the schism. "Although a long-standing desire to study Roman law has led me to Italy," he declared, "the distance has withdrawn the obedience of my body, but has not destroyed my spiritual allegiance."[34]

The pamphlet itself was meant to attack the schismatic pope, but Arnulf directed it against Gerard, bishop of Angoulême, who was the principal supporter of Anacletus. Gerard was bishop of Angoulême from 1102 to 1136; he had been appointed as a papal legate and as vicar of Aquitaine by Pope Paschal II.[35] In 1130 he became Anacletus's legate to France. The character of Gerard is difficult to evaluate fairly, for the story of his legatine service has been told only by those who reacted most strongly to him. One historian has described the sources as "on the one hand a view of a restrained panegyricist and on the other a maliciously slanderous polemic."[36] The panegyric was a flowery nineteenth-century biography.[37] The "maliciously slanderous polemic" was, of course, Arnulf's *Invectiva*. Arnulf justified his approach in this way:

> To be sure, just as the unwearied bishop of Rome takes his position in Italy to resist Pierleoni, so it remains for you in France to resist Gerard, so that the head is united against the head and the right hand against the right hand. For if Peter is the leader and author of his schism, so is Gerard above all others his principal instrument.[38]

Arnulf began his attack on Gerard with some nasty reminders that Gerard was an old man who would shortly have to answer to God for his crimes:

> Do you not see your miserable old age and the imminent failing of your decrepit body from natural necessity and the gaping gates of the tomb? Do you not know that the extension of divine patience is only piling up all around you prayers for your eternal damnation, so that now no excuse will serve to lessen His divine vengeance?[39]

And in Arnulf's eyes, there was no limit to the crimes of which Gerard was guilty:

> All the work and leisure of your accursed body, all the craft of your evil mind, all the time of your detestable life has been expended so that you could appear to be a soldier for the church while you struggled against it. Now, however, God has made clear the plans in your heart. . . . He reveals you to have been a traitor to the church, to which you pretended to be a patron. He reveals you to have been a great hunter of money, who were consecrated as a hunter of souls . . . for which crimes you will be found to be contemptible to men, cursed by the angels, and damned by God.[40]

Arnulf employed one of the hoarier tricks of rhetoric—*praeteritio*—to pretend to spare his audience the pain of hearing the early tales of Gerard's misspent youth: "I do not mention the shameful complaints of your boyhood, the ignominious reputation of your adolescence, the greedy deals of your youth, lest I pollute the ears of those to whom these writings may come with the sordid details of your incontinence and avarice."[41] Having thus "proved" his concern for the sensibilities of his readers, Arnulf proceeded to pull from his collection of rumors the worst possible stories. He told a tale of spiritual incest with obvious enjoyment. According to Arnulf, an archdeacon in Gerard's service had raped the abbess of the monastery of St. Ausonius in Angoulême, and, although she had subsequently given birth to a child, Gerard had taken no steps to punish the guilty archdeacon.[42] Julius Dieterich noted that "it is possible to guess that Arnulf concocted the story from idle rumor, since he knew neither the name of the archdeacon nor that of the abbess."[43] True or not, the story was a necessary component in Arnulf's case against Gerard, for he used it to prove another point. If Gerard were not guilty of all crimes, he was at least capable of them:

> For who, if he is found to be intemperate and lustful in important matters, will restrain himself from minor ones? How so? A man who will not stand aloof from sacrilege or incest, will not hesitate, when he is aroused enough by a passion for luxury or greed, to contaminate his hand or to corrupt his body with simple fornication or rape. Why should he? Because he who is not offended by the filth of someone else's crime, but rather exults in it, will not condemn the experience of his own desire.[44]

Having temporarily finished with his insinuations about the character of Gerard, Arnulf turned his attack to Anacletus. He began by dredging up the story of the Pierleoni ancestry in another example of praeteritio: "It is agreeable therefore to skip over the ancient origins of his birth and likewise his inglorious race, nor would I think of exposing his Jewish name. . . ." But having denied his willingness to accuse Anacletus of being Jewish, he continued his insinuations: "His grandfather, after he had collected an enormous amount of money through usury, damned the circumcision that he had received with the water of baptism."[45] The story was quite true, so far as it went. Peter Pierleoni was descended from a Jewish moneylender named Baruch, who converted to Christianity early in the eleventh century. Thereafter the family became one of the leaders of Roman society and one of the principal supporters of the papacy. According to some sources, Pope Gregory VI was the son of Baruch, and there is a slight possibility that Hildebrand, who became Pope Gregory VII, was connected to the family, if only by marriage.[46] As Engelbert Mühlbacher pointed out, "so long as the Pierleoni remained the loyal vassals of the pope, no one had taken offense at their descent."[47] Arnulf, however, exploited the details, hurling the epithet "Jew" into his argument several times.

Anacletus fared no better when the discussion turned to his morals. Arnulf had merely warmed up on the case of spiritual incest in the diocese of Gerard; now he accused Anacletus directly:

> He is said to have stained his sister Tropea—although it is wrong even to say it—with bestial incest, and to have sons born from this abominable monstrosity, which, having made him the father of his nephews and the maternal uncle of his sons, so confounded the laws of nature that he alternately referred to them as brothers and cousins. So not only a Jew, but worse than a Jew![48]

Nor, according to Arnulf, did Anacletus limit his carnal affections to his sister; he also had a female traveling companion: "A girl was taken around, upon whom he had conferred a tonsure and a kind of vestment that gave her the false appearance of a young man . . . so that while she had the face of a man, she exhibited the other parts of a woman, and both sexes seemed to be set forth in the same body."[49] Thus the slanders, innuendos, and racial slurs multiplied.

That Arnulf was as immoderate in his praise of Innocent II as he was rabid in his denunciation of Anacletus has led many readers to dismiss the pamphlet as almost totally useless. For the historian searching for an explanation of the schism, it contains little fact and even less documentation of its claims. The work has, however, some merit from a purely literary standpoint. Echoes of the rhetorical training that Arnulf had received are apparent. The *Invectiva* begins with an almost direct quote from Cicero: "How much longer, therefore, will you abuse the patience of God?"[50] Few other direct classical quotations appear, but Arnulf vaunted his own education when he criticized the nephews of Gerard for their ignorance of Plato, Cato, and Scipio.[51] Latin figures of speech abound. Besides the instances of *praeteritio* cited above, there are examples of chiasmus, climax, and antithesis. Nor was Arnulf above using the occasional pun to emphasize his point. When he accused Gerard of avarice— "You seek not honesty but full hands"—the impact depended upon a deliberate misspelling.[52] The *Invectiva* may therefore be read for the sheer appreciation of the twelfth-century renewal of classical rhetoric and its effective use.

More significant are the undercurrents of contemporary thought that find written expression in the *Invectiva*. Until recently, historians have tended to gloss over the anti-Jewish feelings that erupted into riot and persecution of the Jews in both France and England at the end of the twelfth century.[53] Here in Arnulf's writing there was an open avowal of the prevailing distrust of Jews.[54] Prohibitions against clerical marriage, a recurrent feature of the canons of twelfth-century church councils, suggest that Nicholaism remained a problem in the French church.[55] Arnulf's accusations of clerical immorality may have been occasioned by the young reformers' attitude toward the marriage of priests.[56] The challenges of rival monastic institutions provided additional fuel for the arguments between papal parties. Arnulf's praise of the Cistercian movement reflected the bias of the party of Haimeric.[57] Thus the *Invectiva* can be seen as more than an isolated attack on individuals. It was an expression of a paradigm that Arnulf shared with many of the younger leaders of Christendom.

Even the most outspoken critics of Arnulf's "dirty stories" have recognized that the *Invectiva* was an effective piece of political propaganda and that it was well accepted by contemporary churchmen, many of whom shared its views.[58] Bernard of Clairvaux received an early copy of the pamphlet and was so impressed with its vigorous arguments that he helped to distribute it throughout Europe.[59] It was only eight years after its publication that Arnulf was promoted to the bishopric of Lisieux, with the full approval of his archbishop and the pope. Both Bernard of Clairvaux and Peter the Venerable commended his election. Since the supporters of Innocent II welcomed and valued Arnulf's contribution to their cause, one can only assume that his *Invectiva* provides a glimpse into their real motives and attitudes.

Although it is crucial to an understanding of many of Arnulf's attitudes, the influence that St. Bernard of Clairvaux had upon the young archdeacon has not been fully recognized because there has been no firm evidence of the date of the first meeting between Arnulf and Bernard. No correspondence between them has been preserved. Frank Barlow proposed that the two men met for the first time in 1135 at the Council of Pisa; his only evidence, however, was a letter from Peter the Venerable, which stated that John, bishop of Sées, had traveled to the council with Bernard. Barlow assumed that Arnulf would have taken the oppportunity to visit his brother there and to meet the famous abbot of Clairvaux.[60]

A strong argument can be made for an earlier meeting. In May 1131, Henry I of England met with Innocent II at Rouen. In attendance were most of the people who would play major roles in Arnulf's career. Among them were Hugh, archbishop of Rouen, who ten years later consecrated Arnulf as bishop of Lisieux; John of Lisieux, Arnulf's uncle and predecessor in the bishopric; John of Sées, Arnulf's brother and his immediate ecclesiastical superior; Geoffrey of Chartres, who was his teacher and the inspiration for the *Invectiva*; Abbot Suger, who would later employ Arnulf as an envoy for the French court; and Bernard of Clairvaux.[61] Arnulf's name does not appear as a witness on any document from this meeting, but that does not preclude his presence as a humble clerk and observer. He had not yet begun his studies in Italy; he was the clerk of Geoffrey of Chartres and archdeacon of Sées. In either capacity, his natural place would have been at the side of his superior. It is extremely likely that Arnulf went to Rouen in 1131 and that his admiration for Bernard, as well as his decision to compose a pamphlet in support of Innocent II, stemmed from this meeting.

Herbert Bloch has suggested that Bernard picked up from Arnulf the idea of attacking Anacletus on the basis of his Jewish ancestry.[62] The instance in question is a letter written by Bernard to Lothar in 1134, in which he stated, "It is obvious that it would be an insult to Christ to allow the son of a Jew to occupy the papal throne."[63] The dating of this letter, however, does not necessarily prove that Bernard's anti-Jewish feelings were something new in 1134. In fact, there is ample evidence that resentment of Jews pervaded most of northern Europe in the twelfth century.[64] Bernard was in a much better position than Arnulf to know the scandals and rumors of the papal city. It seems more reasonable to assume that it was the older, morally righteous Bernard who influenced the young archdeacon to exploit the anti-Jewish mood in his attack. This assumption is strengthened by other echoes of Bernard in the phrasing of the *Invectiva*. Even in the preface addressed to Geoffrey, Arnulf defined his purpose in Bernardian terms: "I have joined together in my argument the character of the pope, the order of his election, the approval of the emperor, the consensus of the people, and more than anything else, the unopposed authority of all those who fear God."[65] Henri Pellerin has drawn attention to the great similarities between the *Invectiva* and a letter written by Bernard to the bishops of Aquitaine in 1132. In the two documents he sees the same thoughts, the same use of dialectic, the same objectives. In fact, he suggests that "the lampoon against Gerard is so exact a response to the letter of Saint Bernard that one is almost led to question whether the two men had not consulted and acted in unison."[66]

Arnulf should be seen as a spokesperson for the party of Innocent II, and particularly as an advocate of the position of Bernard of Clairvaux. One real contribution of the *Invectiva* was that it expressed publicly the opinions Bernard and other like-minded clerics held in private. Arnulf was a young man, probably still relatively innocent of the ways of the world and convinced that the answers to all questions came in clearly defined categories of right and wrong. It should come as no surprise that the portraits he painted were in black and white. In the *Invectiva* he overextended his arguments and sacrificed accuracy for the sake of emotional appeal. Yet by his own statement he was transmitting widely accepted views: "I have written nothing that I did not know for myself or did not hear from a reliable authority, or that, at least, public opinion does not confirm."[67]

For Arnulf, the schism of the 1130s constituted a crucial stage in the development of his personal world view. Following the examples of other members of his family, he had already set upon a dual career of ecclesiastical and royal service. He now firmly established himself as a member of the faction within the church that had supported the claims of Pope Innocent II. The influence of the young reformers in the party of Haimeric had strengthened his attitude toward the proper relationship between secular and spiritual responsibilities. The moral example of Bernard inspired many of his theological views. The paradigm by which Arnulf would test his future actions was essentially complete.

II.

The Search for Political Allegiance

Arnulf completed his formal education in 1136 and returned to his duties as archdeacon of Sées. An archdeacon was usually a member of the clergy, in deacon's orders but not an ordained priest. His primary responsibility was to serve as an administrative assistant to his bishop, handling, in many cases, those temporal duties with which ordained priests did not wish to deal. He might collect taxes from the secular estates that belonged to the bishopric, enforce discipline in the cathedral chapter, and preside over court cases involving corporal punishment.[1] Because of the secular nature of many of his duties, he was frequently viewed with scorn or cynicism. John of Salisbury once described archdeacons as clerics for whom "every road to salvation was closed."[2]

For many clerics, however—and Arnulf was certainly one of them—the post of archdeacon was a finishing school for those who aspired to episcopal office. Arnulf's archdeaconry at Sées was designed to acquaint him with the day-to-day functioning of a diocese. The prebend that accompanied the office of archdeacon financed Arnulf's studies in Paris and Italy. His contribution to the cause of Innocent II during the schism of the 1130s brought him to the attention of the church hierarchy. By 1136, the only element missing from his preparations to qualify for the office of bishop was a period of experience at the royal court, which would introduce him to the wider world in which clerics interacted with secular rulers.

The Anglo-Norman kings had traditionally relied upon the clergy for support. Over half of all bishops in the reigns of William I and his sons had been drawn from the circle of their own royal clerks, and at one point in the reign of Henry I as many as sixteen English sees were occupied by such curial bishops—men who had been trained at the royal court.[3] The pattern was even more obvious in Normandy. Of the eleven bishops confirmed by Henry I, ten had either gained their experience at the royal court or were related to other curial bishops.[4] Under normal circumstances, Arnulf would have sought to complete his training by gaining experience and recognition at the Anglo-Norman court. But 1136 was not a normal year. Henry I had died on December 1, 1135, leaving his kingdom with a disputed succession. There followed a nineteen-year period of disorder and civil war, and so long as it raged, Arnulf's future career hung in the balance, awaiting the outcome of a conflict between elective and hereditary monarchy.

The principle of hereditary monarchy seems to have developed through the acceptance of customary usage and may have been firmly accepted in France as early as the eleventh century.[5] Every French king, from Hugh Capet in 987 to Louis VII in 1179, designated his oldest surviving son as his heir. In most cases, the heir was actually crowned and participated in royal acts during the lifetime of his father, although such early associations in power were often precipitated by the king's illness or proposed departure on a dangerous expedition. Examples include the coronation of Robert II in 987 when his father was planning an invasion of Spain, the coronation of Philip I in 1059 before his father left for Normandy, and the coronation of Philip Augustus in 1179 when Louis VII was too ill to rule. French historians have generally seen the practice of anticipatory association as a sign that the hereditary tradition in France was not strong enough before the time of Philip Augustus to assure the automatic succession of the oldest son.[6] Nevertheless, there can be little doubt that Capetian kings inherited their thrones without opposition or the need to resort to formal election.

Anglo-Norman kings were more susceptible to challenges against hereditary monarchy because they had failed to establish such clear precedents. The early Norman dukes, from Rollo in the 920s to Robert I in 1035, had made it a practice to designate their sons as heirs and to associate them in the rule of the duchy, even when, as in the case of Richard I and William I, these sons were illegitimate. The only exception was Richard III, whose reign lasted only a year before passing to his brother Robert.[7] The invasion of England, however, disrupted the traditions of orderly succession. The claim of William I to the throne of England was, of course, based on a weak claim of heredity. Emma, the mother of Edward the Confessor, was the daughter of Richard I of Normandy and therefore the great-aunt of Duke William. Young Edgar the Atheling, grandson of Edmund Ironsides, had a better hereditary claim to the throne, although there was little likelihood of his pressing the point from his exile in Hungary. Harold Hardrada, king of Norway and successor to Cnut the Great, could also base a claim through Emma.[8] In the eyes of most of his contemporaries, William became king of England by right of conquest, not right of blood. William even gave tacit expression to the difference by associating his oldest son, Robert Curthose, in the rule of his hereditary duchy in 1080, while designating his second son, William Rufus, as his successor to the conquered land.[9]

Subsequent events did little to stabilize the hereditary nature of the English throne. When William Rufus was killed in a hunting accident in 1100, his younger brother Henry seized the English treasury and had himself crowned king in defiance of the hereditary rights of Robert Curthose. Henry then challenged Robert for possession of Normandy in 1106 and effectively disinherited not only Robert but also his legitimate heir, William Clito. Most historians credit Henry with considerable political acumen in thus restoring the unity of the Anglo-Norman empire created by his father.[10] Still, the precedents for an orderly hereditary succession had been shaken. When Henry's only legitimate son died in the sinking of the White Ship in December 1120, the problems of succession loomed even larger.

Henry attempted to secure the throne for his only remaining heir, the dowager-Empress Matilda, by forcing his barons and bishops to take an oath of loyalty to her on Christmas Day, 1126. The exact terms of that oath remain unknown; contemporary accounts shed little light on what actually happened. The Norman chroniclers were particularly taciturn. Orderic Vitalis mentioned it only as a justification of David of Scotland's later invasion of England. Robert of Torigni spoke of Matilda's return to England but not the oath. English records, too, tended to mention the oath only in passing. *The Anglo-Saxon Chronicle* stated that Henry "caused archbishops and bishops and abbots and earls and all the thegns that were there to swear to give England and Normandy after his death into the hand of his daughter Athelic [Matilda]." The *Gesta Stephani* told the story in more detail, but only to stress that an oath extracted by force was not valid.[11] The clearest description is to be found in William of Malmesbury:

> After much consideration and debate, he called into council all the nobles of England, along with the bishops and abbots, administered an oath and required that, if he should die without a male heir, they would at once receive his daughter Matilda, the former Empress, as their queen without any hesitation . . . since the succession ought to belong alone to her, both from the reigns of her grandfather, uncle, and father and from her maternal descent from many kings.[12]

No complete list of those who took the oath exists. William of Malmesbury gave only the names of William, archbishop of Canterbury; David, king of Scotland; Stephen, count of Mortain; Robert, earl of Gloucester; and Roger, bishop of Salisbury.[13] Some chroniclers seemed to suggest that the oath was administered only to English barons.[14] But in a kingdom in which most of the major lords, including the bishops of Normandy, held land on both sides of the channel, such a distinction would have been difficult, if not impossible, to maintain. Certainly several Norman bishops were at Woodstock for Henry's Christmas court in 1126. Among them were Geoffrey, archbishop of Rouen; Ouen, bishop of Evreux; and John, bishop of Lisieux.[15] Further, William of Malmesbury indicated that the bishop of Lisieux was one of the few who were privy to the plans to marry Matilda to Geoffrey of Anjou.[16] It is difficult to avoid the conclusion that at least some of the Norman episcopate had taken the vow to support Matilda. Nevertheless, at the death of Henry I, most of the Norman bishops and barons ignored or repudiated their obligations to support the daughter of Henry.

A few Norman castles, among which were Domfront, Argentan, Exmes, Ambrieres, Gorron, and Columbiers, immediately opened their gates to Matilda and Geoffrey. But at the same time an assembly of barons of Normandy sent word to Count Theobald of Blois that they were prepared to turn Normandy over to him. They had assembled at Lisieux to make their allegiance official when word arrived from England that Stephen of Blois, brother of Theobald and nephew of Henry I, had been elected as king by the people of London and anointed by the archbishop of Canterbury. Without further discussion, the Norman barons, too, acknowledged him.[17]

The Norman bishops were unanimous in their support of King Stephen. Stephen assembled a great council at his Easter court in 1136, one that was designed to demonstrate that he had the backing of magnates from every part of his kingdom. It was a crucial assembly; one modern historian has remarked, "If it was the anointing that had made him king, it was the Easter Court that showed that he *was* king, and accepted by his kingdom."[18] Archbishop Hugh of Rouen and four of his six suffragan bishops—Ouen of Evroux, Algar of Coutances, Richard of Avranches, and John of Sées—attended.[19] For the two who were missing, there could be several explanations. John of Lisieux never returned to England under the reign of Stephen, but there is no question of his loyalty to the king. He continued to function in his capacity as one of Normandy's chief administrators and may well have felt that his permanent presence in Normandy was required.[20] John was one of the last holdouts among the supporters of Stephen and did not surrender to Geoffrey of Anjou until shortly before his death in 1141.[21] Richard of Bayeux presents more of a problem. He had been consecrated just before the death of Henry I and may not have been willing to leave his new diocese so soon. But more important, he was the son of Robert of Gloucester, Matilda's half-brother and most ardent supporter.[22] Nevertheless, Richard was firmly in Stephen's camp by 1137, witnessing royal charters in both England and Normandy.[23]

The factors that determined the choices made by the clergy in this struggle were as often political as religious. The chroniclers would have had their readers believe that the Normans rebelled against Matilda because of her husband and the reputation his people had for cruelty and violence. Orderic Vitalis was particularly vehement on this point, describing their attacks on the church and other "unspeakable crimes."[24] But the quarrel between Normandy and its southern neighbors also had roots in the schism of 1130.[25] The house of Blois had supported Innocent II during that schism; the Angevins and Poitevans had often sided with Anacletus. Arnulf himself had attacked the Count of Poitiers in his *Invectiva*, calling him "a man addicted to pleasure, a human being of animal-like sensuality, incapable of attaining any measure of spirituality."[26] Now those same ecclesiastical differences strongly influenced the political preferences of the Norman and French clergy. Throughout the period of the civil war, the clerics who had served the cause of Innocent II aligned themselves with Stephen of Blois in his claim to the English throne. These same clerics almost unanimously opposed the pretensions of Geoffrey of Anjou. Peter the Venerable noted that the whole church of God regarded the count of Anjou as an enemy.[27] Bernard of Clairvaux called him "the hammer of goodness, an oppressor of the peace and of the liberty of the church."[28]

The choice was relatively simple for established bishops. A hostile monarch might make life uncomfortable for them, but they had no fear that he would be able to remove them from their sees. For a young aspirant to the bishopric, however, the choice carried much more serious consequences. The settlement of the Investiture Struggle had lessened the threat of lay control of episcopal elections, but, particularly in France and England, the monarch retained the right to confirm such elections and to invest the newly consecrated bishop with his temporal possessions. No candidate for a bishopric could realistically hope to gain his diocese without royal consent. Arnulf had three choices. He could follow the rest of the Norman clergy in their support of Stephen. He could support Matilda and her husband, Geoffrey of Anjou, hoping to receive some reward from them in Normandy. Or he could shift his loyalties southward and seek preferment at the French court, where he was already known and admired by the ecclesiastical advisors of the king. During the following years he would try all three solutions, each in its turn. Each brought him its own particular form of disillusionment.

At the outset of the civil war, Arnulf chose to be guided by the decision of the Norman bishops. The first record of his participation at a political level shows him firmly ensconced at the court of King Stephen. His name appeared in the record of a plea brought before the king's court at Westminster sometime between Christmas 1136 and March 1137. He was included among those who were "assisting and aiding" the prior of Holy Trinity in a case against the castellan of the Tower of London: Queen Matilda, Algar of Coutances, Roger the chancellor, William Martel the dapifer, several barons, and many of the citizens of London.[29]

Young Arnulf soon learned that the king whose court he frequented expected him to use his ecclesiastical position in the service of the crown. In 1139 the two claimants to the English throne brought their case before the pope at the Second Lateran Council. Matilda's spokesperson was Ulger, bishop of Angers from 1125 to 1148. Stephen's delegation consisted of Roger, bishop of Chester; Lupellus, a former clerk to the archbishop of Canterbury; and Arnulf. Although he was still only an archdeacon, Arnulf was chosen to argue against the claims of Matilda—surely a heady experience for a young cleric! The arguments may have been presented in a private session, for records of the Council do not include an account of the proceedings.[30] Arnulf's speech before the pope has been preserved only indirectly through a letter of Gilbert Foliot and the comments of John of Salisbury. Both accounts agreed that Arnulf charged Matilda with illegitimacy, basing his argument on the old story that Maud, the wife of Henry I, had been a nun before her marriage. Therefore, he concluded, the oath extracted by Henry was invalid because the Empress Matilda was not his legal heir. Further, according to Salisbury, Arnulf claimed that Henry had changed his mind on his deathbed and had released his barons from their oath of allegiance to Matilda.[31]

Gilbert Foliot's account ended there. There was no response, he said, from the other side. Salisbury, however, recorded an acrimonious response from Ulger:

> I marvel, Arnulf, at your presumption in attacking now he is dead the man whom you and your fathers and brothers and whole family worshipped as long as he was alive; the man who raised you and all your kindred from the dust. I would marvel at the shamelessness of your lies were it not that your whole race is garrulous and deserves to be held up as an example of sinful life and skill and effrontery in lying. In these arts you are conspicuous even among the Normans. Further, by treacherously accusing your dead lord of incest, you lift up your heel against your mother, the holy Roman church . . . for it was not a secret marriage contracted in the darkness dear to the works of men like you. . . . As for your statement that the king changed his mind, it is proved false by those who were present at the king's death.[32]

Salisbury's account was, of course, simply another attack on Arnulf's duplicity. Salisbury was not present at the hearing, as Gilbert Foliot had been, and he wrote his version some twenty years later. Ulger's purported response seems much more reflective of Salisbury's animosity than of the reasoned arguments of a wise and respected bishop.[33] Nevertheless, Arnulf's attack on the legitimacy of Matilda's birth had no real basis in fact. The question of whether the queen of Henry I had at one time taken the veil had arisen before their marriage, but Anselm, the venerated archbishop of Canterbury, had satisfactorily cleared her of the charges.[34]

Arnulf employed the charge of illegitimacy here in the same way that he had used rumor and innuendo against the supporters of the antipope Anacletus. Both arguments allowed him to denounce such sinful behavior and then use the teachings of the church as an indictment of political ambitions. Just as a rhetorical ploy had effectively destroyed the papal claims of Anacletus, so once again it worked against the regal claims of Matilda. Innocent II did not rule in favor of Stephen at the council itself but simply dismissed both sides. Later he expressed his support of Stephen by recognizing his occupation of England and Normandy, thereby settling the question of succession so far as the church was concerned. After 1139, Stephen's charters legitimately included the statement that his election had been confirmed by the pope.[35]

For Arnulf, however, the issue was not to be so easily resolved. In Normandy, the successes of Matilda and Geoffrey of Anjou continued despite papal disapproval. Angevin forces had attacked Lisieux in September 1136, and the Breton defenders of Lisieux set fire to the city to prevent its falling into Angevin hands.[36] John of Lisieux was caught in the middle of an ongoing political power struggle. After holding out for some time despite the destruction of his cathedral, the bishop surrendered the city and all the powers of the count of Lisieux to Geoffrey, count of Anjou, in April 1140.[37] John died shortly thereafter, a death, one chronicler suggested, brought on by exhaustion and despair over his inability to continue the fight against the Angevins.[38]

The chapter of Lisieux elected Arnulf to succeed his uncle as bishop, and Hugh, archbishop of Rouen, consecrated him in his office. Understandably, however, Geoffrey of Anjou objected to the elevation of the outspoken young cleric who had attacked his wife's legitimacy at the papal court. For two years and three months, Geoffrey refused to recognize Arnulf as bishop of Lisieux and held on to the temporal possessions of the diocese. The message he sent to Arnulf was clear: anyone who seeks ecclesiastical preferment must bend to political realities. And the political reality was that Geoffrey of Anjou ruled the diocese to which Arnulf aspired.

Much of what is known about the election of Arnulf comes not from Arnulf himself but from the correspondence of others. Bernard wrote to the pope in 1142, defending Arnulf's election and urging that he be consecrated despite Geoffrey's opposition:

> If you consider the person [i.e., Arnulf], he is your beloved son, in whom you have been well pleased; if you consider the affair itself, it was conducted with full holy orders and according to canonical liberty; if you consider the originator of the deed [i.e., Hugh, archbishop of Rouen], he is a holy and God-fearing man; if you consider the enemy of the deed [i.e., Geoffrey of Anjou], behold a man who has not placed his trust in God, a public foe of the church and an enemy of the cross of Christ.[39]

Peter the Venerable also petitioned the pope to recognize Arnulf's past contributions to the church by confirming his election:

> The clergy and people of Lisieux, as I have heard, when the church was devastated by the death of its bishop, unanimously elected Arnulf, the archdeacon of Sées, to be its priest and pastor, and they caused him to be consecrated according to ecclesiastical custom by the bishop of Rouen, who conducted the consecration according to canon law. The church chose him, I believe, and caused him to be consecrated, not only because he is a man of the best and unique witness among them, not only because he is well-known for his literary ability, not only because his wisdom and activity on your behalf has not gone unnoticed, but because he is your special son, and a disciple recognized by the Roman church from his youth.[40]

Pope Innocent did confirm the election, but Arnulf was forced to recognize the political ascendency of Geoffrey of Anjou. Loyalty to King Stephen, no matter how well-intentioned, could not gain him his bishopric. It was, in fact, becoming more and more obvious that Stephen intended to let Normandy go its own way. In his only visit to Normandy in 1137, the English king had been singularly ineffective in opposing Geoffrey. He had retired from the field after only a few months, seemingly willing to return to England and let the Angevins have their way in Normandy. Arnulf could not hope that Stephen would come to his defense. If he wanted to be bishop of Lisieux, he would have to give his political allegiance to Geoffrey of Anjou.

The lesson was a costly one. Arnulf paid a fine of over nine hundred pounds for the return of his temporal possessions.[41] The cost in terms of the loss of idealism must have been even higher. Arnulf seldom referred to the incident, except for a letter to Pope Celestine II in 1144. He apologized for not coming to Rome to extend his congratulations on the pope's elevation, pleading that his recent confirmation by Geoffrey had left him short of time, energy, and money.[42] His lack of energy may have stemmed from a certain disillusionment—a first realization that the paradigm by which he governed his life might not always offer the best solution to the types of problems that faced a bishop. He had assumed that it was not only possible but even desirable that a bishop should serve his monarch as well as the church. He was not fully prepared for the possibility that his monarch's interests might clash with the interests of his diocese.

In Normandy, the civil war was effectively over soon after Arnulf assumed his seat as bishop. The last opposition to Geoffrey faltered in 1144, when the city of Rouen surrendered and the archbishop of Rouen formally recognized him as duke. His acceptance by Norman bishops and barons, however, was more an acquiescence to the status quo than wholehearted support. The French king viewed the expansion of power by one of his more troublesome vassals with trepidation. France stopped short of intervention in Normandy, but French forces hovered near the borders, ready to step in if Geoffrey showed signs of weakness. In England the civil war raged on. Matilda had seemed to be on the verge of success in early 1141, only to be driven out later that year by Stephen's supporters. English barons and bishops vacillated; only ten of thirty-one prominent English barons remained consistently loyal to one side during the period from 1136 to 1153, and none of those ten were bishops.[43] The political activities of the new bishop of Lisieux have left little mark, perhaps because his political allegiances wavered. He witnessed no royal documents and took little part in the affairs of the world outside his own diocese. There is almost no charter evidence of Arnulf's activities as bishop before 1147, except for one instance in 1142 when he witnessed a charter issued by Hugh of Rouen confirming the establishment of canons regular at St. Lô.[44]

In Lisieux, however, Arnulf faced several problems. Besides the usual adjustments to a new responsibility, he had also inherited a diocese plagued by financial difficulties and greatly in need of reconstruction. During the seige of 1136, both the cathedral of Lisieux and its bishop's residence had been burned. Bishop John had done little to repair the damage. The task of restoring the episcopal buildings would fall to Arnulf, even though the fund for the fabric of the cathedral was severely depleted. In later years Arnulf revealed that there had been only seventeen marks in the cathedral treasury when he became bishop.[45]

Arnulf was also concerned with developments in the diocese of Sées, in which he had been educated. In 1144, his brother John of Sées died and was succeeded in the bishopric by a certain Gerard. Arnulf, along with Rotrou of Evroux, had been invited to supervise the election of a new bishop, but the cathedral chapter moved quickly to choose a candidate before their arrival.

Arnulf disapproved of the election on several grounds, partly because it had not followed canonical rules but more because of Gerard himself. John had made a strong effort to reform the chapter of Sées by filling it with canons regular to replace the secular clergy. Arnulf feared that if the new bishop were not a canon regular, the gains made by his brother would be lost.

The situation was complicated by the interference of Geoffrey of Anjou, who was by this time recognized as duke of Normandy. He opposed Gerard because he had not been consulted in the election. In an attack on Sées, Geoffrey caused widespread confiscations of church property, and his henchmen horribly mutilated the new bishop himself.[46] Arnulf's reaction reveals his continued mistrust of Geoffrey. Reluctant to support the duke's interference in ecclesiastical affairs but also unwilling to defend an unsuitable episcopal candidate, Arnulf delayed his protest against the election until Geoffrey and Gerard were reconciled in 1146. Then Arnulf wrote to Pope Eugenius III asking that the election be nullified. He did not argue against freedom of election but rather that the privilege of election would itself be threatened by a successful but unsuitable candidate.[47] The letter charged that the pope's decision had been swayed by sympathy for Gerard because of the injury done him by the Angevins. But even more serious, it accused Geoffrey of getting off too lightly:

> The count pleads his innocence for the rest of what was done, so much so that he has given up the perpetrators to the church court for punishment, as if the church should be grateful to him; and so that he will not be accused of working against the freedom of the church, he has turned over the administration of the universal church to our archbishop and even to the advice of bishops.[48]

The words are scornful, the attitude uncompromising.

Once again Bernard of Clairvaux lent his support to a cause espoused by Arnulf. In a letter to Eugenius, Bernard attacked Gerard and urged the pope not to be deceived by him:

> An evil man came to you. . . . Do not let the pitiable face of this man, his cheap habit, his humble expression, his downcast eyebrows, his humble words move you; even his tears, running down to his nose, as they say, are produced only to lie. . . . Therefore do not pay attention to his words, nor to the studied gestures of his body; ask about his deeds.[49]

Bernard also praised Arnulf because he had "spared neither purse nor body" to thwart the ambitions of Gerard and to preserve the legacy of his brother.[50] Arnulf even traveled to Rome to make his protest in person. Nevertheless, Gerard received his bishopric, and Geoffrey of Anjou received no reprimand for interfering with an episcopal election. Arnulf accepted the papal decision, although he later compared the consecration of Gerard as bishop of Sées to the act of a worker affixing a brass head to a golden statue while the master was absent.[51] Nor did Arnulf ever again publicly criticize Geoffrey. But the split between the bishop and the duke was both obvious and permanent.

During this same papal audience, Arnulf asked to be relieved of his bishopric so that he could enter a monastery. The request was rejected because, as Arnulf later admitted, he was still "of robust age and strong in body, and no physical defects had yet contributed to failings in knowledge and memory."[52] Was he reacting in despair to what was happening in Normandy, or was he moved by the example of predecessors such as Anselm, who had used the threat of resignation to put pressure on kings and popes? There is no certain answer. One can only assume that a fairly new bishop, still trying to organize his diocese, would not normally have been eager to leave it. But to a cleric influenced as Arnulf had been by an older generation of curial bishops, service to the church implied service to his monarch, and Arnulf had found no reception for his political loyalties at the Angevin court. Arnulf delayed his return to Normandy until the following spring and was present at Vézelay when Bernard preached the Second Crusade. He immediately took the cross.[53] The exact nature of Arnulf's role in the Crusade has been questioned. Apparently he held the position of papal legate in charge of the Anglo-Norman contingent; his counterpart in charge of the French forces was Bishop Godfrey of Langres.[54] Unfortunately, the two bishops were incompatible. John of Salisbury blamed the lack of discipline within the French army on quarrels between the two legates:

> Whatever one recommended the other decried; both were smooth-tongued, both extravagant, both (it is said) mischief-makers, devoid of the fear of God; butofthetwothebishopofLangreswasmorepruudentanndmmorehigh-mindded. Few if any haave brought moore harm on the Christtian army and whole community. Each had his own following who believed in him, and both received large sums of money from the sick and dying whom they attended and absolved in the name of the pope, claiming to be his representatives. Indeed they are believed to have accumulated more wealth during the expedition than they paid out of their own pockets.[55]

Arnulf himself never described his experiences in the Crusade, perhaps because he found them disappointing. His only reference to the journey appeared in an 1180 letter to Pope Alexander III, in which he indicated that "the holy father Pope Eugenius sent me against my will."[56] In light of Arnulf's desire to resign his bishopric, it may well be that the pope had suggested the Crusade as an alternative more suitable than taking monastic vows. The journey to the Holy Land provided more than an opportunity to extend the boundaries of Christendom. It offered Arnulf a chance to find a place for himself in the entourage of the king of France. Perhaps even more important, it exposed him to one more example of a cleric who dictated the opinions and deeds of a king. The influence that Abbot Suger wielded over Louis VII strengthened Arnulf's conviction that his paradigm of dual service to church and crown was valid.

Arnulf expended much effort in making himself indispensable to the French king. When Louis needed an ambassador to placate the irascible emperor of

Constantinople, he turned to Arnulf. After being kept waiting for two days at the imperial court without either food or bed, Arnulf put the king's case before the emperor with at least some degree of success:

> ... with wise and gentle eloquence the bishop would have rendered the emperor tractable if that serpent could have been charmed by anyone; but deaf and swollen with poison as an adder, he had changed from the man whom they had seen before. . . . Nevertheless, the bishop was insistent, and he prevailed in part; the army obtained a market, and a way of departure lay accessible to the pilgrims who had lost their goods. . . .[57]

When Louis needed money to continue the Crusade, Arnulf was there to provide it. Louis acknowledged this loan in a letter to Abbot Suger:

> May you know that Arnulf, bishop of Lisieux, in a time of great need, gave me as large a sum of gold and silver as he was able, whence I owe him 104 marks of silver. I therefore order that you, without any delay or excuse, repay these to him as soon as you receive these letters, so that he will have no cause to be disturbed or offended by me. Know you also that I have signed a pledge to him for this money.[58]

Arnulf also attempted to advise the king in matters of strategy, but in this area he was less successful. Throughout the journey Arnulf had found himself at odds with Godfrey of Langres over the goals of the Crusade. At Constantinople it was Godfrey who urged Louis VII to complete the destruction of Constantinople before moving on to Jerusalem. Arnulf questioned his motives:

> At this time we can attack the richest of the Christian cities and enrich ourselves, but in so doing we must kill and be killed. And so, if slaughtering Christians wipes out our sins, let us fight. And so, if harboring ambition does not sully our death, if on this journey it is as important to die for the sake of gaining money as it is to maintain our vow and our obedience to the supreme pontiff, then wealth is welcome; let us expose ourselves to danger without fear of death.[59]

Arnulf's sarcasm made its point this time, but at the Council of Acre in May 1148, King Louis was less inclined to accept moderate advice. Godfrey of Langres argued that the Crusade be continued at all costs, while Arnulf and the count of Flanders favored a quick end to a venture that was rapidly turning into a disaster.[60] Louis VII took the advice of those who favored an attack on Damascus. Arnulf apparently left the Crusade in disgust shortly after the failure of the siege, although John of Salisbury, by omitting Arnulf's name from the list of those who joined the general exodus, implied that he had departed sometime earlier.[61]

Despite the disappointments of the Crusade, Arnulf seems to have at least toyed with the idea of maintaining his allegiance to the king of France after his return to the Continent. In 1148 Suger employed him as an ambassador from the French throne to the Angevin court. War between Normandy and France seemed imminent, and this embassy was a last-ditch effort to avert it. Arnulf carried his message to Matilda and her son Henry. In a letter to Suger, Arnulf reported that the empress had offered him support and encouragement. She had immediately sent a message to the count of Anjou, urging him to enter into peace negotiations concerning Normandy.[62] Geoffrey, too, acknowledged Arnulf's diplomatic efforts, even though he did not promise an immediate end to hostilities.[63] On a broad political level, the embassy may have been successful. War between France and Normandy was at least temporarily avoided, although there is no evidence that Arnulf played a further role in the negotiations.

For Arnulf, however, his visit to the Angevin court had long-ranging significance. Ever since the death of Henry I, Arnulf had been searching for a political allegiance, one in which he could exercise the same moral influence that his uncle and his brother had displayed in the Anglo-Norman court. King Stephen had failed to conquer Normandy, and Arnulf had no hope of holding onto his bishopric on the Continent while serving an insular king. Geoffrey of Anjou held Normandy in his wife's name but could not command the undivided loyalty of the Norman barons. Geoffrey was still one of the hated Angevins, and his heavy-handed attempts to control the Norman clergy had made it impossible for a Norman bishop to support him wholeheartedly. The king of France might have been a viable alternative for Arnulf's loyalties, but in the 1140s Louis VII, guided by Bernard and Suger, had no real need for more ecclesiastical advisors. During this entire period, Arnulf had been an almost apolitical bishop, not by his own choice but because the secular world offered him no outlet for his political ambitions.

At the court of Matilda and her son, Arnulf found the political role he had been seeking. Matilda had always claimed the hereditary rights of her son Henry, along with her own, to the throne of England.[64] Perhaps as early as 1144, Geoffrey had associated his son in the administration of Normandy.[65] By 1147, Henry was issuing charters in his own name as son of the duke.[66] It was clear that Geoffrey and Matilda intended Henry as their joint heir. Arnulf must have seen in him obvious parallels to the young Louis of France, whom Abbot Suger had taken under his protection in 1119, and to Henry I of England, whom Arnulf's uncle John had guided through the difficult first years of his reign. Here at last was a potential monarch who could use Arnulf's assistance. Young Henry was in need of experienced advisors and was still malleable to the suggestions of loyal bishops. Arnulf was in an enviable position as a diplomatic envoy to Henry's court, and he took immediate steps to make himself indispensable to the young heir apparent.

Ironically, Arnulf, who had argued against the hereditary right of Matilda in 1139, found it necessary ten years later to argue in favor of the hereditary claims of her son. As early as the summer of 1149, Arnulf began petitioning for recognition of Henry in England. In a letter to the newly elected bishop of Lincoln, Robert de Chesney, he asked Robert to "favor our duke, to whom the right of hereditary succession to the throne of your kingdom ought to belong, insofar as you are able to do so, saving your honor."[67] The question of when Henry actually became duke of Normandy has long been the subject of debate, although most scholars now agree that he did not assume the title until 1150.[68] Frank Barlow, however, adduced this letter as proof that Henry was already recognized as duke in 1149.[69] It seems more likely that Arnulf was simply indulging his habit of stating as fact what he hoped would come about. With his own hopes for secular preferment tied to the royal aspirations of Henry, Arnulf probably gave him the title of duke prematurely.

Events proved Arnulf's presumption correct. By 1150 Henry was duke of Normandy; in 1151 he succeeded to his father's title of count of Anjou. For the next four years Arnulf was seldom far from the side of Duke Henry. Charter evidence proves that he traveled with Henry throughout his continental possessions, witnessing documents as Henry reconfirmed the rights of his people and clergy. Their journeys took them to Rouen, Fontevrault, Perigueux, Le Mans, Torigni, Argentan, Lisieux, and Tours.[70] Lisieux became a center of Angevin support. It was there that Henry first intended to call his supporters together on September 14, 1151, to plan an invasion of England, and there that he introduced Eleanor of Aquitaine as his wife when the nobles finally met after Easter 1152.[71] When King Stephen died on October 25, 1154, Lisieux was the point from which Henry and his entourage, including Arnulf, set out to claim the throne of England.[72]

Nor did Arnulf's efforts go unrewarded. Some time between 1151 and 1153, Henry granted Arnulf the revenues from the fairs at Touques and Nonant, a grant that would increase both the wealth of his diocese and his personal influence.[73] During the same period Henry appointed him as chief justiciar in Normandy.[74] This was a major step for Arnulf, for he now held under the young duke a position very similar to the one that his uncle had occupied under Henry I. Arnulf had been raised within the church to believe that members of the clergy had a dual responsibility, to serve not only as the head of a spiritual community but also as the moral conscience of the secular ruler. Arnulf's exemplars had fulfilled that dual function—the bishops John of Lisieux and John of Sées under Henry I, Abbot Suger and Bernard of Clairvaux under Louis VII. Arnulf thus assumed under Duke Henry what he viewed as the proper province of a bishop. He would serve both church and monarch, contributing his moral guidance to both and ensuring the proper cooperation of the realms of God and king. But this part of the paradigm would be more difficult to accomplish than Arnulf realized in 1154.

III.

The Bishop as Baron

Arnulf would have been a wealthy man and a powerful secular lord even if he had not established a political allegiance to Henry II. The diocese to which he was elected in 1141 was rich in temporal possessions, and his ecclesiastical office carried with it the title of count of Lisieux. By attaching himself to the new ruler of the Angevin empire, he created an opportunity for even greater activity in the secular world. Henry repaid his service with grants of land and revenues in both Normandy and England. The office of justiciar, to which Arnulf had been appointed while Henry was duke of Normandy, acquired additional importance when Henry became king of England. As Henry established his position among the secular and spiritual rulers of Christendom, he frequently needed the services of a cooperative bishop. As count of Lisieux, English baron, chief justiciar in Normandy, and special envoy to the pope, Arnulf would find many opportunities to test the assumption implicit in his paradigm that the exercise of secular power need not detract from the spiritual influence of a bishop.

The bishoprics of Normandy had traditionally been treated as ecclesiastical baronies. The early rulers of Normandy had recognized the advantages of working hand in hand with the church and strengthened their control by assuming the right to appoint the archbishop of Rouen and his suffragan bishops. One device used by the Norman dukes to manage their land was the creation of *comtés*. The dukes granted these border territories the privilege of self-government, while the counts who held the lands assumed responsibility for their defense. Under Duke Richard II (996–1026), two bishoprics had already become *comtés*. Archbishop Robert of Rouen, the brother of Richard II, held the *comté* of Evreux, and Bishop Hugh of Bayeux, his cousin, held the *comté* of Ivry.[1] Other ducal relatives achieved similar status in the following years. In 1049 Duke William II appointed his half-brother Odo as bishop of Bayeux and a second cousin, Hugh, as bishop and *comté* of Lisieux. John, the younger brother of this Hugh of Lisieux, became bishop of Avranches in 1061 and then succeeded to the archbishopric of Rouen in 1068.[2] The dukes of Normandy saw these appointments as a convenient way to assert their authority over the territorial churches while keeping strategic locations under family control.[3] But for the Norman church they had far-reaching effects. Land given to a bishop remained, in most cases, a part of the temporal possessions of the diocese in succeeding generations. The diocese of Lisieux, for example, was termed an *évêché-comté*, or ecclesiastical barony, until its dissolution in 1790.[4]

Although records from eleventh-century Normandy are sparse, it is possible in a few cases to determine the extent and value of such episcopal land holdings. At Bayeux, for example, the bishop compiled a list of the lands of his bishopric in 1035 to prevent them from being claimed by the powerful lay nobility.[5] The possessions of Bayeux were plundered after the imprisonment of Bishop Odo in 1083 but were restored by King Henry I, who ordered a full inquest of the revenues and ancient possessions of the bishopric.[6] If this Bayeux Inquest of 1133 may be used as a guide for Norman bishoprics in general, a bishop who held temporal lands and enfeoffed them to his followers was entitled to extract from each of his fees an aid of twenty shillings any time he went on crusade, traveled to the papal see, or needed to repair his cathedral or episcopal buildings. At the death of a tenant he was entitled to a relief of fifteen pounds per fee. In addition he held the usual feudal rights to rents, aids, escheats, and wardships.[7] Such temporal rights were an important source of episcopal income.

Unfortunately for historians of the diocese of Lisieux, no similar records of its temporal possessions before 1172 have survived. The lack of documentation may, however, be an indication that the diocese, unlike Bayeux, seldom suffered from attempts to plunder its riches. Orderic Vitalis, who wrote his monumental *Ecclesiastical History* at his monastery of St. Evroult within the diocese of Lisieux, was more interested in the character of his bishops than in their land holdings, but his comments give brief glimpses of the abundance of wealth they controlled. He commended Hugh d'Eu, bishop from 1050 to 1077, for the construction of the cathedral of the diocese, because he had "spared no pains to adorn it, dedicate it with all ceremony, provide it with clergy, and enrich it abundantly with all manner of vessels for the service of God."[8] Orderic's description of Gilbert Maminot, bishop from 1077 to 1101, although less than flattering, portrayed him as a wealthy and generous man who "gave alms generously to the poor, and had a high reputation for an open-handedness and hospitality appropriate to his station."[9]

In the early twelfth century, Lisieux suffered from a series of totally unqualified bishops imposed upon it by Ranulf Flambard, whom some historians have called the "evil genius" of William Rufus.[10] Gilbert Maminot was succeeded first by Flambard's brother William, whom Orderic Vitalis described as "almost illiterate," and then by Flambard's twelve-year-old son, Thomas.[11] It was obvious to his contemporaries that Flambard, deprived of the revenues of his bishopric of Durham by King Henry I, was recouping his losses by despoiling the conveniently vacant and wealthy see of Lisieux. The appointments caused a scandal; Bishop Ivo of Chartres denounced the appointments in letters to Pope Paschal II; William, archbishop of Rouen; Gilbert, bishop of Evreux; and Robert, count of Meulan.[12] Orderic lamented the incident: "So Lisieux was without a bishop for about five years, and the Lord's flock, deprived of a worthy shepherd, was ravaged by wolves. . . ." [13] When Flambard regained his position at Durham, he abandoned his efforts to divert the revenues of Lisieux. Henry I appointed John, archdeacon of Sées, as bishop of Lisieux in 1107. John was an efficient and dedicated prelate, and Lisieux seems to have recovered its financial stability under his guidance. Despite the burning of the town and its cathedral during the civil war, John left to his successor an extremely valuable temporal estate.

With the episcopacy of Arnulf, conjecture gives way to certainty. For the first time, it becomes possible to determine the extent of the temporalities of the bishopric. In 1172, Henry II commissioned an inquest into the holdings of knight's fees in Normandy. Those charged with conducting the inquest were to determine the number of knight's fees each tenant-in-chief of the king held, the number of fees each had enfeoffed for his own service, and any recent changes in these holdings.[14] The resultant list was similar to, and in many respects completed, the *Cartae Baronum* that had produced a similar record of military fees in England in 1166.[15]

The Inquest of 1172 reveals much about the workings of feudal society in Normandy and thus goes far to identify Arnulf's secular role within his diocese. It began with a listing of the major ecclesiastical and baronial holdings:

> The Bishop of Avranches holds 5 knight's fees for Avranches and 5 for the honor of Saint Philebert.
>
> The Bishop of Coutances has 5 knight's fees, and in his own service, 18 more.
>
> The Bishop of Bayeux holds 20 knight's fees, and in his own service, 120.
>
> The Bishop of Sées has 6 knight's fees.
>
> The Bishop of Lisieux has 20 knight's fees, and in his own service, 30 and 3 parts; and beyond that, he has 10 knight's fees in the banlieu of Lisieux who serve as a guard for the city unless they are summoned as part of the whole body of vassals, and then they go at the expense of the bishop. He also has 2 knight's fees as a gift from King Henry, son of Matilda, namely in Le Mesnil-Eudes and Courbéspine.
>
> The Archbishop of Rouen sends no knights.
>
> The Bishop of Evreux sends no knights to the duke.
>
> The Abbot of Fécamp has 10 knight's fees and 13 and 3 parts in his own service.
>
> The Abbot of Bernay [Lisieux] has 2 knight's fees.
>
> The Abbot of Jumièges has 3 knight's fees; and in his own service 1 knight's fee in Esmaleville, which Hugh Bigod withholds from him.
>
> The abbot of St. Catherine du Mont in Rouen has 2 knight's fees and four parts of one fee.
>
> The Abbot of Mont St. Michel has 6 knight's fees in Avranches and Coutances, and 1 knight's fee in Bayeux, who serve as vavasors or subtenants unless they serve in the army.
>
> The Abbot of Caen has one knight's fee from the fief of Tallebois.
>
> The Abbot of St. Evroult [Lisieux] has 2 knight's fees, and besides this the fief of Roger Golafre, which William Paganus holds from Roger in bail, whence he ejected the servants of the abbot.

The Abbot of St. Wandrille has 4 knight's fees.

The Abbot of St. Ouen de Rouen has 6 knight's fees, and in his own service, 14 more.

The Abbot of St. Denis has 1 knight's fee in the fief of Bonaville.

The Abbess of Montivilliers [Lisieux] has 3 knight's fees, and in her own service, 5 and three parts of a fee.

Count John has 20 knight's fees, and in his own service, 111 more.

The Count of Meulan has 15 knight's fees, and in his own service, 63 and a half.

The Count of Chester has 10 knight's fees from St. Severus and Brichesarde; and in his own service 51 and a half, plus a fourth and an eighth.

The entry for the bishop of Lisieux was the longest individual account given. A comparison of Arnulf's holdings with those of the other barons of Normandy provides some interesting conclusions about his position within the secular hierarchy. First, these figures confirm his statement that possession of his temporalities cost him over nine hundred pounds. Excluding the two fees given to Arnulf by Henry II, the diocese held sixty and one-third military fees. At the standard rate of fifteen pounds per fee, his relief when he succeeded to the diocese would have amounted to 905 pounds. Only three lords owed as many as twenty military fees in the service of the duke—Arnulf, John of Ponthieu, and the bishop of Bayeux. Among all those who held fees in personal service as well as of the duke, Arnulf ranked seventh. It is also noticeable that he was the only individual for whom a recent gift from King Henry was included. There can be no doubt about his wealth and power in Normandy.

This survey offers a general guide to the financial world of the bishopric, but it fails to provide details. Because the Inquest of 1172 was little more than a tally, it gave no description of the lands held and assigned no values. Further, no records from the Norman Exchequer have survived for the period before 1180 to fill in the picture. It is possible, however, to supplement this bare outline from somewhat later records. When Philip Augustus assumed control of Normandy in 1205, he authorized a new survey of military fees. His list of those who owed him military service from the diocese of Lisieux totaled twenty fees, evidence that the fee structure had not changed.[16] The twenty knight's fees held by the bishop of Lisieux were distributed among sixteen feudal manors that were enfeoffed to subtenants. Their distribution shows that the bishop controlled the lands surrounding the banlieu of Lisieux, along with other estates scattered throughout his diocese (map 1). The manors that can still be identified with existing Norman villages include Piencourt, 1 fee, held by John de Asneriis; Mesnil Godomen, 2.5 fees, held by a king's man; Fonte-le-Lovet, 1 fee, held by John Lovet; Espreville, 1 fee, held by John de Espreville; Bonneville-le-Lovet, 1 fee, held by Geoffrey Lovet; Glos, 2.5 fees, held by Hugh Tirel; Cortonne-la-Meurdrac, 2.5 fees, held by Hugh Tirel; Malloc, 1 fee, held by William de Malloc; Mesnil-Eudes, 1 fee; Houblonniere, 1 fee; and Gonneville, 1 fee. Those whose locations are no longer evident include the land of Reginald Chaperon, 1/2 fee; la Coeria, 1/2 fee, held by

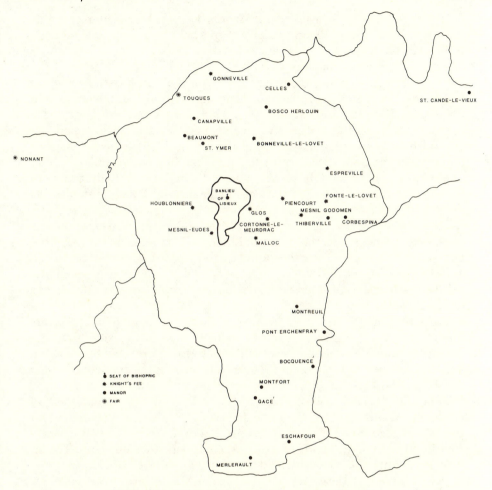

1. Holdings of the Bishop of Lisieux in His Diocese

Oliver de Albigny; the castellany of Gallon, 1/2 fee; Margileium, 1 fee; la Boissiere, 1 fee; and unidentified land, 1 fee, held by Henry de Quesneto, William de Granville, and Matthew de Favo.

Arnulf's temporal holdings as count of Lisieux comprised seven large baronies. Primary among them was the Barony of Gacé, assigned to the bishops of Lisieux by Duke Richard II beginning in 1015. It included five major fiefs—Gacé, Bocquencé, Echaufour, Merlerault, and Montreuil—all located in the southern end of the diocese. By Arnulf's time, the barony had apparently expanded to the entire archdeaconry of Gacé. Arnulf claimed temporal jurisdiction over the lands of St. Evroult, such as Pont Erchenfray and the priory of Montfort, and donated the church of Saint-Pierre-de-Gacé to the canons of St. Victor in Paris without opposition.[17] Duke Richard II also presented the diocese with the barony of Touques, located at the mouth of the Touques River, a holding that may have contained as many as forty-seven separate fiefs. His charter specified that the bishop of Lisieux held possession of town, port, and forest, with rights over the churches and high justice. When Henry II granted permission for the bishop to hold an annual fair in the town on July 22, the feast day of St. Maria Magdalena, he simply topped off Arnulf's financial control of this area.[18]

The dates at which the other baronies were added to the *comté* of Lisieux are less certain, but the bishops claimed to have held them from "time immemorial." Bonneville-le-Lovet, near Pont-l'Évêque on the Colonne River, supplied the diocese with high revenues from its mills.[19] Canapville, located in the deanery of Vimoutiers, had been detached from the barony of Gacé early in its history.[20] Glos contained seven parishes, along with the valuable fiefs of Canteloup, Courtonne, and St.-Germaine-de-Livet.[21] Nonant contained four parishes located in the diocese of Bayeux and exempted from that bishop's control; all were in the hands of the bishop of Lisieux by 1050.[22] And Thiberville, near Fonte-le-Lovet, contained the fiefs of l'Epervier and l'Hôtellerie.[23]

Determination of the value of these holdings is ultimately an insoluble problem. Total income from the temporalities depended on several variables, including the death rate, the frequency with which aids were demanded, and even the productivity of the land from year to year. Besides the periodic death reliefs and feudal aids, the bishop was entitled to draw rents and tithes from the land he had enfeoffed to the laity. These tithes were imposed upon crops such as corn, wine, flax, fruit, and other types of foodstuffs.[24] No estimate of payments is possible for the twelfth century, but some idea of their scope and nature can be gained from a later comparison. The chapter of the cathedral of Lisieux imposed small rents on seventy-four houses located in the village and banlieu of Lisieux. In 1321, the bishop's income from these properties totaled £175.2s.2d., and included rents in kind of 150 eggs, 52 and 1/3 (!) capons, 3 hens, 1 goose, 36 bushels of cheese, and 18 bushels of oats.[25] Another tantalizing hint of the extent of the bishop's financial influence comes from a fragment of the record of the Norman Exchequer of 1180. It shows a tithe of seven pigs paid to the bishop of Lisieux from the *porcaria* of Les Essarts in the forest of Lillebonne, north of the mouth of the Seine.[26]

Beyond these bits and pieces, no records of Arnulf's personal wealth or land holdings have survived. Some idea of the relative value of the diocese, however, may be gained from a statement made by Arnulf's successor. When Ralph de Varneville succeeded Arnulf as bishop of Lisieux in 1182, he is reported to have said that the loss of his office as chancellor of England had been fairly compensated for by the inheritance of great wealth.[27] The temporal assets of the bishop were vast and varied. But the most important aspect of the bishop's position as count of Lisieux was the personal nature of his lordship.

Arnulf's tenants inhabited the hilly but fertile lands through which he had traveled since childhood. Local Norman names, such as de Asneris, Lovet, Tirel, d'Aubigni, Caisneto, and Granville, figured prominently among Arnulf's friends and ecclesiastical associates. Several of the men who held fiefs from the diocese in 1205 were the sons of men who had signed Arnulf's charters a generation earlier. Along the Rue de Char, houses that owed their rents to the chapter of the cathedral were inhabited by people who worshiped in that catheddral. When a tenant delivered a rent of one goose, the chances were good that Arnulf not only knew the tenant personally but perhaps even knew the goose. Within the lands of Lisieux, it was possible for Arnulf to live up to part of the paradigm he had adopted for himself as bishop: "paying attention both to the holiness of the office and the power of the honor, from the one I hoped to discover holiness for myself, from the other to attain magnificence."[28]

Across the channel, Arnulf's situation was much different. At one time the bishops of Lisieux had been considered large landowners in England. Domesday Book listed Gilbert Maminot (1077–1101) as the holder of over thirty manors located in twelve English shires. Gilbert, companion and personal physician to William the Conqueror, began to accumulate properties even before his consecration as bishop, for in some Domesday entries he was listed under his own name as a tenant of Odo of Bayeux. The other entries specified that the manors were held in chief by the bishop of Lisieux, a designation indicating that the lands were ecclesiastical rather than personal property. Within a few years of the Domesday survey, however, almost all of these properties had been alienated. Some lands held of the bishop of Bayeux were lost when Odo fell from favor, some were repossessed by the king, and others passed into lay hands as part of Gilbert's personal estate. By the time Arnulf succeeded to the diocese, few English properties remained in the bishop's possession. Arnulf held one piece of property near Knaresborough in York, for which he owed a scutage of one hundred shillings in 1161–1162, the equivalent, apparently, of one knight's fee.[29] He also held the manor of Kingston Deverill in Wiltshire in joint custody with his canons. This manor had the longest continuous history as a property of the bishop of Lisieux. A writ of King Henry III, dated June 18, 1230, declared that those who were renting the land could not treat it as heritable property because it belonged to the bishop of Lisieux.[30]

Just as Henry II had rewarded Arnulf with fairs and knight's fees in Normandy, so he granted him additional holdings in England. The chapelry of Bosham and its manors of Thorney and Farington comprised an ancient and valuable holding in Sussex. Originally Edward the Confessor had given the fief of Bosham to his Norman chaplain, Osbern. When Osbern became bishop of Exeter, the property was attached to that diocese.[31] In 1154, Robert, the bishop of Exeter, had been assessed £16.13s.4d. for his *servitium debitum* of twenty knight's fees.[32] Sometime between the coronation and Michaelmas 1156, however, Bishop Robert had angered Henry II by taking a plea to the pope. For his punishment, Henry took Bosham away from him and presented it to Arnulf for an assessment of £7.10s. for seven and a half knight's fees.[33] From then on the chapelry was charged a fixed assessment of ten pounds for seven and a half knight's fees, a sum that was regularly pardoned.[34] Arnulf employed a proctor to manage the estate, pay out the customary alms to the Abbey of Godstow, and send the rest of the proceeds to Normandy.[35]

The Pipe Rolls reveal little more about Arnulf's land holdings, but they do clarify his standing within the English baronage. Arnulf's total English responsibility for eight and a half knight's fees was not large as military fiefs went in England. It could not compare, for example, with the 79 knight's fees of William de Ferariis, or the 97 fees of the Count of Essex, or the incredible 215 fees held by Reginald of Cornwall.[36] It was enough, however, to qualify him as an English baron, and Henry II specifically recognized him as such in 1159 and 1170.[37] Nor were his financial responsibilities very great. His lands in Wiltshire were probably held in frankalmoin; the Pipe Rolls show only one small general assessment of 5s.5d., which was then pardoned by king's writ.[38] His land in Yorkshire was part of the *terrae datae*, i.e., lands given by the king and no longer accountable to the sheriff.[39]

Arnulf's name appears more frequently in the rolls for Hampshire because the manor of Farington in Neatham Hundred was attached to the chapelry of Bosham.[40] In 1159–1160, Arnulf was amerced seven shillings for *murdrum*, a fine levied on an entire hundred when a secret murder had been committed.[41] The amercement was pardoned, however, because of Arnulf's position as a member of the king's court.[42] Similarly during the period between 1166 and 1170, the accounts of the sheriff of Hampshire showed that Arnulf owed one mark for a fine imposed by the Court of Regard on the manor of Farington. This court handled pleas concerning infractions of the forest law—cutting wood, poaching, collecting honey, selling bark, allowing farm animals to stray, assarting new clearings from the forest, or the running of unlawed dogs in the forest.[43] None seems likely to have been a crime of which the bishop of Lisieux would have been guilty. It is probable that the fine resulted from the behavior of an active and ambitious estate manager, for whose actions Arnulf was legally responsible. Still, the matter was carried on the sheriff's books until 1170, when once again Arnulf was exempted from payment.[44]

More important to Arnulf's financial interests in England were the lands held by monasteries within his diocese. The period of the Norman domination of England had corresponded to a time of monastic resurgence in Normandy, as many cross-channel lords endowed Norman monasteries with gifts of English manors. Several monasteries within the diocese of Lisieux profited from this impulse. The Abbey of St. Evroult, home of Orderic Vitalis, received Rowell, in Gloucestershire, from William the Conqueror himself, along with gifts of land from Count Roger of Mortain, Earl Roger of Shrewsbury, Hugh de Grantmesnil, Earl Hugh of Chester, and many others.[45] William also favored Bernay, founded in 1008 by Judith, wife of Richard IV, Duke of Normandy, by presenting it with lands at Creeting in Suffolk.[46] The great lords of Normandy followed the royal example. Cormeilles, founded shortly before the Conquest by William Fitz Osbern, received many of his manors as a gift from his son and heir. The most prominent of these was Newent, where Earl William was buried.[47] Grestain, founded in 1050 by Herluin de Conteville, second husband of the mother of William the Conqueror, profited enormously, receiving lands from both his sons, Bishop Odo of Bayeux and Count Robert of Mortain.

Few Norman monasteries established real conventual priories on the lands they were granted. English manors were regarded as profit-making endowments; they were often managed by just one or two monks who acted as bailiffs for the Norman abbots.[48] The interest of a Norman bishop in these cross-channel possessions was limited to a proprietary one. Matters of discipline or administration came under the control of the local English bishop or the king's agent. The English manors remitted a fixed payment to the mother house each year, a sum that could then be tithed by the bishop of the Norman diocese. These payments, or *apports*, were sometimes quite high. Although no figures are available from Arnulf's time, records show that in the thirteenth century the Abbey of Cormeilles received £40 a year from Newent, Grestain received £100 from Wilmington, and St. Evroult received £166.13.4 from Ware.[49] Some idea of the total value of these holdings can be derived from the records of Archbishop Eudes of Rouen (1248–1276). During his visitation to the diocese of Lisieux in 1249, he found that the combined tithable incomes of twelve monastic institutions there amounted to £13,880.[50]

The most noticeable difference between Arnulf's positions as count of Lisieux and as an English baron was the lack of personal influence over his English possessions. He was very seldom in England, and when he did cross the channel, his activities were centered at the royal court. There are no records to show that he ever visited the English lands from which he collected the revenues or that he knew any of the people who lived on his lands, except for a certain William, the vicar of Farington, whom Arnulf professed to have appointed.[51] A Norman bishop had little opportunity in England to combine the holiness of his ecclesiastical office with the magnificence of secular power. In England he was a magnate and a member of the royal court, but the king did not expect him to exercise his secular or episcopal rank in anything but a symbolic fashion.

Neither a bishop's holiness nor his magnificence interested the young King Henry II during the early years of his reign. He was more concerned about establishing royal power, proof of his legitimacy as king, and control over the barons who had grown independent and ambitious during nineteen years of civil war and anarchy in England. Civil and judicial administration had virtually ceased to function. England bristled with unauthorized castles. Mercenaries hired by recalcitrant supporters of King Stephen still held various outposts. Land titles were confused. Some fiefs were claimed by two lords, others by none. To achieve the reorganization the country so desperately needed, Henry moved to centralize his power. In effect, Henry was setting into motion a paradigm shift in which the very nature of kingship would be redefined. And he chose as his instruments a cadre of young supporters who would be willing to work with him. Among them were laity and clerics, Normans and Anglo-Saxons, supporters of Stephen and supporters of Matilda, barons and commoners. Despite their differences, however, they shared the very characteristics that were necessary to encourage a paradigm shift: youth, loyalty to a new monarch, personal ambition, and education.

During the crucial first three months of his reign, Henry was almost constantly in the saddle, passing from London to Oxford, Silverton, Northampton, Peterborough, Ramsey, Thorney, Spalding, Lincoln, York, Scarborough, Nottingham, Burton upon Trent, Alrewas, and Radmore. Attending him and witnessing his charters were the archbishops of Canterbury and York, along with the bishops of Bayeux, Winchester, Chichester, Ely, Evreux, London, Lincoln, Durham, Carlisle, Chester, and Lisieux. Bishops played an important role in Henry's new court because, besides their qualifications of knowledge and loyalty, they lent an air of legitimacy to the reign. Henry needed his bishops for their authority, not for their spiritual guidance.

That becomes increasingly clear to anyone examining the charters issued by Henry from December 19, 1154, to March 27, 1155. Charter evidence, of course, may be misleading. First, one can never assume that all charters from a particular period have come to light. The most one can hope is that those documents that have survived the vicissitudes of fire, time, mildew, warfare, and human carelessness are fairly representative of the whole. Second, the preservation of twelfth-century documents has been skewed in favor of ecclesiastical interests. Particularly in Normandy, the archives contain almost exclusively monastic cartularies; no public records exist from earlier than 1180. Even so, it is possible to draw some preliminary conclusions by noticing what the extant documents do *not* show.

There is no discernible pattern of testimony that would indicate that the new king was using his bishops only to assist him with church-related matters. Of forty-eight charters known to have been issued in this period, thirty-six dealt with ecclesiastical affairs, while twelve were purely secular in content.[52] Historians have sometimes assumed that witnesses to a charter or writ were those who had a particular interest in its content.[53] The early charters of Henry II, however, do not support this contention. Most charters were randomly signed by both bishops and barons, following what seems to have been Henry's general practice of drawing his witnesses from those who happened to be present at the time. An examination of the witness lists reveals both a secular appointment witnessed by five bishops and an ecclesiastical grant witnessed only by secular officials.[54] The only consistent policy within the charters was that the signatures of archbishops and bishops took precedence over those of barons and members of the king's household.

The charters attested by Arnulf support these general observations. His name appears as a witness on eighteen charters. Five of them were purely secular—recognitions of the rights of the cities of Lincoln and Essex and three restorations of lost titles and properties in England, to none of which Arnulf had any property-based ties. Seven dealt with church affairs in England, including grants to the bishops of Lincoln and Winchester. Six concerned abbeys located in Normandy, although none were in his own diocese. Two others dealing with the Norman church, however, did not bear his signature. For five of the charters, Arnulf was the first or primary witness; in the others he took second place to an English bishop or to Philip of Bayeux, who preceded him in wealth and date of confirmation as bishop. There are thus few patterns to explain Arnulf's position at the court. Henry may well have regarded Arnulf merely as a tool—someone to be used when convenient but not a vital element in the administration.

Arnulf quickly became aware of the limitations to effective action, as well as the temptations, faced by a cleric in the service of the king. When Thomas Becket received the office of chancellor in 1155, Arnulf wrote him a congratulatory letter, but he included a caution that the applause and flattery so available at court could "pass more swiftly than they come."[55] Heeding his own warning, Arnulf returned to Normandy shortly after the Great Council of London, held on March 27, 1155. There he hoped once again to be able to combine his two roles as bishop and as a servant of the king. During the period before Henry's coronation, Arnulf had served him as justiciar in Normandy. He now returned to that office.

The office of chief justiciar had its inception during the reign of Henry I.[56] At one time historians assumed that the chief justiciar was the equivalent of a regent, acting for the king in one part of his kingdom while the king attended to matters across the channel.[57] More recently Francis West has demonstrated that the seneschal of Normandy was the royal official who held viceregal power in the absence of the king.[58] As justiciar, Arnulf could act for the king, it is true, but only in certain circumstances. He could preside over an assize and determine what taxes were due, but he could not assign new taxes. He could decide between rival claimants to a property, but he could not grant land without the authority of the king. He had little control over matters concerning the ban or hostages; these were the concerns of the senechal and the constable.[59] He was for the most part simply an administrator. He held office at the pleasure of the king; his title was neither hereditary nor feudal. Thus the king retained control over his actions and could dismiss him at will. In Normandy, the title of seneschal was officially held by Robert de Neubourg until his retirement to a monastery in 1159.[60] He was, however, always paired with a bishop who acted as justiciar—a clue, perhaps, to one of the differences between Norman and English administration. Arnulf fulfilled the role of justiciar until 1157; then he was replaced by Rotrou, bishop of Evreux.[61]

Records of several cases handled by Arnulf during this period have survived. The most specific incident in which Arnulf acted as justiciar for the king occurred in 1155 at Domfront. The abbot of Mont St. Michel and William of St. John disagreed over the location of a trial by battle, which was planned to settle a dispute between them. The case was brought before the assize being held by Arnulf and Robert de Neubourg. The judgment of the court affirmed the right of Norman barons to insist that trials by battle be held at their chief residences, even if such a location was inconvenient to the other party.[62] Although the litigants in this particular case happened to be clerics, the decision profoundly affected the lay lords of Normandy. It seems clear that Arnulf was acting in a purely secular capacity as the king's justiciar.

Arnulf also contributed his opinion to cases that touched the conflicting interests of laity and ecclesiastics. Robert de Neubourg presided over the assize held at Caen in 1157, with Arnulf acting as justiciar. At this assize, the abbot of Mont St. Michel won a judgment against a penitent who tried to attach conditions to a gift. The court ruled that once an endowment was given to an abbey, the giver retained no rights except prayers.[63] On another occasion Robert and Arnulf, both titled justiciars, issued a writ in their own names, ordering surety to be given by Robert of Thaon for the restitution of tithes and lands to the Abbey of Savigny. At the same time they placed Robert's brothers under the king's ban.[64] Arnulf participated in a meeting of Henry's court at Argentan, which ruled that John, count of Ponthieu, owed a candle a year to the church of St. Mary's in Evreux. Notice of the settlement was addressed to Arnulf, as the official who would enforce compliance.[65] And at Rouen, he contributed to a judgment in favor of the abbot and monks of St. Evroult in their suit against Robert Curthose concerning the church of St. Peter of Sap.[66]

Arnulf may have ceased to act as justiciar after 1157, but his interest in the activities of the royal court continued. In at least two later cases, he attended the court sessions that settled disputes brought before the king. At Tours in 1159 he was present when the case of Garin, abbot of St. Julian's, against Robert, abbot of Vendôme, was settled peacefully.[67] And in October 1167 he witnessed the settlement of the argument between the abbey of Troarn and Count John of Ponthieu over the boundaries of their property.[68]

One suspects that Arnulf enjoyed his experiences as a justiciar. The activities of the royal court gave full scope to his legal education and allowed him to serve both *regnum* and *sacerdotium*. Once again it must be noted that surviving documents are not a reliable guide to the extent of Arnulf's judicial activities. Because the Norman archives contain little other than monastic materials for this period, cases dealing with purely secular matters may be grossly under-represented. Further, the compilers of monastic cartularies had no reason to preserve records of cases that went against them. Therefore, the impression given by these documents—that the courts favored ecclesiastical institutions over lay interests—is probably false. There were, however, limitations to a bishop's participation in secular courts. In 1173, Arnulf wrote a letter to Richard of Ilchester, newly elected bishop of Winchester, pointing out the restrictions of canon law. He warned against the temptation to allow himself to be drawn into those secular activities that were unsuitable to a bishop's vocation, since, as he said, "the severity of forensic law does not agree in many ways with the clemency of the compassionate church."[69] There is no indication in the records that Henry and Arnulf clashed over such questions of judicial administration. It is likely that the king respected the bishop's reservations about corporal punishment and did not force him to preside over cases that would require him personally to pass such judgments.

Henry II used his loyal barons and bishops wherever they could be most effective. In Arnulf's case, Henry was able to exploit not only his legal knowledge but also his diplomatic experience. In October 1155, Henry included Arnulf in the delegation he was sending to the pope to gain papal approval of his plans to invade Ireland. The choice was a wise one. Arnulf was a senior bishop, respected at the papal court for his contributions to the cause of Innocent II and well known for his eloquence. In 1160, Henry had Arnulf at his side when he signed a peace treaty with the king of France.[70] Arnulf's long history of friendly contact with the French court made his presence an asset. Henry called upon him again in 1163 to present his pleas for papal approval before he issued the Constitutions of Clarendon.[71] This mission, although ultimately unsuccessful even after six trips to the papal court, had been carefully planned by Henry so that Pope Alexander III would hear the plea from one of his close personal friends. Arnulf was a valuable member of Henry's diplomatic corps, and Henry's use of him, although calculated, was strategically sound.

Arnulf, for his part, gained much from his association with the royal court. Obviously much of his profit was financial, but there were no canonical barriers to episcopal wealth in the mid–twelfth century. A bishop was expected to be wealthy, and if he redirected his wealth to the benefit of his diocese, as Arnulf seems to have done, his magnificence was all the more to his credit. Perhaps even more important to Arnulf was the personal satisfaction he gained from being a member of the king's inner circle. He had a hand in affairs of state and a useful place in the secular administration of Normandy. It was a goal he had long sought.

Arnulf's paradigmatic view of the proper relationship between *regnum* and *sacerdotium* was patterned on the compromise solution to the Investiture Controversy. Throughout his career, he would insist that the interests of the two powers were intertwined. He could not conceive of any political reality that was not based on a united Christendom. Time after time he described the symbiotic nature of the world he thought he knew: "The honor of the church and the honor of the kingdom run hand in hand with each other, since kings cannot obtain salvation without the church, nor can the church find peace without royal protection."[72] In the early years of his reign, King Henry allowed his bishops almost a free hand in Normandy, and Arnulf had found no insurmountable conflict in fulfilling the role of baron as well as bishop. But as Henry II moved to centralize his power, the challenges to Arnulf's paradigm increased.

IV.

The Bishop in the Wider World of Christendom

Arnulf of Lisieux had sought a position in the secular world that would allow him to exercise a dual function as a spiritual leader and as a political advisor. Under Henry II he held positions both as a bishop and as a secular lord, and, at least so long as he remained in Normandy, he saw no difficulty in fulfilling both offices. If he had been able to remain there, quietly serving his God and his king, he might have spent the rest of his life in relative contentment. Henry's political interests, however, extended throughout much of Christendom, and his advisors were required to undertake a correspondingly wide range of activities. Similarly, the church hierarchy was being drawn into political activity, and bishops could no longer be effective if they sequestered themselves within their dioceses. Conflicts engendered by the expansion of both secular and papal goals would severely test Arnulf's ability to adapt to changing conditions.

In constructing his paradigm, Arnulf had envisioned a world in which rulers recognized their own need for salvation, the primacy of the church over all Christian souls, and the wisdom of seeking administrative as well as spiritual guidance from the primates of their realms. He had not anticipated a period of political upheaval during which monarchs would embark upon a course of independent state building, employing professional bureaucracies and centralizing their authority without due regard for the position of the church. The mid–twelfth century, however, was just such a period. Normandy had been wracked by civil war; new dynasties claimed the thrones of Bohemia, Hungary, Brandenburg, Sweden, and Scotland; Rome briefly declared itself a republic under the leadership of Arnold of Brescia. In France, the influence of the church over the reign of Louis VII was greatly diminished by the death of Abbot Suger in 1151. Frederick I Barbarossa came to the German throne in 1152, determined to regain the control over Italy that had been surrendered to the papacy by his predecessors. And in England, Henry II began to draw his advisors from a group of young courtiers who valued political advancement above personal integrity. Few of the new rulers of Christendom seemed interested in the concept of virtuous kingship that Arnulf had inherited from the exemplars of his youth.

The church, too, was changing. Arnulf had identified himself with the party of "young reformers" who had played such a pivotal role in the election of Pope Innocent II. But by the late 1150s, most of them were gone. Haimeric, the papal chancellor, died in 1141, Bernard of Clairvaux in 1153. Only one member of the College of Cardinals of 1130, John of Pastoris, was still serving in 1159. In Normandy, Hugh of Amiens (1130–1164) was still archbishop of Rouen, but none of his six suffragan bishops had occupied a bishopric during the schism of 1130. Of the 222 bishops of England, France, and Germany, 203 had been elevated during the peaceful period of papal politics between 1139 and 1159.[1] The papal chancery had passed to the control of Rolando Bandinelli, who was destined to become the first of the great lawyer popes. Studies at Paris focused on theology and canon law following the appearance of Gratian's *Decretum* and Peter Lombard's *Sentences*. Educated clerics such as John of Salisbury, Hugh of St. Victor, and Peter of Blois urged a restructuring of the old liberal arts curriculum in the schools. The idealistic theologians whose desire for spiritual renewal so influenced Arnulf had almost all been replaced by a new generation that seemed to be concerned primarily with finding pragmatic solutions to current problems.

By 1159, massive changes both inside and outside the church dictated that the concerns of the papal curia turn more and more toward the place of the church among the strengthening secular monarchies. Another paradigm shift was occurring as a growing papal bureaucracy, staffed by graduates of the law schools, sought to extend the juridical authority of the church. Curialists directed their attention to the evils of usury, the interference of lay authority with its attendant temptations toward simony, and the spread of heresy. The attempts of Frederick Barbarossa to reestablish his hegemony in Italy threatened a renewal of the crisis of the Investiture Controversy. None of the church's concerns were really antithetical to Arnulf's personal paradigm, but they were not the issues with which he had been prepared to deal. New problems within the church forced him to reorder his own priorities.

The death of Pope Adrian IV in September 1159 precipitated a new papal schism. A few cardinals who supported a policy of continuing to placate the German emperor favored the candidacy of Octavian, cardinal-priest of St. Cecilia. A majority of the College of Cardinals, however, feared that Frederick Barbarossa was preparing a new challenge to papal supremacy. Their choice was the chancellor, Rolando Bandinelli, who had already demonstrated his ability to deal firmly with Frederick. Under his guidance, Pope Adrian IV had concluded the Treaty of Benevento that effectively excluded the German emperor from Italy.[2] And in 1157, Rolando had pushed the papal claims even further when he met with Frederick at Besançon. There he had infuriated Frederick by describing the emperor's crown as nothing more than a benefice from the pope.[3] The papal election of 1159 began in a canonical and orderly way. The cardinals and bishops assembled at St. Peter's on September 4 and deliberated over the choice for three days. But when the vote was taken, unanimity escaped them. In his *Life of Alexander III*, Cardinal Boso revealed the voting process:

> At length all present, with the exception of the Cardinal Priests Octavian of St. Cecilia, John of St. Martin, and Guy of St. Callixtus, were inspired by God to give a unanimous decision for the person of the Chancellor, Roland. Invoking the favour of the Holy Spirit, and with the assent of the clergy and people, they nominated Roland and chose him to be Pope of the Roman See, Alexander III. (But two of those whom I have just named, John and Guy, eager for the election of Octavian, made so bold as to give their nomination to him.)[4]

Although papal elections must be carried out in secret, there is little reason to doubt the veracity of the contemporary accounts of Cardinal Boso and Gerhoh of Reichersberg. Those who supported the election of Rolando Bandinelli as Pope Alexander III constituted a clear majority and included all but one of the cardinal-bishops. By every provision of the decree of 1059, the election had been properly conducted.

What happened in the few moments after the election is more problematic, for the story was recorded only by the supporters of Alexander. According to their partisan accounts, Octavian refused to let his ambitions be so easily thwarted. When Rolando Bandinelli hesitated in due humility before accepting the papal mantle, Octavian snatched it away, only to have it taken out of his hands by an onlooker. Octavian's supporters then produced another mantle that Octavian had brought with him. In his haste to don the garment, Octavian put it on backwards, and when he could not find the hood in its proper place, he pulled the back of the garment over his head. Despite the ridiculousness of his appearance, Octavian entered St. Peter's and took possession of the papal throne, accompanied by a group of armed retainers hired for the occasion and supported by the cheers of the people.[5]

Fearful of the mood of the crowd, Rolando Bandinelli and his supporters took temporary refuge in the city; later they were forced to leave Rome. On September 20 the chancellor formally accepted the title of Pope Alexander III and excommunicated Octavian and his supporters. Octavian took the name Victor IV on October 4 and promptly excommunicated Alexander. Once again the church was faced with the dilemma of a dual papacy. This time, however, the split was not over questions of morality but rather over politics. Octavian had the support of Frederick Barbarossa, who saw a chance to reassert imperial claims over the papacy. Alexander, as leader of the anti-imperial faction, needed to exploit his political connections with England and France in order to make good his claim to the papal throne. Arnulf of Lisieux was an obvious choice as Alexander's agent. He had the distinction of being one of the few bishops with personal knowledge of the schism of 1130 and was, perhaps, the only survivor from the active participants in the campaign to win the papal throne for Innocent II. His experience was to be vitally important to the cause of Alexander III.

Almost immediately after the schismatic election in September 1159, Arnulf wrote to several Alexandrine cardinals to describe his sorrow that the church had once again been disturbed by internal conflict. But he also spoke of his pleasure at Alexander's election:

> When I learned on whose person almost all the votes had settled, I changed sorrow to joy, lamentation to praise, and wailing to the voice of song. I rejoiced because, even if a few desert the general agreement, none of their number will be able to diminish the universal harmony. I rejoiced, further, that this most important matter has been entrusted to him, through whom it is believed that the freedom and grace of the church will be easily restored.[6]

Arnulf wrote a long letter to Alexander, in which he not only expressed his support but reminded him of the outcome of the previous schism. Schisms had occurred frequently, he consoled Alexander, but God had always prevailed and would again: "Serenity will return soon, God willing, and this small cloud will be dissolved by the rays of the true sun; universal harmony will be restored, and the whole world of the faithful will come together to meet at your feet."[7]

In the meantime, Arnulf assured Alexander that he was taking steps to further Alexander's cause at the English court. Arnulf had served Henry II as an advisor for many years, and he knew that Henry seldom changed his mind after making a decision. But he understood, too, that Henry was more likely to be influenced by the political ramifications of the schism than by purely spiritual arguments. Arnulf was already on guard lest the appeals of the emperor Frederick override Henry's religious scruples:

> As soon as the truth of your promotion and the error of that of your presumptuous opponent reached our ears, I hurried to announce the news to our king, so that I could fill his empty mind with whatever arguments I could muster, lest the skill of the malicious forestall us at a favorable moment. For it is always easier to fill vacant minds than to turn them away from preconceived ideas. He was undecided; but immediately, strengthened by the workings of the Holy Spirit, he vowed himself to support no one other than you, as joyful as he was constant and as constant as he was joyful. . . . Your apostolic authority is unquestioned and firm in his mind; and in whatever way the heart of the king is influenced, I have no fear that he will fall into error. However, it will be my task to observe all those around him with vigilance, lest sinful mouths surround him, and so that, as he began, so may he remain in your obedience.[8]

Alexander was quick to recognize the value of assistance from Arnulf. He could only hope to counter the enmity of Frederick Barbarossa by playing on the political opposition of the French and English kings to Frederick's imperial ambitions.[9] But in order to enlist the support of Henry II and Louis VII, he had to rely on the French and Anglo-Norman bishops to convince their monarchs that he would cater to their political positions. Alexander appreciated the value of Arnulf's experience in the previous schism. On April 1, 1160,

Alexander replied to Arnulf's letter with some specific suggestions about how he could help:

> We have heard that that magnificent and serene prince of the world, Henry King of England, remains firm and steady in the unity of the universal church, and that especially through your efforts he has resolved his mind in favor of our holy cause. We ask, if you will, that you keep up such a careful guard always around him, lest he be tempted through the frequent annoyances of the emperor and his ambassadors to slip away in some way from his devotion to the church and to our cause. (God forbid!) We also wish that you would take it upon yourself to act as an apostle and messenger of the truth among the king and the bishops and neighboring peoples in those parts; that you would exhort the neighboring and kindred bishops, and secular persons as well as ecclesiastic, the distinguished and powerful nobles, to the same stance with all diligence and eagerness.[10]

The hopes of Arnulf and Alexander for a speedy conclusion to the schism proved unwarranted. Nor was Henry quite so committed to the cause of the Alexandrines as they had assumed. Henry had, in fact, sent representatives to the Council of Pavia in February 1160, a meeting that was convened by Frederick to recognize the papacy of Victor IV. In the announcement that this council issued, Henry was listed among the supporters of Victor, having "consented through his legates and his letters."[11] Henry spent the year 1160 on the Continent, and, as he had promised, Arnulf was often attendant on his court. Arnulf signed several charters that have been dated to the first six months of 1160. These included at least three grants issued at Argentan in favor of the Abbey of St. Mary of La Trappe in the diocese of Sées, a judgment addressed to Arnulf from Henry II in favor of the church of St. Mary's, Evreux, and a confirmation of the rights and privileges of the abbey of Holy Trinity, Lucerne.[12] In May he accompanied Henry to a meeting with Louis VII at which a treaty was concluded between the two monarchs. The matters under discussion included the possession of the Norman Vexin, a marriage between the heirs of the two countries, and a year's truce in their ongoing battle over disputed French territories.[13] The schism was not mentioned in the treaty, although the kings may have used the occasion to set plans for a joint synod on the subject.

In the early months of the schism, the English bishops hesitated to support either Alexander or Victor. A letter written to Henry II by John of Salisbury in the name of Archbishop Theobald early in 1160 expressed the split among the English clergy:

> Some of us indeed are preparing to approach or visit Alexander, while others are for Victor, but we are as yet uncertain which has the better cause, nor can we check or hold back by our authority those who fly off to one or the other with such reckless levity. While the matter is in suspense, we think that it is unlawful in your realm to accept either of them, save with your approval. . . . On these matters we await and desire your aid.[14]

Henry responded by giving his permission for the bishops to meet and decide which pope they would prefer to support.

The bishops of England met at the Council of London in June 1160. Neither Henry nor Arnulf attended. In a letter to Henry of Pisa, Arnulf explained his absence only by saying that he "was unable physically to be present."[15] He may well have been reluctant to leave Henry alone before the matter was settled. But whatever his reasons for not attending, he made sure that the English bishops knew his feelings. He addressed a strongly worded letter to the archbishops and bishops of England, enumerating Alexander's qualifications. He described the schismatic election itself, asking how only one bishop and two other cardinals could be taken as representatives of the universal church. He reminded his readers of the armed retainers who were brought into St. Peter's by Octavian and the fear that drove Alexander and his supporters into hiding. His details were dramatic but did not differ in substance from the accounts of Cardinal Boso and Gerhoh of Reichersberg. Next, he turned his attack against the emperor Frederick, and his analysis of Frederick's motives showed a clear understanding of the historical precedents of the emperor's actions:

> In truth, he, . . . out of a desire to finish that which began under the example of his ancestors, joyfully took advantage of the situation. For you know that his predecessors had been trying for a long time past to break away from their subjugation to the Roman church, and that they always either supported or encouraged schismatics against the church. . . .[16]

Arnulf suggested that the French king and his clergy had already decided to support Alexander and that they were only delaying their announcement in deference to Henry:

> . . . they have received and honored his letters and legates everywhere. But because, God willing, a peace has newly been concluded between him [Louis] and our king, they have been pleased for the moment to delay the publication of the announcement of their undertaking, so that our king can consult with the church of his own realm and, when his mind is made up, the acceptance is to be confirmed with your connivance.[17]

The statement was not literally true; the French and English kings had not agreed to do any more than hold a joint meeting to discuss the schism. Arnulf was putting full pressure on the English bishops to convince them that the acceptance of Alexander was a foregone conclusion, and for this half-truth modern historians have criticized him.[18] But despite his lack of veracity, it must be admitted that Arnulf knew his audience well. Shortly before the convocation of the council, Archbishop Theobald revealed to Henry that Arnulf's letter had helped the English bishops to make up their minds:

> The French Church, as we have heard from reliable sources, has accepted Alexander and abandoned Octavian. As far as human judgment may discern,

it has given its adhesion to the better and the sounder party, since it is known to all that Alexander is more virtuous, more prudent, and more eloquent than his rival.... Almost the whole of the Church of Rome is on the side of Alexander; and it is incredible that the other party can obtain its end by means of a man who has neither justice nor the Lord upon his side.[19]

Arnulf had accomplished his task. By early July the English bishops had given their formal approval to Alexander III, although the announcement was postponed until it could be given with the approval of the French and English kings.[20] Henry took full advantage of the delay to strengthen his own position vis-à-vis the king of France, who remained reluctant to oppose Frederick without assurances of English support. Henry and Louis finally issued a joint statement of their support for Alexander before the end of 1160, but not until Henry had used the occasion to extort from Louis an agreement to the immediate marriage of Henry's young son to Louis's infant daughter, along with the simultaneous transfer of the Norman Vexin into Henry's possession.[21]

Despite the agreement of the French and English kings, Frederick Barbarossa remained adamant in his support for Victor. The schism continued for eighteen years, kept alive by Frederick's animosity for Alexander III and by his insistence on imperial control over papal elections. Frederick's cause also received encouragement from the clash between Alexander III and Henry II over the Becket controversy. At the Diet of Würzburg in 1165, Henry's representatives, John of Oxford and Richard of Ilchester, shared the oath of allegiance to Frederick's second antipope, Paschal. The two were excommunicated for their actions by Alexander III, but both later achieved prominence in the English church. John of Oxford was appointed bishop of Norwich in 1175, while Richard of Ilchester became bishop of Winchester in 1174.[22] Perhaps more significant, Henry moved to strengthen his dynastic ties in Germany, opening marriage negotiations with both Frederick Barbarossa and the duke of Saxony. The betrothal of Matilda, the eight-year-old daughter of Henry II, to Henry the Lion, duke of Saxony and the emperor's most powerful vassal, took place in April 1165. For the German emperor, it was a sign that the English king was still wavering in his loyalty to France and the Alexandrine papacy. Although Henry never actually switched his allegiance, he exploited the threat of the schism throughout the decade of the sixties to put pressure on Alexander to grant him his political objectives.

For the English and French clergy, however, the debate over schism was finished by 1161. Their major concern thereafter was to consolidate their forces and to define the papal policies of Alexander III. A common way of doing so was to hold a church council. Since the right of a pope to summon a general council had been established by Gratian's *Decretum*, it followed that a pope could validate his own election by calling such a council.[23] The Council of Tours opened on May 19, 1163, with the approval, though not the presence, of the French and English kings. It was attended by "17 Cardinals, 124 Bishops and 414 abbots, and a very large number of other persons both clerical and lay."[24]

The keynote of the council—the need for the freedom and unity of the church—was sounded by Arnulf of Lisieux. One account listed six speakers at the opening of the council: Alexander; William, cardinal-priest of St. Peter in Vincoli; Henry, cardinal-priest of SS. Nereo and Achilleo; Archbishop Hugh of Rouen; Archbishop Roger of York; and Arnulf of Lisieux, in that order.[25] Since Arnulf's sermon was the only one whose text survived, however, most secondary sources treat it as if it were the only one delivered.[26] Arnulf may have delivered his remarks in one long session or on two successive days.[27] According to the Draco Normannicus, Arnulf's sermon was so full of rhetoric that his exasperated audience finally shouted him down, and he was forced to finish his remarks the next day.[28] The story cannot be confirmed, even though the frequent repetitions and rhetorical embellishments of the text make it plausible. A hint that the sermon was forcibly shortened can be found in its manuscript tradition. One version, based on an early and usually accurate manuscript of Arnulf's work, treats the sermon as a single unit, as Arnulf may have originally intended to deliver it.[29] Later manuscripts broke it into two separate addresses, perhaps reflecting an interruption that forced the conclusion of the sermon to be postponed until the following session.[30] But whatever alterations to the original sermon have occurred, there can be little doubt about Arnulf's message, for he emphasized it again and again:

> Our heritage, however, is the world of the faithful, which is expressed by the name of the church that constitutes catholic unity. God entrusted this to our faith; he commended it to our care. We ought, therefore, with all fear, to bring to bear all our diligence to its care and guardianship. No threat ought to frighten us away, no persecution impede us. Have we been made the partners of consolations? It is just that we also become comrades of sorrows. We must come together to stand up against adversity and to interpose ourselves as a wall for the Lord of Israel. To be sure, He did not promise us that it would be easy; yet is it possible: if we resolve to remain firmly in catholic unity.[31]

Arnulf directed his remarks more to the necessities of the future than to the abuses of the past. He avoided any mention of the details of the schismatic election and referred to the schism itself only obliquely:

> In the same way, dearest lords and fathers, in order to preserve the state of the church unharmed, it is necessary to provide carefully for its unity and liberty. For each of these, in these days and in this storm, as we have so sorrowfully observed, is oppressed by many troubles and attacked by many injuries. For the ambition of schismatics endeavors to separate the one, while the violence of tyrants seeks to extinguish the other. Yet through the grace of God each will prove impossible.[32]

The moderation apparent in the sermon at Tours in 1163 stands in sharp contrast to the exaggerations of the *Invectiva* of 1133. Even when Arnulf referred to Frederick as the only Christian ruler who did not seek the unity of the church, his sentiments were conciliatory rather than inflammatory:

> But even he, through the mercy of God, will be converted and will live: since he is praiseworthy among the princes of the earth for his great wisdom and virtue, unless he should so lessen himself to place his own glory above that of the Divine. We pray that he will submit himself to the power of the hand of God and realize that the dominion of the church outranks his own rule. . . .[33]

There was more involved in the difference than a simple passage of years or the normal maturation that occurred as Arnulf progressed through the church hierarchy. The political considerations involved in the schism of 1159 forced prelates to temper their views for the sake of political expediency. As the young archdeacon of Sées, Arnulf had voiced the immoderate zeal of Bernard of Clairvaux, who sought to implement an idealistic and hierocratic theory of papal government. As bishop of Lisieux, he echoed the conciliatory attitude of Alexander III, who was faced with the practical problems of establishing a papal monarchy and who refused to excommunicate Frederick in the hope that they could be reconciled.[34] The sermon at Tours thus provides a valuable glimpse into the changing political attitudes of the twelfth-century papacy.

Arnulf's paradigm, however, was not so easily altered. He had begun his career as bishop and baron with the firm belief that the universal church encompassed all people and nations. He had seen no limitations to the ability of prelates and politicians to work together for the common good and for the higher goals of Christendom. But the events surrounding the schism of 1159 had made it clear that political advantage was sometimes a more powerful motivation than was religious truth. There were no guarantees that moral good would triumph over secular ambition. Arnulf had learned the painful lesson that secular rulers were more interested in their individual lands than in the unity of the kingdom of God. Worse, he had discovered that his paradigm could not provide satisfactory solutions to all the problems that faced a bishop who tried to serve both church and king.

From the beginning of the schism of 1159, it is possible to detect in Arnulf a certain pulling back from involvement in secular affairs and a corresponding increase in his ecclesiastical responsibilities. A survey of his judicial activities shows him acting more often as an ecclesiastical judge than as a secular justiciar. In some of these church cases he was acting purely in his capacity as a bishop. An argument between Robert Louvet and Master Anquetil over the church of Colleville in the diocese of Bayeux was assigned to Arnulf because the disputed land belonged to the church and chapter of Lisieux.[35] In cases that involved the internal business of a monastery, the concerned parties often preferred the impartial judgment of a bishop from outside the diocese. In this capacity Arnulf ruled in a dispute between the monks and the abbot of Troarn.[36] Similarly he presided over a settlement between the abbey of St. Etienne de Caen and its daughter house of Valle Richeri concerning the right of the smaller house to conduct its own elections.[37]

Current studies of papal decretal collections have discovered only a few instances in which the pope specifically assigned Arnulf as a judge-delegate.[38] As early as the pontificate of Adrian IV, Arnulf had served as a papal investigator. The monks of Jumièges had accused their abbot, Peter of Cluny, of simony, improper use of monastic funds, and unnatural sexual activity. Arnulf visited the monastery to determine the truth of their accusations and then reported to the pope that the charges were based upon the testimony of a single unreliable witness.[39] Decretals addressed to Arnulf by Alexander III covered such diverse subjects as the right of a judge to limit testimony, the inappropriateness of a married person's joining a religious order without the permission of the other partner, the right of a widow to remarry after an appropriate mourning period, and the proper staffing and administration of parish churches.[40] In one particularly complicated case, Arnulf had actively sought a papal ruling that would prevent a convicted counterfeiter from reclaiming hereditary lands in the diocese of Lisieux.[41]

In his letters, Arnulf mentioned several other cases in which he appeared to be acting at the direct request of the pope. Arnulf frequently corresponded with Alexander III or his legates about his judicial findings. In one of his most complete reports on the disposition of a case, Arnulf wrote to Stephen de la Chapelle, bishop of Meaux, concerning a quarrel between the abbot of St. Vincent at Senlis and the priest Garner. Arnulf and his fellow legate, Henry bishop of Senlis, not only found in favor of the abbot but forbade the priest to pursue the matter further.[42] In more complicated cases, however, Arnulf was quick to ask for advice. In a long-drawn-out disagreement between two priests over the cure of the church of Goderville, Arnulf was willing to submit the evidence to the pope so that he could judge for himself, even though the facts seemed quite clear.[43] And in a case that seemed to involve papal letters, he was unwilling to make any decision at all.[44] Arnulf's uncharacteristic deference to the pope's guidance in legal matters cannot be blamed on his ignorance of the law, for his own studies had well equipped him to serve in a judicial capacity. Rather, it seems to be a sign of his support of Alexander's efforts to extend the judicial competence of the papal see.

The struggle over the papal election of 1159 had awakened Arnulf to the dangers of political interference in church affairs and tied him more closely to the interests of the papacy, but it had not destroyed his long-cherished belief that bishops could work with kings to assure a unified Christendom. Arnulf sincerely believed he had a duty to both the church and his monarch. He continued to serve in the courts of Henry II, particularly in cases that pertained to ecclesiastical matters. He frequently attended Henry when the king was in Normandy and served as the king's emissary to the papal court. And if popes sometimes proved to be too litigious and kings too fractious, he could always hope to find solace in carrying out the duties of his diocese.

V.

The Bishop in His Diocese

Travel on the king's business often left Arnulf homesick for the comforts of his own diocese. From Tours, where he had accompanied Henry II to a meeting with Louis VII in February 1156, he wrote to his friend Arnold, abbot of Bonneval, expressing the hope that he would be able to return to Lisieux in time to celebrate Easter. The city itself was his goal, but he would have been content, he said, just to return to his diocese—the familiar landscape he had always called home.[1] Periodically from then on, Arnulf retired to his bishopric, seeking spiritual renewal and release from the demands placed upon him by his political activities.

The diocese of Lisieux lay in the heart of Normandy and at the center of the ecclesiastical province of Rouen (map 2). Defined on the west by the River Dives, on the north by the English Channel, and on the east by the River Risle, it measured 50 miles from north to south and 35 miles east to west, with a perimeter of close to 150 miles. The diocese of Rouen lay immediately to the east; the diocese of Evreux, to the southeast; the diocese of Sées, to the southwest; the diocese of Bayeux, to the west. The city of Lisieux is located at the head of the valley of the Touques River, just a few miles east of a natural fault line that roughly divides the land into Upper and Lower Normandy. Inland, the sandy shores of Lower Normandy give way to fertile farmland. Dense forests and rolling hills cut by deep river valleys mark the landscape to the east. The natural beauty of Lisieux should have made it an ideal refuge from the cares of the world. And certainly there were episcopal duties enough to keep Arnulf busy within the diocese, for it was a well-populated and prosperous area.

The diocese of Lisieux comprised four archdeaconries (map 3). Lieuvin contained the deaneries of Moyaux, Cormeilles, Bernay, and Orbec. The archdeaconry of Pont-Audemer encompassed its own deanery and the deaneries of Touques and Honfleur. In Auge were the deaneries of Mesnil-Mauger, Beuvron, and Beaumont. And in Gacé, the last area added to the diocese, local deans helped to administer Gacé, Montreuil, Vimoutier, and Liverot.[2] Ecclesiastical institutions within these divisions demanded much of the bishop's attention. Foundation dates for individual parishes are elusive, but based on the existence of Latin names rather than fourteenth-century French ones, there appear to have been at least 404 parishes in the diocese

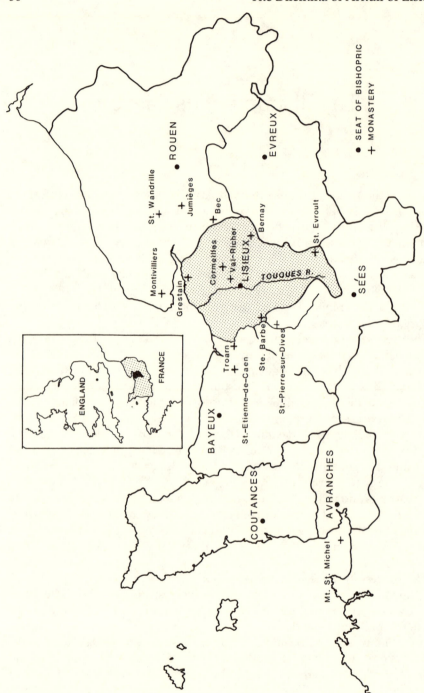

2. Ecclesiastical Province of Rouen

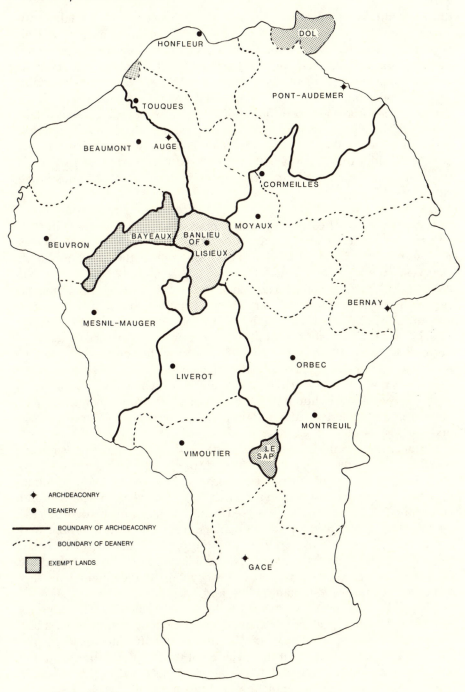

3. Diocese of Lisieux

during Arnulf's episcopate.[3] Arnulf was responsible for an additional twenty parishes that lay outside the borders of the diocese in the exemptions of Dol, Fécamp, Bayeux, Nonant, and St.-Cande-le-Vieux. There were seventy-three monastic foundations, including five major Benedictine abbeys at St. Evroult, Bernay, Préaux, Grestain, and Cormeilles. St.-Désir and St.-Léger-de-Préaux served Benedictine women, while Augustine women maintained a large priory at Ste.-Barbe-en-Auge. Monasteries from outside the diocese had established priories within the diocese of Lisieux; these included houses connected to Bec, Jumièges, St. Wandrille, Montivilliers, St.-Pierre-sur-Dives, Troarn, and Sées.[4] In addition to the many small priories that dotted the diocese, there were fifteen hospitals and lazar houses that fell under the bishop's administrative control.

The duties of a twelfth-century bishop encompassed many purely administrative details. According to the Canons of Lillebonne, passed in 1080 and still very much in effect in twelfth-century Normandy, the bishop was responsible for enforcing the Truce of God, supervising the behavior of both clergy and the lay population, defending church property, and seeing that ecclesiastical justice prevailed. The bishop approved all clerical appointments, purged his diocese of married clergy and concubines, and punished crimes committed by clerics, whether against property, lay interests, or church law. He had juridical competence over the laity in cases of adultery, incest, divorce, necromancy, desecration of churches, robbery committed on church property, and attacks on the clergy. His jurisdiction extended to any case in which a victim was pursued into sanctuary and to any case involving an ordeal by hot iron. His control over church property included the proper maintenance of cemeteries and ecclesiastical buildings and the confiscation of stray animals and lost possessions.[5]

Beyond these administrative matters, a bishop had spiritual responsibilities that derived from the powers of his office. He preached and said mass, helped with the consecration of other bishops, ordained priests and those in minor orders, prepared the chrism used in church rites, bestowed confirmation, and consecrated altars and other objects used in the liturgy. Within his own diocese he was subject only to the pope on matters of ecclesiastical discipline and justice, the filling of church offices, and the proper handling of diocesan property and revenues.[6] On a more personal level, he was to safeguard the faith, promote the spiritual welfare of his people, provide religious instruction, and encourage good morals, piety, and discipline.

Above all, a bishop was expected to lead a pure life. He was to be, as Gratian's *Decretum* specified, prudent, docile, moderate in his habits, sober, careful in his business dealings, humble, affable, merciful, literate, learned in the laws of God, careful about the meaning of the Scriptures, trained in the dogmas of the church, and able to declare the tenets of the faith in simple words.[7] These sometimes conflicting qualities often resulted in a struggle between a bishop's needs to be a good Christian and to be a good administrator.[8] In many cases, bishops were alternately one or the other. A bishop of virtue usually failed to satisfy his diocese in his handling of temporal affairs; the good administrator who replaced him just as frequently fell short in virtue. According to his own paradigm, Arnulf tried to combine the roles of spirituality and administration. His divided efforts, however, seem to have satisfied neither his own spiritual longings nor the administrative demands of his diocese.

Arnulf was sincerely interested in the affairs of his diocese. A survey of his letters and episcopal charters reveals that no matter was too small to escape his personal attention. He kept careful track of church property and, on one occasion, took drastic measures to preserve the movable goods of the diocese. Two priests, Arnulf and Richard, had left the diocese to enter the monastery of Le Valasse, a Cistercian house, but were later expelled from the order. In 1171, Arnulf wrote to Richard de Blosseville, abbot of Cîteaux, explaining why he was unwilling to take them back:

> I am interested for no reason except that it has to do with my church, because one of them, who was withdrawn by revocation, Arnulf by name, pawned a certain book, which a devout collection of the parishioners of his church had contributed, with the advice and assistance of the abbot of Pin, for a pledge of four pounds Angevin, even though I had forbidden him, under pain of anathema, that he neither do this nor presume to carry off anything of the goods of the church without my permission. Therefore, since, although he has been warned and requested often, he has not returned the book of his church, you are given to understand that I have removed him, excommunicated him, and suspended him from all duties of the priestly office, until he makes reparation for his sacrilege.[9]

As an educated man himself, Arnulf was concerned with the education of those under his supervision. Students at the cathedral school received his personal attention; at least one returned home with a personal recommendation from the bishop.[10] On the other hand, he was intolerant of those who would not learn. In 1159, Arnulf received an unfavorable report on a canon of Lisieux studying at Paris with Peter Helias. His response was immediate and harsh:

> If a praiseworthy nature and a hardworking spirit have deserted our young man, I am certain that neither knowledge nor diligence have deserted his teacher. I would have been indebted to you if he had proven himself manageable, but his changeable and contrary arrogance have made me a debtor to many. . . . It is therefore our wish that he return, so that, rebuked both by us and by his father and brothers, he may be able to be returned to you someday with his attitude changed for the better.[11]

Arnulf was equally concerned with the behavior of his parish priests. His correspondence is full of cases in which the bishop became personally involved in disciplining the secular clergy. A letter from Pope Alexander III alerted Arnulf to the presence in his diocese of G. de Lachim, a former

Cistercian, who had run away from his monastery to become a parish priest.[12] Arnulf agreed to send him back to his house under pain of excommunication.[13] Another parish priest, Hamon, was discovered to have "a public concubine, and to have lived with her in the same house and bed and at the same table for more than thirty years, and to have begat many children from her."[14] Arnulf had the priest brought before an assembly of the entire cathedral chapter for disciplinary action as a warning to the other priests of the diocese. He sent away the wife and two daughters, all three of whom, according to Arnulf, "were as delighted to have escaped those hands as if they had escaped from the teeth of a wolf."[15] The priest John de Grimoville was excommunicated for ten years because he had "laid violent hands on a monk, and the holy man, wounded and bleeding in many places, would have died if those who stood with the monk had not forcibly pulled him away."[16]

Arnulf's concern extended to the misdeeds of the laity. Two brothers from Lisieux, Henry and Amfridus, had been found guilty of counterfeiting and passing false coins at Bayeux. Henry was held in chains for many years and then exiled from Normandy; Amfridus, however, was pardoned by Henry II and sought to reclaim his hereditary lands that had been held as a benefice from the bishop of Lisieux. Arnulf refused to allow the claim until full restitution had been made.[17] On another occasion, he took an interest in a paternity suit and wrote to the pope to defend an important man who questioned the legitimacy of a daughter born to his notoriously unfaithful wife.[18]

Such cases comprised only a small portion of the day-to-day activities and concerns involved in administering a diocese, but they serve to illustrate some of the frustrations and disillusionments that plagued Arnulf throughout his episcopate. Arnulf had wanted to be a bishop and he valued his office. He once described the episcopate in these glowing terms: "It is of course fitting that we employ all our diligence, that we support every vexation, that we hazard every danger. For this is the special duty of our profession: we are bishops."[19] But the vexations of being a bishop sometimes overwhelmed Arnulf's finer instincts. His goal of combining magnificence with spiritual glory must have seemed very far out of reach when he contemplated the multitude of petty problems and venial sins that filled his days.

In the darker moments of his episcopal career, Arnulf toyed with the idea of abandoning his bishopric to take up a monastic vocation. The twelfth century witnessed a major revival of interest in the *vita apostolica*, although the correct form of the "apostolic life" was the subject of much debate. The Hildebrandine and Cluniac reformers of the eleventh century had hoped to restore the faded ideals of Benedictine monasticism, and in many ways new orders such as the Cistercians and Carthusians accomplished that goal. They recreated the monastic community described by Peter Damian in which men lived humbly, owning nothing themselves and holding all in common.[20] But the world of the twelfth century, with its growing population, its burgeoning cities, and its increasingly secular focus, required a reinterpretation of the *vita apostolica*.[21] The apostles had been preachers; they had been active in the world, not secluded from it. The Augustinian order attempted to fill the gap left by cenobitic monasticism and worked in the world, using earthly tools to bring the message of Christ to people who lived in a very imperfect world. R. W. Southern described the difference this way: "The monks therefore played the part of Mary, the canons that of Martha in the church. The rôle of the canons was the humbler of the two, but not less necessary."[22] The secular clergy, of course, also worked in the real world, although without the monastic strictures of poverty and community. Which group was following the apostolic path? No one was quite sure, least of all a worldly bishop concerned with his own search for holiness.

Arnulf was in many ways a frustrated monk, and his early training had encouraged that tendency. As an archdeacon in his brother's diocese of Sées, he had witnessed the installation of canons regular in the cathedral and had himself been a member of the conventual chapter. His contacts with Bernard of Clairvaux during the schism of the 1130s exposed him to the credo of the Cistercians and to the same charismatic appeal that lured so many of Bernard's associates to follow him.[23] One passage in Arnulf's *Invectiva* expressed his admiration for the new reformed orders:

> What sort of men are these, who dwell in the perpetual snows of Chartreuse, or those who, flowing from a Cistercian or Cluniac monastery, spread the rays of their light everywhere! For they, removing all earthly matters from their hands and minds, by wise understanding, in rough clothing, with food as rare as meager, and with night vigils and many labors, torment the body, hoping only for that redemption of the spirit of all men that promises grace to those who are diligent. Among them there is holy conversation, wise speech, acute understanding of divine matters, which no cloud of earthy thickness obscures.[24]

At least twice during the first half of his pontificate, Arnulf sought to be released from his bishop's office so that he could become a monk.[25] Canon law specified that a bishop could be released from his office only by the pope; any petition for release had to be made in person unless the applicant was ill. In a letter to Pope Alexander III in 1178, Arnulf revealed that he had made such requests to both Eugenius III (1145–1153) and Adrian IV (1154–1158) during visits to the papal court. On each occasion conflicts between his spiritual and secular duties had led him to doubt that an episcopal career was the correct path to salvation:

> Since, therefore, I sought a remedy, and devoutly longed for consequent salvation, I understood that there is nothing more efficacious, no way more certain, than to follow the doctrine of Christ, to embrace the example of his humility and patience and poverty, rejecting everything that stands in the way of truth, and for me to go so far as to become a brother of some religious order and to enter the house of some religious institution, so that, shut off from what the vanity of the world seems to offer, the temperance of the rule might check my inward wanderings, and, like the little ones dashed against the rock, my constant devotions might regain the strength of integrity.[26]

The first request had been made in 1146, when Arnulf despaired over his quarrels with Geoffrey of Anjou and the general loss of ecclesiastical freedom in Normandy. The second came at the end of 1155, at precisely the time Arnulf was beginning to realize the dangers of becoming too involved in the service of Henry II. During the winter of 1155–1156, both Arnulf and John of Salisbury were at the papal court. Arnulf was a member of a delegation sent to Pope Adrian IV by the newly crowned Henry II to discuss several matters, including Henry's plans to invade Ireland. Salisbury was there in the service of Archbishop Theobald of Canterbury, but he took an active part in furthering the mission of Henry's delegation. In fact, he took credit for securing the document in which the pope ceded Ireland to Henry. This papal privilege was not totally satisfactory, however, for it justified the gift on the grounds that all islands belonged to the pope through the Donation of Constantine.[27] Such a statement posed a real threat to the monarch of an island kingdom. When Arnulf realized that Salisbury's dealings with the pope might not be serving the interests of the king, he faced a very real challenge to his goal of serving both church and king. Very little is known of Arnulf's activities at the papal court, but he must have taken this opportunity to renew his request that he be allowed to retire to a monastery. Once again the pope refused to release him from his duties.

Arnulf returned to Normandy ahead of the rest of the delegation and reported his suspicions to Henry II, who heeded the warning and delayed his invasion of Ireland. Arnulf's subsequent withdrawal from the king's court may be taken as evidence that he recognized the implications of his actions. By supporting the interests of the king against those of the church, he had in some sense betrayed his own yearning for a more spiritual life. Arnulf had sublimated his first impulses toward a monastic career by becoming a soldier of Christ in the Holy Land. But in 1156 there was no outlet for his frustrations except through his episcopal office. If he could not become a monk himself, he could at least take action to see that the reforms he had long admired were properly carried out in the monastic institutions of his own diocese.

Arnulf began his campaign by turning his attention to the canons of the cathedral at Lisieux. The cathedral of St. Pierre was staffed by a chapter of perhaps as many as forty canons who conducted worship services and assisted the bishop in the administration of the diocese. Unlike Sées, where Arnulf's brother had installed a chapter of canons regular in 1124, the canons of Lisieux remained a secular chapter, living more or less unsupervised lives within the city.[28] At least one of their houses was located on the rue de Bouteiller, just two blocks west of the cathedral (map 4).[29] The site later was used by the École Chrétienne and is now occupied by the parish house of the cathedral. The canons also founded a hospital around the year 1160 on Grande Rue.[30] Although most records of the diocese have been lost, it is possible to identify many of the members of the chapter from documentary sources.[31]

Archdeacons had assumed administrative control of their individual regions by the time of Arnulf's episcopacy. They collected secular taxes,

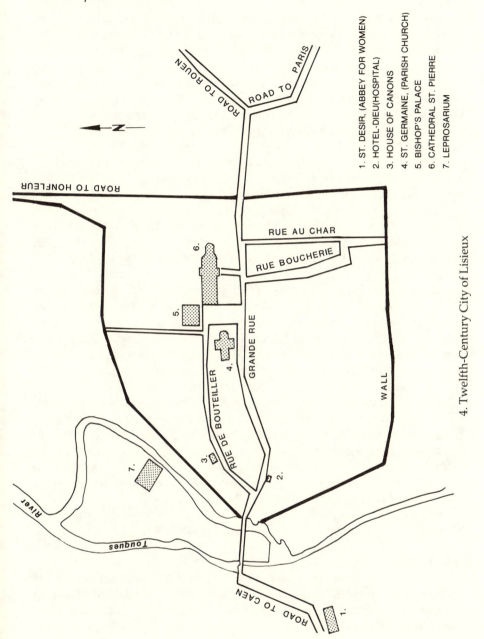

1. ST. DESIR, (ABBEY FOR WOMEN)
2. HOTEL-DIEU(HOSPITAL)
3. HOUSE OF CANONS
4. ST. GERMAINE, (PARISH CHURCH)
5. BISHOP'S PALACE
6. CATHEDRAL ST. PIERRE
7. LEPROSARIUM

4. Twelfth-Century City of Lisieux

presided over local court cases involving corporal punishment, and supervised parish affairs within their archdeaconries. Norman (1139 x 1149) is the only archdeacon who can be identified as a carry-over from the staff of John of Lisieux.[32] After 1157, there were always four archdeacons in office. John (1147 x 1173) witnessed several of Arnulf's charters and sometimes assisted the bishop while he was at the royal court.[33] His duties were assumed by Richard Barre (1171 x 1184), who began his career as a member of the curial staff of Henry II. He seems to have received his archdeaconry as a reward from Henry and Arnulf when he traveled to Frascati to plead with the pope against an interdict in 1171. Although he witnessed at least one diocesan charter, he was most often absent in the service of the king.[34] Robert de Arden (1148 x 1166) served the bishop as his messenger to the pope during the Becket crisis.[35] He was succeeded by Hugh de Nonant (1167 x 1184), Arnulf's nephew, who was specifically designated as archdeacon of Gacé.[36] Gilbert de Glanville (1151 x 1185) was Arnulf's most trusted archdeacon. He was active during the Becket crisis and supported Arnulf's efforts to correct problems in the monasteries of the diocese. He appears as a messenger to the pope in the early 1170s and as one of the mediators of the controversy that arose between the bishop and his canons at the end of Arnulf's life.[37] Hamo de Vinat (1157 x 1190) seems to have limited his activities to diocesan affairs.[38] The names of two additional archdeacons appear at the end of Arnulf's term, but the dates of their appointment are uncertain. William received a papal decretal in January 1182.[39] John de Alençon (1182 x 1195) began his career as a canon of Lisieux. His appointment as archdeacon may not have come until after Arnulf's death.[40]

The internal business of the cathedral was handled by several dignitaries.[41] The dean was the head of the chapter. In a position analogous to that of a prior in a monastery or chapter of Augustine canons, he presided over meetings of the chapter canons, enforced discipline, and acted for the bishop in his absence. Two men filled this post during the tenure of Arnulf. Fulk governed the chapter until sometime after 1147.[42] John the Dean replaced Fulk before 1152 and held his office at least until 1198.[43]

The precentor was second in command of the cathedral chapter. His primary duty was to preside over liturgical functions and to supervise the cathedral choir. The only identifiable precentor at Lisieux was Ralph the Cantor (1177 x 1190).[44]

The seneschal was the steward or chief household officer in charge of the wine and food supplies. Roger (1151 x 1171) was Arnulf's seneschal during much of his episcopate.[45] Two other canons, Christian and Oliver, held this title between 1180 and 1190.[46]

The chaplain had pastoral care of the members of the chapter. Walter (1154 x 1170) was the earliest chaplain who can be identified by name.[47] Nicholas de Cust' (1151 x 1181) began his career as a canon. He became chaplain around 1170 and then served as the chapter physician after 1180.[48] Richard the Chaplain appears in a charter from 1174.[49]

The chancellor, often the most highly educated member of the chapter, can sometimes be recognized by the honorific "Magister." He cared for the archives, possessed certain juridical powers within the chapter, and frequently served as scholasticus, or head of the cathedral school. Robert the Schoolmaster (c. 1147?) was Arnulf's first chancellor.[50] Master William de Pavilly (1170 x 1182) succeeded him.[51]

The treasurer supervised the storing of vestments, sacred vessels, and relics and administered that part of the tithes designated for the fabric of the cathedral. He was sometimes referred to as the capiterius or sacristan. Sylvester (1136 x 1190), another of Arnulf's nephews, held the office of treasurer throughout Arnulf's episcopate. He had begun his career under John of Lisieux and was almost constantly at odds with his uncle, encouraging other canons to rebel against Arnulf's attempts to institute reforms and accusing him of having misused cathedral funds. Sylvester never formally relinquished his title of treasurer, but others often fulfilled his duties for him.[52] Among his replacements were Robert de Sancta Honorina, who served as capiterius of the chapter in 1147, and William (1164 x 1171), a canon who temporarily replaced Sylvester when he abandoned his post in Lisieux to follow Becket into exile.[53] John de Constanciis (1182 x 1183) also replaced Sylvester for a time as treasurer at the end of Arnulf's pontificate.[54]

The canons of the cathedral were responsible for the divine offices sung at specified hours. Each canon was allotted one or more prebends from the cathedral lands, the revenues of which provided his support. Among the individual canons who can be identified were Turgis (1147 x 1148);[55] Guarinus (c. 1147);[56] Ralph de Fleuri (1147 x 1148);[57] John, vicar of the archdeacon (c. 1148);[58] William, son of Archdeacon Richard (c. 1148);[59] Gilbert de Furcis (c. 1148);[60] Roger, son of Aimi de Montfort (1148 x 1173);[61] Fulk (1151 x 1171);[62] Hubert (1175 x 1178);[63] Gervase de Saxo (1177 x 1190);[64] Radulf de Saineville, priest (1152 x 1173);[65] Roger Sitaire (c. 1147);[66] Guischard de Marceris (1141 x 1181);[67] Roger of Montgomery (c. 1178);[68] William Rousel (1178 x 1190);[69] Robert of Rouen (1180 x 1190);[70] Fulk Talliefero (1151 x 1190);[71] Arnulf the Priest (1152 x 1173);[72] Eustace (1180 x 1184);[73] and Milo (c. 1164).[74]

Norman Exchequer records list a group of people who were fined for taking part in a duel on the grounds of the cathedral in 1180.[75] Among them are some of the canons already listed and several individuals whose status as canons cannot be confirmed from other records. Until more information becomes available, they may be considered as possible members of the chapter: Robert Carbonel, Radulf de Livet, Roger de Livet, Radulf de SupLouca, Osbert Farout, John de Roca, Hugh de Roca, Bertran, Baldwin Tirel, Roger Fitz Matthew, Tres Urselli, and Durand the Priest.

The size of a cathedral chapter varied from year to year, depending upon such intangibles as the success of recruitment efforts, the death rate, and the number of available prebends. During the late twelfth century, there were probably no more than thirty-eight to forty canons in the chapter at Lisieux. It did not reach its full complement of forty-eight canons until the thirteenth century.[76] By the sixteenth century, the number of prebends available to cathedral canons had reached fifty-three, although there is no guarantee that each was held by a different person.[77] The rate of turnover cannot be determined, but it appears that the major offices changed hands two or three times during the tenure of Arnulf. Thus the fifty-six canons identified so far represent perhaps only half of those who held places in the cathedral chapter between 1141 and 1181. Those whose names have been preserved were, of course, the most active members of the chapter. Several went on to bishoprics or other ecclesiastical offices. Among these were Gilbert of Glanville, who became bishop of Rochester; Hugh de Nonant, bishop of Coventry; and John de Constanciis, bishop of Worcester. Some, such as Richard Barre and John de Alençon, used their positions as stepping stones to royal service. Others were content to serve the cathedral in relative obscurity. Their identities can suggest only some preliminary conclusions. Among the cathedral personnel, there were several who were following a family tradition of service to the church—the Rocas, the Livets, the Glanvilles, sons of former cathedral officials, and Arnulf's own nephews. Most bore Norman names, and many came from local land-holding families. Few, however, were of notable aristocratic extraction. The canons of Lisieux may have seen the cathedral chapter as a vehicle of social mobility, providing career opportunities for those better equipped with education than with inherited wealth. Their ambition, coupled with their relative lack of social position, may go far to explain their constant quarrels with the bishop over money and capitular discipline.

Arnulf had antagonized his canons at the very beginning of his tenure by forcing the members of the chapter to give up their concubines. "I took steps to purge wantonness," he reported to Pope Alexander III, "and to remove the old canons involved in concubinage, which required a hand of necessary severity; so much so that on one day for the assurance of their virtue, I caused eighteen concubines to be publicly adjured by the canons."[78] Arnulf took great pride in thus restoring the moral splendor of his church, but the reforms failed to endure. As the old canons died off and were replaced by younger men, the old temptations reappeared. At first the bishop only suspected that the concubines had returned, for the canons steadfastly defended one another. But by 1160 the truth became obvious. As Arnulf described the situation, "labor pains were making the involvement of the new men most certain, and the whole neighborhood was rejoicing over new cradles."[79]

On this occasion, however, the warnings, threats, and punishments went unheeded, for the sin of fornication involved nearly the entire chapter, and the canons, led by Arnulf's nephew Sylvester, banded together against the bishop. Arnulf despaired over his disloyal nephew: "He, who had been surrounded by many gifts from me from his boyhood, implacable in his hatred of me for certain reasons, does not cease to attack and, deceitful, is not afraid to commit perjury."[80] The quarrels between Arnulf and Sylvester were of long standing. Sylvester had achieved his position as treasurer under John of Lisieux and may well have envied his young uncle's appointment to the bishopric. Arnulf, for his part, felt that he had indulgently heaped honors and kindness upon his nephews and resented Sylvester's lack of gratitude.[81] This time, their mutual hostility spilled over to affect the entire cathedral chapter, with ultimately disastrous results for Arnulf. Good relations between the bishop and his canons were never restored. The conspiracies against Arnulf would continue until at the end of his life the canons were able to drive him out of the diocese.

Frustrated by his attempts to reform his own cathedral chapter, Arnulf turned his attention to the problems of the abbey of Grestain. This Benedictine foundation, located in the far northeast corner of the diocese of Lisieux (see map 2), held extensive properties in England and suffered all the normal consequences of dealing with enormous wealth.[82] The abbot was often absent from his post, and the monks had little regard for discipline or moral order. The monastery was a natural target for a reforming bishop. Arnulf began a direct confrontation with Herbert, abbot of Grestain, in 1165, when he ordered him to return from a fourteen-month sojourn in England.[83] The abbey, he warned, was suffering from both spiritual and temporal losses, and the whole region was being disturbed by the behavior of the unsupervised monks. Herbert returned to Normandy but proved himself unable to restore order. After only a short stay, he once again sailed for the pleasanter lands of England without the permission of the bishop. A second, and much harsher, letter followed:

> Your order is not unaware of how great a scandal and how great a loss to your house has occurred because of your absence. Since this matter is of great concern to us, we order you to restrain your aimless wandering and to provide the proper vigilance over the flock entrusted to you; . . . our territory remains scandalized and the abbey disgracefully defamed. With this letter, therefore, we order you that you return within twenty days of the receipt of this letter, at the first opportunity, unless you are detained by inclement weather or ill-health, God forbid. Otherwise, we warn you that from that day you will find yourself suspended from authority, from officiating at the altar, and from the entry of all churches.[84]

Arnulf had good reason to be upset, for the monks of Grestain were apparently guilty of every sort of crime, from drunkenness to sacrilege and murder. On one holiday all of the monks except for four old men decided that the wine being served in the refectory was inferior to that which they were accustomed to drink in the local tavern. Taking the bell ropes and locking the doors behind them, they moved to the tavern, leaving the monastery silent for several days.[85] On another occasion, their drunkenness resulted in murder. The procurator, who had been left in charge during the absence of the abbot, came into the refectory drunk one night after dinner and attacked two of the brothers with a knife. They retaliated and beat him to death with a club that just happened to be handy.[86]

Such violence would have been serious enough if it had been limited to the brothers themselves. Unfortunately, neighboring people were also involved.

A youth who worked in the kitchen was beaten about the neck with his own pestle until the blood sprinkled onlookers because he had suggested that one of the monks visited his wife too frequently.[87] And a poor woman, already almost dead from cold, was dipped into a well of icy water seven times while the monks sang mysterious songs above her. They hoped to work a miracle and invited the neighbors in to observe it. She died.[88]

Arnulf demanded immediate reform. He transferred the principal perpetrators to other monasteries that would, he hoped, provide a more religious atmosphere in which they would be encouraged to mend their ways. To the pope, he recommended a complete reorganization of the monastery, replacing the Benedictines with canons regular. He may have favored the change because the Austin canons were more receptive to episcopal visitation. This move, he argued, would have several other advantages. Not only would it set a better example of apostolic severity; it would also allow those who wished to join the Austin order to do so without being forced to leave the diocese.[89]

Herbert, as ordered, finally returned to his post as abbot, but not without causing further disruptions. When Arnulf attempted to visit Grestain, Herbert refused to allow him even to speak with the monks who were still there.[90] And when a priest and subdeacon visited the monastery to solicit funds for the reconstruction of the cathedral of Lisieux, the monks attacked them, threw them out of the door, and rolled them in the mud.[91] At that point Arnulf brought the full force of anathema against the monastery. Herbert refused to accept the excommunications and continued to allow masses to be celebrated.[92]

Eventually, Arnulf recognized his own inability to settle the matter and turned it over to the pope: "May it please you to hear us and to apply your hand of resolution, because, so long as he [Herbert] remains in office, monastic order cannot be corrected nor the temporalities restored."[93] Despite the justice of Arnulf's stance and indications in his letters that he had in hand full papal authority to disband the monastery, no known action was taken against Grestain. The modern historian of Grestain admits that new Benedictines restaffed the monastery, but, he says, the order of St. Benedict regarded the suggestion that they be replaced by Austin canons as an insult.[94] Herbert remained in office until his death in 1178.[95]

Episcopal authority within the diocese was further weakened by another type of dispute between Arnulf and his monastic institutions. Although Arnulf had declared himself an admirer of Cluniac and Cistercian reforms, he was unable to accept the full implications of their ongoing campaign for monastic exemption. He was always among the first to support monastic claims of exemption from lay control, but he was too much a bishop to accept a parallel freedom from episcopal supervision. The twelfth century witnessed a renewed effort among some monasteries to exercise certain episcopal rights of administration and jurisdiction over parish churches on their lands.[96] Bishops naturally objected to being deprived of their right to appoint priests and to correct their conduct. At the heart of the dispute, however, lay the issue of whether monks, who had taken a vow of poverty, could collect and use tithes from their parishes or whether these tithes should still accrue to the bishop.[97] Arnulf was in the vanguard of the effort to limit monastic claims of exemption, and his views led him into several conflicts with monasteries that held valuable property in the diocese of Lisieux.

The earliest case involved the abbey of Fécamp, which held the parish of Hennequeville-sur-Mer and claimed that the parish and its cures had been exempted from all episcopal jurisdiction since 1006.[98] In 1159 Arnulf brought suit against the abbot, Henry de Sully, over his right to appoint the priest of an exempt parish. Arnulf was taking on a formidable opponent here, for Henry de Sully was a cousin of King Henry II. The papal judges-delegate who handled the case, however, ruled in the bishop's favor. As Arnulf reported their decision to Hugh d'Amiens, archbishop of Rouen, "the rights that had been usurped should be restored to us, those who had been excommunicated over the matter should be forced to make satisfaction, and a priest offered through whom both the church and its people should be made to obey us as the pastor and bishop of their souls."[99] Arnulf was able to ward off this attempt to weaken his own jurisdiction, but the situation was changing rapidly. By 1186 Fécamp would have restored to it all of its privileges and exemptions.[100]

Much the same sort of problem cropped up in 1170 concerning the nunnery of Montivilliers, just outside Honfleur. The abbess Matilda had interfered in a court case involving the priest of the church of St. Germaine de Vasouy. Once again Arnulf was taking on a member of the royal family, for Matilda was an illegitimate daughter of Henry I by his Norman mistress, Isabel de Beaumont.[101] Matilda claimed that a charter of Robert the Magnificent in 1035 had granted the possessions of Montivilliers absolutely free and immune from all episcopal jurisdiction.[102] The church of St. Germaine de Vasouy was therefore under her personal supervision, and Arnulf had no right to try its priest. Arnulf, however, claimed that the exemption had never been exercised:

> The priests of this church, installed by the hands of our predecessors from the earliest times, and showing all obedience and reverence to our church, have rendered without exception to the bishops and archdeacons of the church of Lisieux all episcopal dues and synodal fines, and have acknowledged the church of Lisieux as a mother with all due and humble reverence. This latest one too, ordained in the priesthood by our church, has obeyed me and my archdeacons for many years with devotion and humility, never refusing to do those things that his neighboring priests were accustomed to do, until, publicly accused in our court of concubinage, in fear of our judgment, he attempted to remove himself from our jurisdiction through improper tricks and carefully chosen lies.[103]

There seems to be little doubt among authorities about the genuineness of the original eleventh-century exemption. Nor is there any need to speculate over which of the complainants was telling the truth, for their claims were not really contradictory.[104] The parish was so small that the church of St. Germaine was not even attributed to a particular village in the original charters.[105] It remained so unimportant, except to Arnulf, that Pope Celestine III omitted it entirely from his bull listing the possessions of Montivilliers at the end of the twelfth century.[106] The full designation—"ecclesiam sancti Germani de Guaswic"—did not appear until a 1203 privilege of Innocent III.[107] At issue there was only a point of honor, one of a series of petty challenges to the power of the bishop. Arnulf may have won a favorable decision from Pope Alexander, but he was forced to admit that it had no real effect.[108] The abbess kept her exemption and the priest his concubine.

Disputes between Arnulf and the monasteries reached their peak at St. Evroult. This famous and well-established Benedictine house had had a long history of disputes with the bishops of Lisieux. Orderic Vitalis recorded a ten-year argument between Bishop Gilbert Maminot and two successive abbots of St. Evroult, during which the abbots refused to promise obedience and the bishop withheld the pastoral staffs that would have marked their consecrations.[109] The abbey has even been suspected of deliberately falsifying its foundation charter to assure its independence from diocesan control.[110] It should come as no surprise that St. Evroult's love of ecclesiastical freedom clashed with Arnulf's desire to exercise his episcopal rights.

The clash began, simply enough, over an unpaid debt. In 1159, Arnulf wrote to the new abbot, Robert de Blangis, warning him that he would be held responsible for all obligations incurred by his predecessor.[111] The creditors of the former abbot, Bernard, who had just been suspended, were pressing Arnulf for repayment because he had guaranteed the abbot's good faith. Arnulf set a deadline after which, if the debts were not paid, he would suspend the house from all holy offices. In the same year, he overruled Robert de Blangis on a judgment passed against one of his monks without a fair hearing, ordering the abbot to reinstate the man upon pain of excommunication.[112]

The crisis escalated, and in 1165 Arnulf made good his threats to excommunicate the abbot. The attitude of the bishop was perhaps unusually harsh: "You ought to know that, in one who has made a profession of religion, disobedience is a crime."[113] But Robert de Blangis was an unusually hostile abbot, "so much so that after his sentence of suspension and anathema, he presumed to celebrate masses and other divine offices for a period of five years and more."[114] Three successive delegations from the pope himself failed to settle the matter, and by 1173 Arnulf's anger extended in general to the brothers of the house. They were guilty, he said, of purchasing parish churches from the laity, collecting the income from altars, tithes, and benefices, and then staffing the churches with priests paid less than a shepherd or messenger, all in defiance of episcopal rights.[115] Arnulf was on firm canonical ground here, for two papal bulls issued by Adrian IV had specifically forbidden the employment of mercenary priests and the acceptance of churches or benefices from lay hands without the permission of the bishop.[116]

Another of his complaints concerned the hermitage of Rupe, which had been held by the bishop of Lisieux and some of his canons. The abbot of St.

Evroult and his monks claimed the land because they had cleared it and farmed it.[117] In this case, as in the others, however, there appears to have been no permanent settlement that would have satisfied the bishop. Alexander was more concerned with property lost to the church than he was with the methods by which its holdings increased. There are, in fact, several bulls addressed to Abbot Robert and the monks of St. Evroult, granting them full possession of all lands that they either tilled themselves or rented to others.[118] Arnulf's last letter to the pope on the subject of St. Evroult expressed his own powerlessness and only a cautious hope that papal intervention would be effective.[119]

These affairs shed light on Arnulf's administrative difficulties within the diocese. Some of his problems arose because twelfth-century bishops did not have a sure means of enforcing their decisions. The ultimate threat of excommunication was ineffective when clerics proved contumacious. Papal authority, although growing rapidly at midcentury, had not yet made itself felt fully in the far reaches of Christendom. Most of Alexander's papal decrees dealt with Italy and southern France—those areas in which he could back up his statements with his own physical presence or that of his legates. During the Becket crisis, of course, he frequently corresponded with English prelates, but his pronouncements seldom included Normandy.

By the 1160s, Arnulf's paradigm was no longer applicable to many of the problems of his changing world. Arnulf was a strong believer in the theories of papal monarchy, even though the papacy was not yet quite strong enough to make the hierocratic theory a reality. As a bishop, Arnulf wanted a strong pope who would personally back up his bishops' decisions—a pope modeled on the pattern of Innocent II responding to the will of St. Bernard. But Arnulf never fully understood the implications of a strong pope backed by a fully developed papal bureaucracy. Alexander, the first of the great lawyer popes, continued to work at building up an ecclesiastical hierarchy of archbishops and papal legates who could extend his control. Arnulf failed to accept the changes that were taking place. He continued to bypass the pope's channels of authority, even after Alexander wrote to Rotrou of Rouen, asking him to remind his suffragan bishops that the archbishop was the proper court of appeal for cases involving excommunication.[120] The results were disastrous, both for Arnulf and for his diocese. Cases that could have, and should have, been settled at a diocesan or provincial level were lost or ignored at the papal court. Thus Arnulf's authority was weakened by his very efforts to strengthen it.

Arnulf's efforts to control the monastic institutions of his diocese also suffered from deficiencies within his paradigm. He admired Cluniac and Cistercian monasticism and supported those who advocated a return to the *vita apostolica*. But at the same time he was bound by tradition and influenced by his exemplars in a simpler age to equate reform with a return to the idealized perfection of the past. In his relationships with secular authority, he had failed to understand that a strong, centralized monarchy would have less need of ecclesiastical support. In much the same way, he failed to see that monastic reform often implied a lessening of local episcopal control. He advocated monastic freedom but was unwilling to give up any of the personal power and authority that came with the office of bishop. The bishop who wanted to be a monk thus found it impossible to be both.

VI.

The Bishop as Builder

A medieval bishop had a primary responsibility to preserve, enrich, and adorn the central church of his diocese. It was the seat, or *cathedra*, from which he conducted episcopal business—hence, his cathedral. A cathedral served many purposes. It was the site of coronations and royal weddings, the altar at which new bishops and priests were consecrated, the repository of holy relics, the burial place of bishops and kings. Townspeople assembled in its nave, merchants set up business in its porticos, criminals sought sanctuary within its walls, and students flocked to its school. For all who entered, the statuary of its portals illustrated the faith and convictions of its bishop. Because a cathedral was the visible symbol of the power and authority of its bishop, its structure and design may yield important clues to the personality of the bishop who authorized its construction.

Bishop Herbert of Lisieux (1026–1050) and his successor, Hugh of Eu (1050–1077), had been responsible for building the first cathedral of St.-Pierre-de-Lisieux, which was begun in 1049 and consecrated in 1055. Legend held that Herbert had torn down the town walls to obtain stone for his cathedral. This legend was tested during archaeological excavations done at the cathedral between 1917 and 1920. The remains of Gallo-Roman walls were found near the southwest corner of the building and in the area of the transept, indicating that part of the wall may indeed have been torn down to make room for the new church. The masonry of these walls, however, differs from that of the eleventh-century foundations of the cathedral; material from the walls was not reused.[1] Still, the townspeople worried about the inauspicious origins of the cathedral. In 1077, lightning struck the cross on the top of the tower, shattering the image of Christ below and killing eight men and one woman among those who had gathered for mass.[2] The congregation took this as a sign that God was obviously displeased with the edifice. An even worse disaster struck in September 1136, when Geoffrey of Anjou led his army into Normandy and the Breton defenders of Lisieux set fire to the city to keep it from falling into Angevin hands.[3] This incident, in which the cathedral was badly damaged, was blamed on Herbert's thoughtless actions, since the destruction of the walls had allowed the invaders to gain access to the city. Rather than repairing the cathedral after the fire, Bishop John spent his remaining years rebuilding the wall.[4] Thus when Arnulf succeeded his uncle as bishop of Lisieux in 1141, he also inherited a badly damaged cathedral and residence.

The twelfth century witnessed a tremendous resurgence of cathedral building. New ideas, new attitudes, and new wealth combined to encourage architectural innovation. Following the lead of the Île-de-France, and in particular the glorious example of Abbot Suger at St.-Denis, French bishops and abbots competed to erect new churches full of light emanating from stained glass windows, soaring lines that drew the eye upward, and altars heaped with symbols of the riches of the world. The new Gothic style of architecture glorified the power of its builder. For a bishop, one French historian has noted, "a new cathedral was a feat, a victory, a battle won by a military leader."[5] The cathedrals most frequently mentioned as examples of twelfth-century Gothic architecture are Chartres, Noyon, Laon, Paris, Soissons, and Senlis. But in Normandy, the first, and perhaps the finest, example of an early Gothic cathedral was erected by Arnulf of Lisieux. The title of "bishop-builder" is still applied to Arnulf by the people of Lisieux. A small park at the southeast corner of the cathedral has recently been dedicated to *Arnoul, Évêque-Bâtisseur de Lisieux*.

The cathedral of St.-Pierre-de-Lisieux stands in almost the exact center of town, commanding the same pride of place as it did in the twelfth century (see map 4). Yet time has altered both its aspect and its importance. One approaches the cathedral across a wide square, the Place Thiers, now given over to parking and, on Saturdays, to an open-air farmers' market, complete with squawking chickens. Both the square and the cathedral are surrounded by modern shops, rebuilt after the Allied bombings of 1944 destroyed most of the town. The cathedral itself, which ceased to be the seat of a bishopric in 1789, is still in use, though seldom visited by tourists.

St.-Pierre-de-Lisieux, however, has much to offer those who take the time to explore its secrets. The view toward the east from the Place Thiers offers a history lesson in microcosm (plate 1). The original twelfth-century structure is now obscured on both sides. Chapels added in the fifteenth century jut out from the southern exposure and partially obscure the Paradise Door leading into the transept. On the north, a bishop's palace built in the early seventeenth century abuts the cathedral. It blocked off the original windows and made the interior of the church so dark that the remaining stained glass was replaced with clear panes. The north tower dates from the thirteenth century. The south tower bears the clearly visible date 1579, marking the completion of the spire, and a plaque at its base commemorates its restoration in 1901. The central portal of the western façade has been stripped of statuary. The first mutilation was perpetrated by Huguenots in 1562; the second, by revolutionaries in 1793. Traces of red, white, and blue stain the arch where the supporters of the Second Republic painted their tricolored symbol in 1848.

By its size alone St.-Pierre-de-Lisieux dominates its surroundings. The cathedral measures 110 meters (361 feet) from the west portal to the apse. The original width was 18.5 meters (61 feet); with the addition of the chapels on each side it now measures nearly 28 meters (90.5 feet). The vaults of the nave are twenty meters (66 feet) high, while those under the lantern measure thirty meters (99 feet). The towers of the west façade extend forty meters (131 feet) above the square, and the south tower is topped by a spire that stretches it to sixty meters (197 feet).[6]

To discover the original twelfth-century cathedral, the visitor need only step inside the west portal (plate 2). The air is cold and filled with dust and the slightly sweet odor of mildew and must. A few candles flicker, and occasionally an elderly parishioner slips into a side chapel. Except for some wooden folding chairs and a raised flooring that partially obscures the base of the central pillars, the central structure of the building has been unaltered by time. The narthex, nave, altar, and transepts remain essentially as Arnulf commissioned their design.

The floor plan of the cathedral forms a Latin cross (plate 3). Between the towers of the façade lies the narthex. The central portal is flanked left and right by pillars, the foundations of which date from the eleventh century. An archivolt, decorated with a band of foliage and resting on the acanthus-leafed capitals of the piers, opens into the nave. The nave itself consists of eight bays vaulted by rectangular four-part rib vaults supported by huge cylindrical piers on square bases. These piers also support the pointed arches that separate the side aisles from the nave. Three colonnettes, punctuated by necking rings, rise from the abaci of the piers to receive the spring of the transverse and diagonal ribs. The false gallery consists of bays subdivided into two smaller openings under a relieving arch. At the clerestory level, single lancet windows are partially obscured by the vaults that rise from the base of the clerestory.

The four bays of the choir, the three bays on the east sides of the transept arms, and the bays of the side aisles reproduce the design of the nave. Originally the side aisles provided only a passageway for sacred processions; now they are lined with chapels, although they retain the original design. At the crossing, powerful piers support the two-story crossing tower (plate 4). A square vault with eight ribs rises above the crossing. The choir extends to a semicircular apse, supported by a vault whose ribs radiate to the seven ambulatory bays.

J.-F.-L. Mérimée, a distinguished nineteenth-century painter and outspoken critic of St.-Pierre-de-Lisieux, described it as "resembling an English cathedral as closely as two drops of water. It is huge, cold, ponderous, orderly, and dull."[7] It is that very character, however, that marks this church as a transitional stage between the old Romanesque building style of Normandy and the full flowering of the new Gothic designs originating in Paris.

Dating the construction of a medieval cathedral can be an exasperatingly imprecise science. Most guidebooks give 1170 as the starting date for construction of St.-Pierre, but historians and architects are far from agreement on the matter. Early archaeologists, basing their accounts on contemporary chroniclers, believed that the actual building process was conterminous with the tenure of Arnulf of Lisieux from 1141 to 1181.[8] Architects, on the other hand, argued that the style of the architecture clearly belonged to the early thirteenth century.[9] Modern art historians have attempted to satisfy both sides of the controversy by suggesting that the work was begun under the episcopacy of Arnulf but extended to the middle of the thirteenth century.[10] Historians of the diocese, however, have maintained that construction began around 1170 and was completed before the end of the twelfth century.[11] Clearly a new synthesis is needed. The evidence of contemporary chronicles and archaeological discoveries can be brought into some sort of agreement with modern historical chronology and the architectural features of the cathedral itself. The key lies in understanding the degree to which the "bishop-builder," Arnulf of Lisieux, used the construction of the cathedral as an expression of his own paradigm.

A letter written by Arnulf to Pope Celestine II on the occasion of the pope's elevation in the spring of 1144 contained an early mention of the cathedral. In it Arnulf apologized for not coming to Rome to offer his congratulations in person, pleading that he had been too busy with the funeral of his brother, the dispute with Geoffrey of Anjou, and the need to repair his church and residence.[12] This letter has been cited by Serbat, Vasseur, and others as proof that the rebuilding of the cathedral began in 1143, but such a conclusion misinterprets the evidence.[13] Arnulf's use of language was always precise, and the word he used was *resarcio* (to patch or mend). In his later discussions of the construction of the cathedral, he used the terms *reedificio* or *construo* (to build or construct).[14]

It is much more likely that Arnulf contented himself in these early years with simple reparations that would render the cathedral usable until he could find the time and money to rebuild the entire structure, and there is archaeological evidence that such repairs did take place in the first half of the twelfth century.[15] A cathedral was primarily meant to serve as the seat of the bishop; the sanctuary was reserved for his use, while the canons of the chapter had their seats in the choir. The people were restricted to the nave and side aisles, where they could assemble on feast days or conduct community business. Since masses were also sung in the several parish churches of the town, the religious needs of the people could be met elsewhere. So long as the sanctuary and choir of the cathedral could be used for the bishop's private masses or official ceremonies, there would have been no rush to complete construction of the nave.

Arnulf's activities during the early decades of his tenure as bishop left him little time to do more than patch up the old Romanesque structure. It was not until 1157 that all elements came together to make construction of a new cathedral possible. Arnulf's travels were reduced in that year, when he ceased to serve as Henry's chief justiciar. Further, his second request to be released from his episcopal duties to enter a monastery had just been refused by the pope. Now he had both more time to spend at Lisieux and more certainty that he would be bishop long enough to accomplish something remarkable within his diocese. The crucial factor, however, may have been money. When Arnulf had succeeded to the diocese, he had found a greatly depleted treasury and had faced the burden of paying Geoffrey of Anjou a fine of over nine hundred pounds for the possession of his temporalities. It would have taken some time to recoup those expenses and to rebuild the treasury. According to the old Carolingian system of tripartite division of episcopal tithes, one-third of the bishop's income should have been earmarked for the repair and upkeep of the cathedral fabric, but such a fund could not have produced enough money to embark on a major construction project.[16] The turning point in the financial situation of the bishop seems to have come with the increase of his personal land holdings. Henry II had rewarded Arnulf in 1153 with the rights of fairs at Nonant and Touques and in 1155 with the valuable chapelry of Bosham in Sussex. Revenues from these new holdings would have provided the necessary funds to begin construction.

There exists little documentary evidence of the actual progress of the construction. Two letters, however, describe Arnulf's ongoing efforts to raise additional funding through the establishment of confraternities dedicated to the construction project. One reference to the financing of the cathedral occurs in a letter to Baldwin, bishop of Noyon, concerning some fund raisers working at Lisieux. The letter explains that Arnulf retained four priests from the diocese of Noyon to establish confraternities and to make collections because they had previous experience in these duties. After they passed through the diocese they remained in Lisieux, staying at a local inn, where they ran up a rather large debt by naming Arnulf annd another priest of the diocese as surety. Then they absconded, leaving their guarantors to absorb the debtt. Arnulf paid the creditorssomethirttypounds,buutthepriest,probablyRalphhdeSaineville,still owed seventy sous. The bishop was not seeking a repayment of the money, but he thought the fund raisers should at least be punished for their misdeeds.[17] Since there were two Baldwins at Noyon (the first presiding from 1167 to 1174 and the second succeeding him in 1175) and Arnulf gave no indication to which man he was writing, the letter proves only that the confraternities existed after 1167.[18]

A second letter can be dated more closely. In the fall of 1166, Arnulf wrote to Pope Alexander III with a catalogue of complaints against the Abbey of Grestain. Not the least cause of his anger was the refusal of the monks to contribute to his building fund. When a priest and a subdeacon of Lisieux visited Grestain to solicit contributions, they were unceremoniously ejected and rolled in the mud, from which they suffered serious injuries.[19] This letter is crucial to the dating of construction, for it contains the clause "the construction of our church, which we have begun from the foundations." Arnulf's use of the perfect tense leaves no doubt that the building process had already begun at the time of the writing of the letter. And since it was common practice for a building bishop and his canons to demonstrate their good faith by taking on at least three years of construction before the pope would allow the establishment of such confraternities, the construction can be assumed to have begun no later than 1163.[20]

A third contemporary account adds both additional evidence and more confusion to the problem of dating the construction of the cathedral. William of Canterbury included in his stories of the miracles attributed to Thomas Becket the tale of a young man who survived being buried alive while working on the cathedral of Lisieux.[21] A certain Roger was occupied in digging out the foundations of the cathedral. When he reached a depth of twenty-two feet, the excavated dirt suddenly collapsed, burying him deep inside the ditch. A fellow worker managed to free himself by rowing his arms through the dirt, but Roger's feet were caught under a mass of rock. Roger had no hope but to pray to the martyred Thomas, promising that he would make a pilgrimage if he were saved. It was, however, only a silent prayer, for every time he opened his mouth, more dirt fell in. Bishop Arnulf was present, and when he realized how slim the man's chances were, he addressed his prayers to the patron saints of the cathedral. Thus inspired, as well as fearful that the entombed body would endanger the foundations, the people of the congregation rushed for tools to exhume him. At last they reached the man, and even though the diggers had accidentally struck him three times on the head with a mattock, he was able to climb a ladder to safety.

Whether or not one believes that Roger was saved through the intercession of the martyred Becket, the incident seems to have been well attested. There is evidence that a cult of St. Thomas developed in Lisieux very soon after his death.[22] But since Becket was killed on December 29, 1170, this particular miracle could not have occurred before spring 1171. Its inclusion at the beginning of book II of William of Canterbury's work, written between May 1172 and February 1173, makes it not the first of the miracles attributed to Thomas but certainly one of the earlier ones.[23] Several authorities, therefore, point to this story as evidence that construction did not begin until 1171.[24] Such a conclusion depends on the assumption that the collapse occurred at the beginning of the construction process.

Architectural evidence shows that the foundations on which Roger was working were actually located in the area of the transept. At the western corner of the south arm of the transept, there is a flaw in the foundations that not even modern construction techniques have been able to overcome. The original stonework has suffered a slippage of at least six inches (plate 5). Diocese records indicate that repeated efforts were made to repair the damage caused by this weakness in 1370, 1481, 1802, 1840, 1905, and 1951, all without lasting results.[25] Scaffolding was up once again in the south transept during the summer of 1986. No other area of the foundation has shown a similar weakness. It is likely that Roger's accident occurred at this spot that remains plagued by subterranean instability. Most cathedrals were built from east to west, but at Lisieux, construction began at the western end of the nave and moved toward the transept.[26] This unusual progression resulted from the nature and extent of the destruction of the original building. Roger's story may therefore be taken as an indication that work had progressed at least as far as the transepts by 1171. Construction must have begun many years earlier.

Most of the evidence concerning the construction of a medieval cathedral lies concealed within the building itself. Architects can tell much about the time of construction by examining structural features such as arches, piers, and buttresses. Art historians find their clues in iconography and stylistic devices. By studying small changes in design, it is possible not only to determine the direction in which construction proceeded but also to identify the individual marks of different master builders. Those who seek to discover the secrets of a building from its masonry, however, must be careful not to overlook the very real human influences that determined its essential character. In the case of St.-Pierre-de-Lisieux, several attempts have been made to date the construction by a careful physical examination of the cathedral. No one has yet adequately explored the role played by the bishop who commissioned it.

Georges Duval, an internationally known architect and a lifelong resident of Lisieux, studied the cathedral for his doctoral thesis at the University of Paris in 1956.[27] He concluded that the cathedral had been built in two stages. The first, which included the nave, the narthex, the transepts, and the first two bays of the choir, he assigned to the last ten years of Arnulf's episcopacy, 1170 to 1180. Duval did not, however, give more than lip service to Arnulf's role in the construction. His sources included only modern works; most of what he knew of the bishop came from secondary references. The rest of the choir and the apsidal chapels he assumed to have been constructed in the first quarter of the thirteenth century. The major architectural influences, he said, came from Paris. Duval was correct in seeing the eastern end of the cathedral as a thirteenth-century structure, although he failed to mention the stylistic similarities between the eastern end of the cathedral at Lisieux and other thirteenth-century Norman Gothic churches, such as those at Rouen and St.-Etienne-de-Caen. His major contribution to the accurate dating of the cathedral was to point out the break in construction that occurred between the second and third choir bays. The most obvious change appears in the piercing of tympani of the tribune arches with trefoils (plate 6).

An American art historian, William W. Clark, revised Duval's dating scheme in 1970. His careful study of the architectural features of the cathedral revealed the existence of an intermediate stage of construction between the work of the nave master and that of the builder who completed the choir. Names of master builders were seldom recorded in the twelfth century. Clark identifies the nave master at Lisieux only as a Norman who gained his training in the shop that built the second level of the Tour Saint-Romaine at Rouen.[28] Clark used the letters of Arnulf to prove that construction began on the nave around 1160, and, relying heavily on Barlow's introduction to his edition of the Arnulf correspondence, he assumed that work on the cathedral might have stopped as early as 1175 because of the bishop's financial difficulties.[29] He then projected a second campaign, extending from 1185 to the end of the century, during which the transepts, the first two choir bays, the narthex, and the façade were constructed. Among the indications of this second campaign, he pointed to certain changes in the arrangement of columns and a slight shifting of the axis in the transept. Once again the differences are fairly easy to spot. In the nave, every line of support may be traced from vault to floor; in the transept, there are several columns that are corbeled into the wall at the second story level (plate 7). The shifting of the axis has resulted in a transept that is half a meter wider at the north end than at the south end. The shift amounts to no more than two degrees to the south and is usually not shown in diagrams of the cathedral plan. It is obvious enough, however, to cause a slight feeling of disorientation to a viewer standing at the western end of the aisles.

A major problem with Clark's theory is that the similarities between his first and second campaigns are more pronounced than their differences. The aisle bays on the eastern side of the transept reproduce those of the nave. The capitals of the columns in the nave and transept are nearly interchangeable. The floor levels and the elevations are very similar, except for the terminal walls of the transept. Even the stone-cutting techniques are the same. Clark handled the problem by surmising that the second builder had been trained in the shop of the first master and was using materials that had already been prepared before a lack of funds brought the first campaign to a close.[30]

The theory that work on the cathedral stopped at an early stage because of the financial difficulties of its builder should be laid to rest. Barlow's introduction to the Arnulf correspondence stated that by 1178 "the builders had not been paid for several years."[31] That interpretation is unlikely; workers who had not been paid would have immediately moved on to another job, for their services were much in demand during this peak building period. The letter to which Barlow refers says only that Arnulf's creditors had stood surety for the expenses of construction and other church needs for a long time without receiving any interest on their money.[32] There can be little justification for equating, as Barlow seems to do, the creditors with the builders of the cathedral, especially since this passage indicates that the creditors had been paying for expenses other than construction. The mention of interest is unusual in this context, but it seems to indicate that the creditors had been acting in good faith rather than as usurers.

According to his own statement, Arnulf financed much of the building from his personal resources. In a letter to Pope Alexander III at the end of his career, he rendered the following account in answer to charges that he had mishandled diocesan funds: "I laid out twelve thousand pounds on the existing buildings, and the same amount on the episcopal church, for the most part supplied from my own possessions and property."[33] Figures such as these must, of course, be viewed with suspicion, for people often overestimate their expenses and charitable donations. The sum of twelve thousand pounds for rebuilding the cathedral within a twenty-year period is not, however, too far out of line. Construction costs for the cathedral at Autun, including materials, supplies, and labor, have been estimated at over four hundred pounds per year over a period of nearly thirty years.[34]

Architects, as such, did not make their appearance until fairly late in the development of high Gothic style. In the twelfth century, construction of a cathedral was a cooperative venture between those who commissioned the work and those who performed it.[35] The bishop and his canons were usually responsible for making the major decisions concerning the size and iconography of the cathedral. The master builder then used his technical skills and experience to design and construct the building. The master builder's individuality may be evident, for example, in the technique he used to spring an arch or in the detail of his carvings. But it was the bishop and his canons who determined how many arches occurred and which images were portrayed.[36] In the case of Lisieux, of course, Arnulf's poor relationship with his canons and their hostility toward his building campaign make it likely that the bishop acted alone.

It is clear that two different builders supervised the construction of the nave and transepts, but there is little or no evidence of a time lapse between the first and second campaigns. On the contrary, the unity of design from portal to choir argues for a continuous effort. Custom and professional courtesy decreed that a new builder would not make any changes in the work that had been done by his predecessor, although he was free to introduce new features in his own part of the building. As a result, many Gothic cathedrals built over long periods or under the direction of several different people display a variety of techniques and decorative features within a single structure.[37] The similarities between the first and second campaigns at Lisieux, therefore, indicate that the second builder was being guided by the same hand that had directed the nave master—presumably Arnulf of Lisieux. I believe construction began shortly after 1157 and continued without a break, except for a change in master builders, until 1180 or 1181. By the time work came to an end, the façade, the narthex, the nave, the transepts, and the first two bays of the choir were essentially complete. The entire structure had been overseen by a single individual who knew exactly how he wanted his cathedral built.

It is safe to assume that Arnulf kept close watch over the construction. His correspondence demonstrates that he was a busybody and a stickler for detail. He knew the private affairs of his parishioners and clergy. He kept track of the possessions of outlying parishes and of debts owed by monasteries within the diocese. He followed up on decisions he made as a judge and did not hesitate to castigate Henry de Sully for paying a fine with worthless coins.[38] He even knew which of the citizens of Lisieux was raising his Christmas goose. It is almost inconceivable that such a bishop would spend twelve thousand pounds of his private income to build a cathedral without personally dictating aspects of its design and supervising its construction. St.-Pierre-de-Lisieux may therefore be best understood by viewing it as an iconographical explication of its bishop's personality.

Arnulf left his mark on the cathedral in many ways. The criticism leveled against St.-Pierre-de-Lisieux—that it is huge, cold, ponderous, orderly, and dull—has validity. But what Mérimée saw as a similarity to English cathedrals might be more accurately described as the characteristic restraint advocated in Cistercian thought. Arnulf had two strong French influences in his life: he admired the secular accomplishments of Abbot Suger, and he longed to be more like the saintly Bernard of Clairvaux. It would have been difficult for anyone to emulate two such opposites as Suger and Bernard, but nowhere did their differences become more obvious than in their attitudes toward the decoration of churches. Suger's great abbey church of St.-Denis glowed, not only from the light of his stained glass windows, but also from a profusion of gold and jewels and painted statuary. Bernard harshly criticized such ostentation:

> O vanity of vanities, but not so much vanity as insanity! The church glitters on every side and exists among paupers. It clothes its stones in gold and abandons its sons to nudity. A banquet for the eyes is served up to the hungers of the poor. Curiosity seekers find much that delights them, and the sufferers find nothing to sustain them.[39]

Characteristically, Arnulf may have sought a middle ground at Lisieux by copying Suger's new architectural style in the Île-de-France while practicing the decorative restraint advocated by Bernard. The result was a curiously plain Gothic cathedral (plate 8), similar in some ways to the cathedral of Sens, built some twenty years earlier and also influenced by Cistercian attitudes.[40]

Arnulf had long been torn by opposing political allegiances. He had early ties to England and France, as well as to his Norman homeland. It should come as no surprise, therefore, to find elements of French, Norman, and English styles intermingled in his cathedral. Duval's assumption that the major architectural influence came out of France was both logical and based on observable similarities. St.-Pierre-de-Lisieux resembles the early Gothic architectural style of the Île-de-France in many ways. It contains three stories, pointed arches, ribbed vaults, a simple lean-to roof over the aisles rather than a fully developed gallery, high clerestory windows, and cylindrical piers with foliated capitals. Even small details, such as the grape motif that predominates in the friezework of St.-Pierre-de-Lisieux, were borrowed from the Île-de-France (plate 9). Pilasters decorated with grapes may be found at St.-Denis, on the west portals of Sens, and at Notre-Dame-de-Paris. Grapes also adorn the porch of the north transept at Chartres,[41] the tomb of John of Salisbury, and the remains of a house discovered under the parvis at Chartres. As new Gothic ideas appeared in France, they too were immediately adopted at Lisieux. The flying buttress, developed and used for the nave of Notre-Dame-de-Paris in the early 1170s, was probably incorporated into Lisieux by the second builder when he vaulted the nave around 1180 (plate 10). Duval believes that the flying buttresses were added at the end of the twelfth century to replace the original wall buttresses, but Clark's investigations proved conclusively that the nave buttresses were not later additions to the construction. He suggests that the idea of flyers was transmitted first from Paris to Mantes and then to Lisieux.[42]

Other stylistic elements at Lisieux were specifically different from the French. The four-part rib vault was an old Anglo-Norman device, first used in England in the aisle vaults of Durham in 1093 and developed at Rouen and Fécamp.[43] It contrasted sharply with the six-part vaults of twelfth-century France, such as the nave vault used at St.-Etienne-de-Caen in the 1120s, which required an entirely different system of supports. The design of the central portal of the façade at Lisieux was also Anglo-Norman in character. Although the portal sculptures were destroyed during the French Revolution and the tympanum and lintel replaced by a clear window after a fire in 1808, it has been possible to determine their original composition from surviving documents.[44] A letter written by Dom Prosper Tassin in 1729 described the tympanum as containing a Christ in Majesty, surrounded by the human figures of the Four Evangelists, each of whom bore the head of his symbolic animal.[45] The portrayal of the Evangelists as human bodies bearing animal heads is an unusual iconographic device, found most frequently in English manuscript illuminations of the twelfth and thirteenth centuries.[46] The *Maiestas* theme is not normally thought of in conjunction with a fully developed Gothic style, although it was used in the central tympanum on the west façade at Chartres. There, however, the evangelical figures were represented by their animal symbols, not human bodies with animal heads.[47] The portrayal of Christ in Majesty was common in Normandy from 1140 to 1170, then almost completely disappeared to be replaced by themes of the Virgin and the Last Judgment.[48] Design features of the cathedral thus reflect a bishop who was equally familiar with France and England but most at home in Normandy.

Almost every description of the cathedral has noted the symmetry and simplicity of its design. Yet clustered around the main piers that separate the narthex from the nave are several sculptured heads that seem to be contemporary with the twelfth-century construction but out of keeping with the foliage that otherwise predominates. At the junctures of the foliated archivolt of the narthex with the pillars on either side are the crowned heads of a man (plate 11) and a woman (plate 12).[49] At the top of a column in the interior of the arch, directly behind the head of the woman, there are five tiny heads, almost concealed among the leaves of one of the capitals (plate 13). On the other side of this southern pile, facing the side aisle, is a somber face with head bared to show carefully carved hair and beard (plate 14). In a similar position facing the north aisle, a kindly face is topped by what appears to be a scholarly cap or a bishop's mitre (plate 15).

The existence of these heads was noted by Hardy, but he professed not to know their identities. Most other descriptions of the cathedral fail even to mention them. Duval follows local legend in identifying two of the larger heads with Henry II and Eleanor of Aquitaine and the smaller ones as their children.[50] One of the most persistent traditions of the cathedral of Lisieux is that Arnulf performed the marriage of Henry II and Eleanor of Aquitaine there on May 18, 1152. Contemporary records confirm the date of the marriage but contradict the location; by several accounts the ceremony actually took place in Poitiers.[51] Legends do not often spring up spontaneously; most have some basis in fact. In this case, it seems likely that the legend of the marriage ceremony arose out of a need to explain the existence of the heads of Henry and Eleanor in the cathedral.

If the legend can thus be dismissed, the existence of the heads cannot. Capitals decorated with figures were a familiar feature of Romanesque style, while Gothic favored foliated capitals. Sauerländer noted this basic difference and cautioned that "figures or cycles actually incorporated into the structure remain an exception, and in each case call for special explanation."[52] Every capital at Lisieux, except for the one bearing the five small heads, conforms to Gothic foliate design. Heads used as corbel decoration were also rare in twelfth-century Gothic churches; when heads did appear, they were non-human or grotesques.[53] The overall Gothic impression of this cathedral thus draws attention to sculptures that seem out of place. Because the naturalistic heads at Lisieux are the only human representations carved into the original structure and because the small heads comprise the only lack of symmetry, one must assume that they had a special significance for the builders of the cathedral.

Attempts to attach specific identities to the heads in the cathedral of Lisieux have generally been rejected by art historians because realistic portrait sculpture did not develop until the thirteenth century. Clark, for example, completely discounts the legend that the two central heads of the archivolt were meant to be Henry II and Eleanor of Aquitaine, preferring to identify them only as "a queen" and "a king."[54] Certainly it would be futile to try to prove facial resemblances between these stylized sculptures and the people they may have been meant to portray. They merely follow iconographical conventions—a king and a queen, both crowned; five children, shown smaller than the accompanying adults; a bareheaded workman; and a mitred bishop.

But despite the tendency of modern art historians to dismiss twelfth-century sculptures as merely generic, there are many examples of living persons whose figures adorned contemporary ecclesiastical buildings. Statues of kings and noblemen frequently joined ecclesiastical figures as part of the accepted iconography of twelfth- and thirteenth-century churches.[55] The Royal Portal at Chartres can be cited as an attempt to prefigure the relationship of *regnum* and *sacerdotium* in its Old Testament statues.[56] Real persons appeared in the crusading window of St.-Denis by 1158; both Robert of Flanders and Robert of Normandy were shown fighting in the First Crusade.[57] The tympanum of the Portal of Saint Anne at Notre-Dame in Paris shows the figures of Maurice de Sully, the bishop who began construction, and his king, Louis VII.[58] The Portal of the Coronation of the Virgin at Notre-Dame originally contained a monumental statue of the young Philip Augustus in commemoration of a miraculous rescue from a forest shortly before his coronation in 1179.[59] The crowned heads of a king and queen found in the twelfth-century church of Notre-Dame-du-Bourg at Langon, near Bordeaux, have been popularly identified with Henry and Eleanor, who visited the area in 1155.[60]

Studying iconographical conventions is one way to determine the date at which a sculpture was carved.[61] And once the date of its creation becomes clear, it is possible to determine the historical events that may have inspired it. The king's head at Lisieux has much in common with the Old Testament figures on the right portal of Chartres-West (ca. 1155).[62] In size, the square shape of the face, the treatment of the sharply ridged eyebrows and carefully delineated eyelids, and the placement of the crown, the Lisieux king most closely resembles the head of King David from a jamb statue on the Portal of Saint Anne at Notre-Dame, which was carved between 1165 and 1170.[63] The same characteristics may be seen in a collection of twelfth-century sculptures discovered under the parvis of Notre-Dame and now on display at the Cluny Museum in Paris (plate 16). The treatment of softly flowing hair and beard is clearly more advanced than that on heads that have been identified with the original portal sculptures at St.-Denis (ca. 1140).[64] But the Lisieux head does not demonstrate the same individuality of features and elongated shape that appear in the Moses head at Mantes (ca. 1180) and in the sculpture of the central portal of the north transept at Chartres (ca. 1205–1210).[65] The head of the king at Lisieux thus displays several characteristics that indicate it was carved between 1160 and 1175, the period of construction over which Bishop Arnulf exercised the most control. Although sculpture from this period cannot be expected to present a pictorial likeness of its subject, it is hard to escape the conclusion that the bishop was thinking of Henry II when he commissioned the carving of this head.

Throughout his career, Arnulf adhered to the belief that kings and prelates should work together for the common good of Christendom. His paradigm assumed that the church could not survive without the support of its monarchs and that there was no salvation for a king outside the church.[66] This idea had a long history of acceptance. Bishop Ivo of Chartres had argued the same point during the Investiture Struggle, as had Abbot Suger earlier in the twelfth century.[67] The members of the party of Haimeric had assumed that the best solution to the conflict between *regnum* and *sacerdotium* was a form of compromise that would allow the two powers to cooperate. Despite changes in the nature of kingship in the second half of the twelfth century, Arnulf saw no reason to alter his paradigm.

The bishops of France included Capetian kings in their sculptural programs whenever there existed a special relationship between the king and a particular church. During the thirteenth-century rebuilding program at St.-Denis, kings and queens of the Capetian dynasty were added to many of the keystones.[68] But unlike the Capetians, who had usually maintained a good relationship with the church, the Plantagenets were often at odds with ecclesiastical authority. Arnulf had realized as early as the schism of 1159 that there was a real danger of Henry II's splitting away from the church for his own political advantage. By the mid-1160s, the Becket controversy made that danger even greater. Arnulf could not control the actions of his king, but he could symbolically freeze Henry within the church by having his image carved into the structure of the new cathedral.

Once the identity of Henry is accepted, there can be no doubt that the queen's head was meant to represent Eleanor of Aquitaine. That makes it possible to fix a date after which these sculptures would not have been produced. By Easter 1173, the older sons of Henry II were in revolt against their father, with the active encouragement of their mother. By the end of that year, Eleanor herself was Henry's prisoner, and they were never thereafter reconciled. It would have been a foolhardy bishop indeed who would have portrayed the queen after the middle of 1173. The identity of the five small heads is more problematic, since Henry and Eleanor had eight children. If the sculptures were meant to represent the five living children of the king and queen, the carving would have been planned after the birth of the young Eleanor in 1161 but before the birth of Joanna in October 1165. If they represent the five Plantagenet sons, including the first-born William, who died at age three, the carving must have been designed after the birth of John on Christmas Eve 1166. Further, the lack of a crown on any of the children's heads would indicate that the carving was done before the crowning of the Young King on June 14, 1170. The heads in the narthex arch thus help to confirm the dating of construction and strengthen the argument that Arnulf used the cathedral as a personal statement of his loyalties.

The identities of the corbel heads in the north and south aisles cannot be definitely established. During this period, it was common practice to have the likenesses of both the instituting bishop and the architect carved into a commemorative stone located in the center of the labyrinth of the nave. If such a stone existed at Lisieux, it has long since disappeared under the elevated floor.[69] If a cathedral did not have a labyrinth, the portraits of bishop and builder often appeared somewhere else in the cathedral in recognition of their accomplishments.[70] Students of St.-Denis have located no less than four portraits of Abbot Suger in its sculpture and stained glass.[71] Arnulf himself was often accused of egotism and self-aggrandizement, and he knew Suger and his abbey church well. To incorporate his own portrait into the fabric of his cathedral would have been entirely in character. The bishop who oversees the north aisle, therefore, may well be Arnulf. As for the image of the master builder, one could argue that the exquisite detail of the sculpture of the south aisle bespeaks a self-portrait.

Whether or not the mitred head was meant as a portrait of Arnulf, there can be little doubt that the cathedral as a whole reflects his personality, his experiences, and his attitudes. Even more, it displays as much evidence of his willingness to compromise as of his steadfastness and bears the marks of his doubts as well as of his beliefs. Arnulf was often eager to welcome new ideas while remaining hesitant about the value of the changes they brought about. He had longed for a strong centralized monarchy but feared the subsequent loss of ecclesiastical influence. He had worked for the expansion of papal bureaucracy while regretting the loss of personal contact with the pope. He had urged monastic reform, but only so far as it did not impinge on his own episcopal privileges. In much the same way, he admired the appearance of the new French cathedrals but was reluctant to abandon the Romanesque structures that had served the Anglo-Norman world so well.

St.-Pierre-de-Lisieux has long puzzled architects and art historians because it is a mixture of Gothic design and Romanesque structure. Visually it is Gothic; the eye of the observer is quickly drawn to its pointed arches and soaring vaults. But it also has a heaviness uncharacteristic of Gothic architecture. The cylindrical piers of the nave are massive, measuring nearly eight feet in diameter. The galleries are closed. The windows, even now with their clear glass, provide little light. The single-wall construction and four-part vaults are confining rather than liberating. Clark has described the effect as that of "a Romanesque structure in a Gothic guise."[72] The description is apt. More important, it is equally applicable to the cathedral and to the bishop who built it.

1. Exterior of St.-Pierre-de-Lisieux.
(Photo: Floyd Schriber)

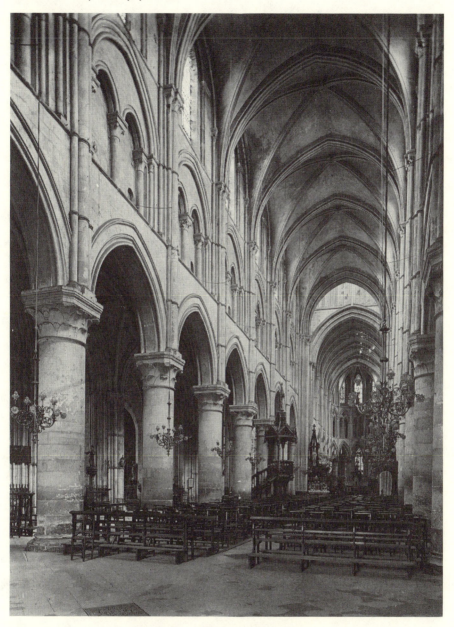

2. Interior of St.-Pierre-de-Lisieux.
(Copyright ARS N.Y./ARCH. PHOT. PARIS, 1990)

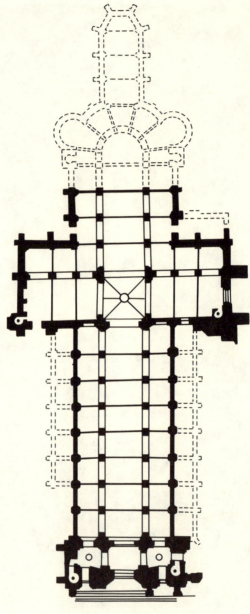

TWELFTH-CENTURY FLOORPLAN

- - - - - LATER ADDITIONS

3. Floor plan of St.-Pierre-de-Lisieux.

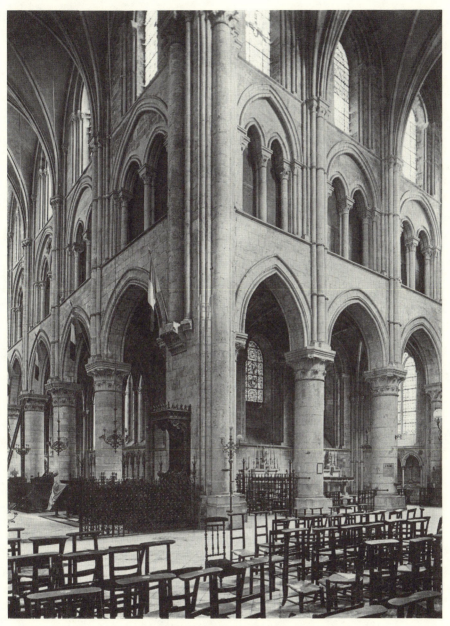

4. Southeast corner of crossing tower.
(Copyright ARS N.Y./ARCH. PHOT. PARIS, 1990)

5. Deterioration of south transept.
(Photo: Douglas Schriber)

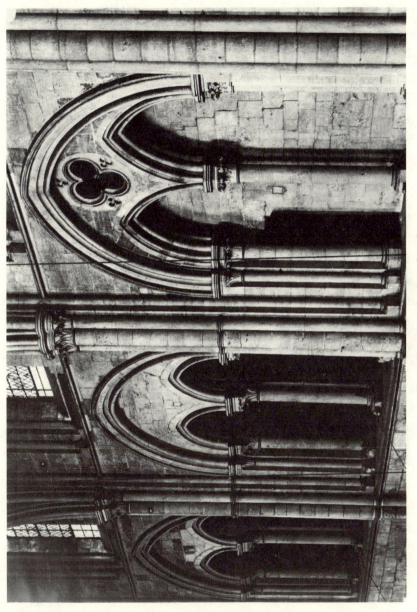

6. Second and third north choir bays.
(Copyright ARS N.Y. / ARCH. PHOT. PARIS, 1990)

7. Corbeled column in north transept.
(Photo: Douglas Schriber)

8. Nave and south aisle.
(Copyright ARS N.Y. / ARCH. PHOT. PARIS, 1990)

9. Detail of grape motif from north portal.
(Photo: Douglas Schriber)

10. Flying buttresses above south aisle.
(Copyright ARS N.Y. / ARCH. PHOT. PARIS, 1990)

11. Head of a king on archivolt of narthex.
(Photo: Floyd Schriber)

12. Head of a queen on archivolt of narthex.
(Photo: Floyd Schriber)

13. Five children's heads in narthex.
(Photo: Floyd Schriber)

14. Head of a workman in south aisle.
(Photo: Floyd Schriber)

15. Head of a bishop in north aisle.
(Photo: Floyd Schriber)

16. Heads at Cluny Museum, Paris.
(Photo: Douglas Schriber)

VII.

The Pivotal Crisis
The Becket Controversy

For almost a quarter of a century, Arnulf had managed his episcopal career through a series of compromises predicated upon the paradigm he had adopted in his youth. He had recognized Geoffrey of Anjou as Duke of Normandy, even though he mistrusted him, in order to secure his own appointment to the bishopric of Lisieux. He had switched his political allegiance to the Empress Matilda and her son when it became evident that such a move could assure his own political influence. He had absented himself from the primary duties of his diocese in order to solidify his position as an advisor of the young Duke Henry. And he had taken leave of the English court when it appeared that he could play a more influential role in the reign of Henry II by returning to Normandy as a bishop-justiciar. Periodically he had sublimated the desire to take up a monastic vocation by channeling his efforts toward other manifestations of religious devotion—going on crusade, reforming the excesses of his diocese, and beginning the construction of a fine new cathedral.

Even his most firmly held beliefs had been subject to modifications required by the exigencies of the moment. He had professed admiration for the Cistercian ideals of poverty while accepting valuable gifts of land that would increase his personal wealth and the income of his diocese. He had deplored the interference of the German emperor in the papal election of 1159, even while he used every trick at his disposal to assure Henry II's support of Pope Alexander III. His efforts to improve the standards of religious life within his diocese had stopped short of any reform that might threaten his episcopal revenues. He had served almost simultaneously as an instrument of Henry's efforts to extend his system of courts and as a papal judge-delegate charged with protecting the jurisdictional rights of the church.

Such compromises and vacillations make Arnulf vulnerable to modern charges of untrustworthiness, but they accurately reflected the period in which he had been raised and educated. He was a student of the same new scholastic method of thought that had produced Abelard's *Sic et non* and Gratian's *Concordance of Discordant Canons*. He had been trained to recognize that there were two sides to every issue and that the proper duty of an educated individual was to create a synthesis of truth out of contradictory opinions. His mature years had brought him a long way from the immoderate excesses of youth and the intemperate accusations of his *Invectiva*. Yet the spirit of balance and compromise that so characterized Arnulf's career as a bishop was not yet universally recognized as a virtue, and the moderation that led him to seek a middle ground in any dispute was apt to earn him as many enemies as admirers, particularly in a situation that raised fundamental issues of right and wrong. Such an incident occurred in the Becket years, and the clash between the rights of a king and the privileges of the church shook the very foundations of Arnulf's carefully balanced episcopate.

The dispute that arose in 1163 between Henry II and Thomas Becket, formerly royal chancellor and now archbishop of Canterbury, had repercussions that reached far beyond the original boundaries of their personal quarrel to touch the lives of clergy and laity alike. For Pope Alexander III, already challenged by the schismatic Victor IV, this dispute posed the possibility of a further erosion of the influence of the Roman church. For Louis VII, whose former wife, Eleanor of Aquitaine, had married Henry and borne him five sons after producing only daughters for the throne of France, this was a long-awaited chance to frustrate the ambitions of his archrival by allying himself with Henry's opponents. The Anglo-Norman nobility realized that many disputed land claims depended upon the outcome of the struggle between ecclesiastical and temporal powers. Clerics of every degree faced a conflict between allegiance to their king and obedience to their holy vows. Perhaps no one felt more strongly the dangers of the conflict than did bishops such as Arnulf of Lisieux.

Arnulf's relationship with Henry had been a complicated and difficult one. Arnulf had always been an ambitious man, and he had sought an outlet for that ambition at the English court. It had long been his hope that his early devotion to Henry would be repaid by a prominent place at the king's side. Henry, for his part, had once regarded Arnulf as a valued senior advisor, but by 1163 Arnulf had been shunted aside by younger claimants to the king's favor. Some chroniclers seem to indicate that Arnulf was actually out of favor with the king at the time the Becket controversy arose. William of Canterbury said that Arnulf had fallen from the king's friendship. Edward Grim stated that the king had been hostile to the bishop for a long time. And Anonymous I indicated that Arnulf had offended the king.[1] None of them, however, offered an explanation that would reveal a real clash between the two men, and there is no documentary evidence to support the suggestions of a quarrel. Arnulf had, for example, attended the king's court at Domfront in 1162, where he witnessed a confirmation of an agreement concerning the priory of Viry.[2] Most of his attention after 1159, however, had been devoted to the settlement of the papal schism, and Henry may well have resented the bishop's interference in a matter that seemed to the king to have purely political significance.

Arnulf maintained a more rewarding association with Pope Alexander III. He had offered unquestioning support of Alexander during his disputed elevation in 1159. Frank Barlow has commented that "the tone of some of the bishop's letters to the pope suggests that he considered himself another St. Bernard and Alexander another Eugenius."[3] The two men carried on a voluminous correspondence, and no matter how blunt Arnulf might have been in criticism of the pope's actions in handling ecclesiastical matters, their personal friendship had seldom suffered.

Arnulf's life was also closely tied to that of Thomas Becket. The Becket family was of Norman extraction; Thomas's mother came from Caen and his father from the region around Lisieux.[4] While geographic coincidence does not prove long-standing acquaintance, it may help to explain why a Norman bishop took a special interest in the career of a relatively unknown English clerk. Arnulf, in fact, may have been one of the first to bring Becket's abilities to Henry's attention. Anonymous I credited Arnulf and Philip of Bayeux with recommending Becket to Henry for the position of chancellor. Other chronicles, however, do not confirm the story.[5]

When Becket was appointed royal chancellor in 1155, Arnulf wrote a congratulatory letter, in which he declared himself to be "delighted to be greeted among those who had first claim to your early favor and friendship, a friendship not destroyed by the distance between our locations nor extinguished by frequent business dealings."[6] Arnulf adopted a fatherly attitude and warned the new chancellor that it would not be easy to keep Henry's approval. The statement would prove prophetic for both men:

> Therefore [at court] everything is twisted, and one must hide an angry countenance and mental anguish beneath a numbing gaiety and cover hidden enmity with deceitful flattery. Further, if the favor of the king turns against someone and he begins to regard him with a harsher eye, he, upon whom the pleasure of being a boon companion, applause, and the zealous deference of all were once lavished, goes out immediately, bereft of all consolation.[7]

Arnulf wrote again when Becket became archbishop of Canterbury in 1162. This letter was uncharacteristically short for the voluble bishop and perhaps, as Barlow suggests, tinged with jealousy at Becket's rapid rise to preeminence.[8] The tone was still warm: "We received the news of your consecration with such great delight, the more so because we knew that the news arrived out of the more abundant richness of your affection."[9] Nevertheless Arnulf could not resist another opportunity to counsel his young correspondent. In an obvious reference to Becket's penchant for high living, he wrote: "We urge you to observe the proper limits, so that piety shall not take away your magnificence, nor your splendor diminish your holiness, but that they may run together as horses in stride, and that they may sanctify and glorify the priest in the divine image of Christ."[10]

Thus in 1163 Arnulf of Lisieux faced a conflict, not just between ecclesiastical and temporal loyalties but among three people whose friendships he had cultivated. He was a loyal liegeman of Henry II, always striving to prove the worth of his services to the English court. He was a devoted and obedient servant of Pope Alexander III, supporting the privileges of the church above all others. And he was the personal friend of Thomas Becket, ever willing to guide the younger man's career by his paternal advice. It was inevitable that Arnulf should become involved in the dispute; what remained in doubt was which side he would support.

Arnulf's position in the Becket controversy was complicated even further by his own view of the double role of a bishop. From the beginning of his ecclesiastical career, he had believed it to be his duty to support and advise his monarch. He was firmly the king's man, as eager for political influence and secular responsibility as for ecclesiastical prominence. In these loyalties, he was completely faithful to the examples set for him by his family of curial bishops. At the same time, he recognized the dangers the church faced from overly ambitious rulers. In his sermon at the Council of Tours in May 1163, he had warned his fellow bishops that they must make every effort to counteract secular encroachments on the spiritual authority of the church. His special target at Tours, of course, was the Emperor Frederick, but he expanded his comments to include all princes who, he said, "held their power from no other law than that which was granted only by the grace of the holy Roman church."[11]

Most theologians involved in the Becket controversy stood fast to their principles, which dictated that the primary duty of a prelate was to defend the liberties of the church against all attacks of anticlerical princes.[12] There can be little doubt that Arnulf believed in the primacy of canon law and ecclesiastical jurisdiction over the actions of all Christians. But he was unprepared for a situation in which the church's liberty was challenged from outside by secular authority while its unity was being threatened from within by conflicting opinions about the proper relationship between *regnum* and *sacerdotium*. For the first time, the moral obligations of his faith conflicted directly with his loyalty to his monarch and his vows of obedience within the church hierarchy. Arnulf was not alone in facing this conflict, but his inherent preference for compromise and expediency isolated him from those other prelates who took refuge in a strict interpretation of canon law.

The split between Henry and Becket became apparent at the Council of Westminster in October 1163. Henry wished to restore to the crown those privileges that had allowed his grandfather, Henry I, to exercise a high degree of control over ecclesiastical affairs. Becket refused to accept any agreement that lessened the powers of the church, and his suffragan bishops supported him. Arnulf arrived at the council in time to hear Becket announce his willingness to obey the king in all things, "saving our order." But he also noticed, as apparently Henry did not, that Hilary, bishop of Chichester, took the oath without that temporizing clause.[13] Arnulf approached Henry with a plan that might fend off the impending clash and at the same time restore Henry's confidence in him. He suggested that Becket's greatest strength arose from the support of his suffragan bishops and that Henry's attack should begin with them: "Therefore, even if you cannot separate all of them from him, you might somehow try to win some of them over to your side; once this has been accomplished, the remainder will not easily sustain their firm opposition."[14]

The chroniclers are unanimous in their view that Arnulf acted out of self-service, and Becket scholars have almost unanimously condemned this proposal as "double-dealing."[15] Henry, however, recognized the practicality of the suggestion and immediately put it into effect. Frank Barlow has speculated that all of the bishops yielded to Henry, using as evidence the argument that the chroniclers do not mention any exceptions.[16] The account of William of Canterbury may confirm this opinion, for he simply stated that the bishops were converted.[17] Anonymous I and Edward Grim were specific, however, in naming the converts: Roger of Pont l'Évêque, archbishop of York; Robert de Chesney, bishop of Lincoln; Gilbert Foliot, bishop of London; and Hilary, bishop of Chichester.[18]

When the bishops reconvened at the Council of Clarendon in January 1164, Henry presented them with a list of sixteen principles that, he declared, were merely restatements of the ancient customs of the land. Becket, opposed to any document that might result in the weakening of ecclesiastical power, took the required oath but immediately repudiated it. Because Henry could not countenance any such show of insubordination, the battle lines were drawn. In October at the Council of Northampton, Henry called upon Becket to answer a variety of charges concerning the administration of his baronial estates. Brandishing his archiepiscopal cross in front of him like a weapon, Becket refused to listen to a verdict of treason and fled into voluntary exile in France.

Henry was not the sort of person from whom one could walk away with impunity. He marshaled his support and, almost in defiance of his own Constitutions, set out to gain the support of the pope. Arnulf was one of the delegates sent to the Continent to obtain papal confirmation of the Constitutions of Clarendon as well as a legateship for Roger of York. In all, Arnulf made six trips between the English court and the papal seat at Sens in 1163 and 1164, but the pope remained obdurate.[19]

By the end of 1164, both sides had had an opportunity to explain their positions to the pope, and Alexander had remanded Becket to the abbey at Pontigny. Henry, who was never known for his moderation when his temper was aroused, had begun reprisals on Becket's adherents and was extending tentative feelers toward an alliance with the schismatic German emperor, Frederick Barbarossa. Arnulf experienced a gradual change of allegiance. In a letter written at Christmas 1164, Nicholas of Rouen informed Becket that he had visited Arnulf at his manor of Nonant and found him sympathetic toward Becket's cause.[20]

In March 1165, Arnulf wrote a long letter to Becket, praising him for tempering his zeal for justice with proper humility. He explained in some detail what people were saying about Becket in England—their criticism of Becket's pride, of his desire for power, of his ostentation, and of his attempts to destroy the royal authority:

Some people—those whose malice has been accustomed to invent what it did not know—think that your work grew out of pride, not true virtue;—that you hope to regain your former chancellor's duties and to serve in that position, too, so that no one would dare to resist your power or will; . . . that you want to be highly placed and advanced to a higher divine eminence, not just to observe the assembly on a footstool or from the side, but to seek a crown for your own head, because so much depends naturally on your authority that it ought to belong to you in the first place for your duty and the sealing of your duty;—that for that reason you order the seizure of royal prerogatives so that in this matter the world might appear to be taken by storm, since no confidence will remain for those who resist, when royal commands are not able to prevail.[21]

Arnulf also offered a very telling portrait of Henry. The king, he said, was feared by everyone because he was so unused to failure that he could not accept any defeat or criticism:

In truth he may at one time or another show himself yielding to humility and patience, but he does not allow himself to be conquered by strength, but whatever he does openly must seem to have resulted from his own will, not from weakness. He seeks more for glory than success, which in a prince might be commendable enough, if truth and virtue, not vanity and the sweet flattery of his followers, furnished the material of that glory. He is great, and much greater than most; because he has neither a superior who terrifies him, nor a subordinate who opposes him, nor has he been defeated by foreign injuries by which his inborn wildness might have been tamed.[22]

All of this led up to the real purpose of the letter, which was to impart some advice:

In the meantime, if anyone suffers to appeal to your serenity, your good sense should not spurn the occasion, but you should accept the offer with a ready hand. More than that, if he should attempt to delay, don't be willing to discuss small points of excessive hair-splitting; because hair-splitting encourages strife, and truly strife kindles and enflames the sleeping embers of hatred just as surely as a wind. It will not be for you to fail over single matters, but to stick more diligently to the generalities, because that is a healthy thing, unless the agreements clearly and especially destroy freedom. For if we confess our faith, owing reverence and divine services, if we offer goodness and our persons to honor and its uses for the sake of expending them, if we promise to observe the royal dignities and ancient customs in which the laws of God are not opposed, it will not hurt, because in these things we are by no means obligated against our vows. If, therefore, divine goodness provides peace for you and yours under this or a similar wording, save the interpretation of words for a future time.[23]

Arnulf's moderate view here was clear: that it was perfectly possible to acknowledge royal dignities without violating one's holy vows or the laws of God. But as Smalley has observed, "'Put your principles in your pocket' is unhelpful advice to one who takes them seriously."[24]

The letter ended with the assurance that Arnulf was fully in support of Becket's cause and that he would do whatever he could to be of assistance:

> I, as devoted as I am helpful, shall faithfully provide service in the cause of your peace; since I sympathize, God knows, with your trouble, and I sincerely embrace your person and your cause with loving arms. . . . Accordingly there will be much for me to do, so that on the face of things I may show myself unfriendly to you; because in showing myself to be a friend, no one would have faith in me or reveal an approach. A friend might be able therefore to serve zealously by the pretense of seeking favor [with the king], so that he might attack the excellence of your work and the diligence of your conversations carefully to your own advantage.[25]

Arnulf seemed to have switched his stance from advocacy of Henry's claims to full championship of Becket. Yet this letter was larded with small slivers of warning and conditions. He cautioned of the dangers of excessive zeal, the ease with which argument can flare into hatred, and the temptations of secular office. His offer of support was carefully worded; he intended to serve Becket, but only "in the cause of peace." Arnulf understood well the personalities of both protagonists, and his main goal was somehow to bring their conflicting elements to a peaceful settlement.

During the ensuing years, that goal seemed to grow more elusive. The questions at issue shifted, and as the claims on both sides escalated, the chances of a peaceful settlement diminished. The dispute spilled into Arnulf's own diocese, for several members of his cathedral chapter had joined Becket in exile, and the canons who remained in Lisieux used the affair as one more weapon in their ongoing dispute with their bishop. Two archdeacons of Lisieux—Hugh de Nonant, Arnulf's nephew, and Gilbert de Glanville—were members of the circle of *eruditi* who made up the itinerant household of the archbishop. To their number may be added Arnulf's other nephew, Sylvester, the treasurer of Lisieux, who witnessed at least two documents for Becket during this period.[26] Arnulf certainly regretted the king's harassment of Thomas's supporters, just as he grew impatient with the pope's failure to act and deplored the arrogance of Thomas's intractability. By June 1166, he was once more willing to act on the king's behalf, if there was any hope of bringing the matter to a sensible conclusion. He traveled with the king's delegation to Pontigny, where he proposed to forestall Becket's threat of excommunications with a personal appeal. Becket avoided the meeting, and the mission failed.[27]

For a time Arnulf buried himself in administrative details within his diocese, but deteriorating health and the frustration caused by the protracted ecclesiastical dispute reawakened his desire to retire to the more peaceful atmosphere of a monastery. This effort was more serious and more justified than his previous attempts to be released from the episcopacy. He was in his early to mid-sixties and had served in his office for over a quarter of a century. True even in old age to the model that St. Bernard had set in his youth, he had chosen the Cistercian house of Mortemer as the site of his retirement and had authorized the construction of a modest set of lodgings for his use.[28]

Twice during the fall of 1166, Arnulf approached Henry with a request that he be allowed to leave Normandy for a year in order to recover his health and recoup some of his financial losses by avoiding the expenses associated with the day-to-day responsibilities of a presiding bishop. At the end of that time, he proposed, he would be free from debt and able to retire honorably to a monastery. An anonymous correspondent immediately reported the story to Becket as a warning that Arnulf might not remain trustworthy if he accepted favors from the king.[29] On the first occasion at Touques, Henry promised only to speak to Arnulf's creditors and to lighten his work load. Later, at Caen, he offered Arnulf money to pay off his debts but provided only sixty of the two hundred marks that Arnulf requested. On neither occasion did he give any indication that he would consider a request for retirement, for the king could ill afford to lose the services of a skilled diplomat during this time of political crisis. Further, Henry immediately engaged the abbot of Mortemer in an argument over the land on which Arnulf was building his retirement home. The exact nature of the dispute is clouded by Arnulf's rather hysterical reaction, but it is clear that the king was claiming ownership of the land that the abbot had granted to Arnulf.[30] The royal stratagem worked, construction stopped, and Arnulf once again abandoned his plans to leave the episcopate. To the Becket forces, however, the episode merely confirmed their suspicions that Arnulf could not be trusted. The friend who reported the arrangement to Becket warned:

> Would that he had not accepted the tainted money of the king, since the king now believes that he has purchased a man who seemed to be in need, and he will use him as an instrument for the accomplishment of his evil ways. For the king will perhaps believe him now more readily, and the bishop, I fear, will be all the more faithful in his infidelity.[31]

Arnulf continued his efforts to encourage all sides to come to a reasonable settlement, but his patient diplomacy reached its breaking point in September 1169. He had attended the reconciliation talks conducted by the papal legates Gratian and Vivian, following them as they moved from place to place. The discussions broke down when the legates refused to accept Henry's insistence that they include the phrase "saving the dignity of the kingdom" in the agreement. Arnulf reacted by writing in fury to the pope. The settlement had been a fair one, he said. The king had agreed to restore the archbishop's holdings in England, and the legates were prepared to absolve all those who had been excommunicated during the dispute. Quibbling over words was both silly and futile. Arnulf continued with a brief but clear statement of his understanding of the relationship between the church and royal power. He remained adamant in his belief that neither was able to exist without the other:

> In our observation the freedom or dignity of the church was in no way oppressed by the dignity of the kingdom. Indeed, the honor of the church promotes royal honor more than it takes that honor away, and royal honor has been more

accustomed to preserve the church than to remove its liberty; and indeed the honor of church and realm run hand in hand with each other, since neither can kings obtain salvation without the church, nor can the church find peace without royal protection.[32]

This last passage was characteristic of Arnulf's view of his own dual role as baron and bishop. He ended abruptly with advice for the pope and his legates: "We humbly and urgently beg that your wisdom not be led to embrace the diacritical marks of the letters and the legal forms of the words as more important than the matter itself."[33] Despite his loyalty to the church, Arnulf had been forced back to the side of the king by the stubbornness of Becket and the papal legates.

By the early months of 1170, it was obvious to all that the situation could not be allowed to remain unresolved for much longer. Yet Henry was characteristically unable to concede without making one final grand nose-thumbing gesture. In June he went ahead with plans to have his eldest son crowned by the archbishop of York, an insulting usurpation of the traditional coronation right of the archbishop of Canterbury. But this time Henry had gone too far and he knew it. The action met with howls of protest from Louis VII, whose daughter Margaret, wife of the young Henry, had not been included in the hurried-up consecration, and by renewed threats of an English interdict from Becket. A reconciliation between Henry and Becket was effected in July at Fréteval, under exactly the terms Arnulf had been advocating for so long. Henry agreed to allow Becket to return to his former position with powers undiminished. The troublesome phrases were omitted from the agreement. Becket prudently refrained from demanding the kiss of peace. The bishop of Lisieux had reason to be proud of the rational restraint of both king and archbishop.

His relief was short-lived. Almost immediately upon his return to England, Becket unleashed another series of excommunications, this time directed at all those who had the audacity to participate in what he considered an uncanonical coronation of the king's son. Shocked by the resumption of hostilities, Arnulf wrote several letters to the pope in defense of the anathematized churchmen. He summed up his analysis of the situation in a personal and angry letter to Alexander. Arnulf was eloquent in his description of the gratitude felt by the world at the news of the reconciliation. His praise for Henry's actions was unstinting; his condemnation of Becket was brutal.

> For the most powerful king conquered his anger, he conquered his hatred, and at last he conquered himself at your pleading, and mercy changed the entire course of the preceding calamity on account of his devotion to your fatherhood; he even surprised himself that he was able to command himself or to lay out such a high price for someone else. . . . Thus in my presence were peace and favor restored to the archbishop. . . . He, however, about whom we are not able to speak without sadness and shame, carried fire and sword in his hands; and he who was hoped to have come as a blessing was seen to have undone the tranquil beginnings of peace with his abuses.[34]

Arnulf went to great lengths to assure the pope that the coronation of the Young King had been perfectly legal from a canonical point of view and that the excommunicated bishops had done nothing more than carry out their ecclesiastical duties. Arnulf's greatest fear was that this incident presaged further trouble:

> Therefore we pray . . . that your authority . . . may hold back and keep within bounds the animosity of this priest, lest the unexpected happiness of an un-hoped-for peace, which we have received from your kindness, should increase the insolence within him, so that as a result, confidence in your favor may lead him to war with kings and kingdoms; because it is my fear, and the fear of many, that this little spark may grow into a blaze, unless prudent sternness quickly tempers the passion of this man and curbs his audacity.[35]

Arnulf's disillusionment with Becket is apparent in his choice of words. At the beginning of the letter, Becket was referred to as *archiepiscopus*; later he became *sacerdos*; by the end of the letter he was called *homo*. Obviously, in the eyes of Arnulf, Becket the man had sacrificed all claim to the reverence due an archbishop or even a priest.

Now firmly committed to the justice of Henry's cause, Arnulf was with the king at Argentan when word of Becket's assassination reached the court. Arnulf's letter to Pope Alexander, describing Henry's reaction to the news, has been frequently quoted.[36] Arnulf deplored the rash and violent actions of the assassins, but the letter was curiously lacking in grief, almost as if Arnulf were unsurprised by Becket's fate. His real sympathy and concern were for the king's excessive anguish:

> For three whole days he was shut in his room, neither able to take food nor admit comforters; but his grief at the disaster seemed obstinately to impose a voluntary destruction upon himself. The face of these things was bad enough, and our anxiety was sorrowfully increased, since we who first mourned the priest now began to fear for the health of the king, and we believed neither one to be more lamentable than the other.[37]

Arnulf's plea for the pope's understanding and forgiveness was all but a whitewash of Henry's responsibility for the tragedy.

> He understood that he might have caused new enmities through recent injuries and frequent ill deeds, . . . and that it would be suspected that it was his own idea; but he called upon Almighty God to bear witness that he had committed this crime neither by his will nor by his knowledge, nor had he sought it through cunning, unless by chance he was guilty in this, that he was believed to be less than forgiving. On this account he places himself utterly before the judgment of the church and will humbly accept whatever is honestly decided. . . . We therefore pray that, in so far as possible, according to the spirit of understanding and bravery given to you by God, your severity will pay back to the creators of this crime the inhumanity of their deed, and that your apostolic piety will wish more affectionately to restore to the king his innocence in his own position.[38]

In later years Arnulf may have regretted his impassioned defense of Henry, for he deliberately excised this letter from the second edition of his correspondence. The letter was preserved only through the manuscript collections of the Becket correspondence, which accounts for the oddities of spelling that distinguish it from the Arnulf manuscripts.[39] But in the months immediately following the martyrdom, Arnulf continued in his support of Henry. He accompanied Rotrou, the archbishop of Rouen, to Sens in late January, where a large delegation from the king failed to prevent the archbishop of Sens from placing an interdict on Henry's continental possessions. The delegation then determined to carry their appeal directly to the pope at Frascati. Arnulf was not well enough to accompany the group on this arduous midwinter journey, but he was represented by his archdeacon, Robert de Arden.[40] Arnulf continued to write letters on behalf of the king and his supporters through the summer of 1171.[41] At Savigny on May 17, 1172, he witnessed the meeting between Henry and the papal legates Albert and Theodwin, who had been sent by Alexander to make a final determination of responsibility for the murder of Becket. Henry was characteristically obstinate, and the meeting would have broken up had it not been for the intercession of Arnulf. Several sources named him as the architect of the final settlement that took place at Avranches two days later.[42] Arnulf himself, seldom inclined to modesty about his accomplishments, described the settlement to the pope:

> Since the matter, on which [the legates] had come, had turned into a deplorable parting of the ways, and all who had intervened had departed, despairing of harmony, I alone approached them in such a great fervor of love, and having examined and predicted with all your legates the usefulness of dragging out the matter, I called back the king, already preparing to return to England, from that journey, and divine grace persuaded him to the benefits of peace through my intercession.[43]

Thus the great crisis came to an end, and most of the participants were able to salvage something beneficial from the wreckage.[44] Pope Alexander III had patiently outwaited the advocates of drastic action and had accomplished most of his goals without sacrificing his principles. Perhaps more important, he had avoided driving Henry into the ranks of the antipope. As a result of the settlement at Avranches, appeals from Anglo-Norman courts to Rome increased, and decretals issued to English judges-delegate brought England firmly into the mainstream of papal jurisdiction. The dedicated partisans of Becket eventually achieved their own prominence within the church. Among the *eruditi* who had accompanied Becket into exile, several became bishops in the following years. Among them were John of Salisbury at Chartres, Gilbert de Glanville at Rochester, Gerard la Pucelle at Coventry, and Hugh de Nonant, who succeeded Gerard at Coventry.[45] And if not all of the goals of Thomas Becket were realized at the end of the twelfth century, the blame seems to lie more with the weakness of his successor at Canterbury than with the terms of the original settlement.[46]

Henry had agreed to renounce the "new customs" he had introduced and to grant freedom of appeals to Rome. But he never formally renounced the "old customs" on which the Constitutions of Clarendon were purportedly based, nor did he grant papal legates the privilege of entering England without his permission. He retained the right to receive the homage of bishops for their secular possessions and the right to take for himself the revenues of vacant sees. Even after he made further concessions to the pope in 1176, Henry continued to exercise a subtle but pervasive influence over the church in England.[47] Henry's most loyal supporters also benefited. Roger of York (d. 1181) and Gilbert Foliot (d. 1187) retained their bishoprics without serious loss of reputation, and between 1173 and 1175 four other enemies of Becket received bishoprics—Richard of Ilchester at Winchester, Reginald Fitz Jocelin at Bath, Geoffrey Ridel at Ely, and John of Oxford at Norwich.

But for Arnulf of Lisieux the end of the Becket controversy marked the beginning of a long slide into despair and disrepute. Although the settlement at Avranches reflected almost exactly the attitude of compromise that he had advocated throughout the crisis, neither side was particularly grateful to the bishop who dictated the terms. Henry had little further use for the aging prelate who had orchestrated his public concessions to the pope. He kept Arnulf away from the royal court whenever possible and seldom consulted him. One measure of Arnulf's fall from favor may be found in the number of times Henry called upon him to act in an official capacity. Of 114 extant royal charters witnessed by Arnulf from 1150 to 1181, only eleven, or fewer than ten percent, occurred after the meeting at Avranches. Alexander III also seemed to pull back from his former close friendship. The pope frequently failed to respond to Arnulf's requests for help with diocesan problems during the 1170s and only rarely addressed him as a papal judge-delegate. In extant decretals, Arnulf was delegated only once, while the archbishop of Rouen received five commissions, the bishop of Exeter received thirty, and the bishop of Worchester received forty-three.[48] The staunch supporters of Becket, of course, could not forgive Arnulf for what they considered to be a betrayal of their cause. The canons of his cathedral continued to conspire against him as an unfit bishop, and John of Salisbury never tempered his judgment that Arnulf was "the hammer of iniquity bent on the destruction of the church of God."[49] Arnulf's opponents on both sides of the issue believed that he had betrayed them by negotiating with their enemies.

For Arnulf, his negotiations had been nothing more than the culmination of a lifetime of principled compromise. The paradigm he had adopted in his youth had encouraged conscious imitation of the accomplishments of his predecessors. He had modeled his episcopacy on those prelates he most admired: his uncle and predecessor, John of Lisieux, the consummate curial bishop; his adored older brother, John of Sées, the successful reformer of his cathedral chapter; Bernard, the instructor of popes and the spiritual leader of his age; and Suger, diplomat, kingmaker, and cathedral builder. Arnulf had attempted to emulate each of these men at some point, striving to combine their finest characteristics into his role as bishop. In each attempt, he had fallen short of his ideal, primarily because his admiration for the past led him to use methods that were ineffective in a rapidly changing world.

So, too, in the Becket controversy, Arnulf had turned to the examples set by Anselm and Calixtus II when they settled the Investiture Struggle through compromise rather than martyrdom. But the forward-looking world of the late twelfth century differed from the one that had welcomed the Concordat of Worms because it offered a peaceful settlement to a difficult question. People in the late twelfth century valued innovation, not discretion. While others sought novel solutions, Arnulf followed an outdated paradigm. He was guilty not of duplicity but of conservatism. He stood on the shoulders of giants, but unlike Bernard of Chartres's dwarf, who could see a little farther from that vantage point, Arnulf faced the wrong way.[50]

VIII.

The Breakdown of a Paradigm

During the Becket controversy, the careful balance Arnulf had achieved between ecclesiastical and royal interests failed to protect him from accusations of double-dealing. The Compromise of Avranches satisfied few of the participants except Arnulf, and in the last years of his episcopacy he experienced a steady and systematic erosion of his ecclesiastical and secular importance. The story of those years has been preserved in a series of letters collected by a clerk of the one friend Arnulf felt he had left, Richard of Ilchester.[1] The letters themselves provide painful and often embarrassing reading. They illustrate the decline of a man who strove to be great, only to discover that his efforts were unappreciated by a world that had passed him by. The letters are frequently repetitious, often querulous, sometimes even maudlin in their self-pity. In his own search for the reasons behind his disappointments, Arnulf dredged up old grudges and replayed, as the elderly often will, the critical moments of his life. In pleas to the king and to the pope, he justified his actions once again, arguing that his choices had been well conceived and guided by the instructive examples of the past. Yet there is little evidence that he understood why the paradigm he had constructed to guide his episcopate was collapsing around him.

Arnulf had always wanted to be a bishop; as a young man, he had idealistic expectations of the advantages of that office and little understanding of the pressures it entailed:

> I hoped on the one hand to achieve holiness for myself, and on the other to be provided with magnificence. I desired, to be sure, that they would run together and work together to the same result of complete virtue, namely that holiness would neither preclude magnificence nor magnificence destroy holiness, but that each glory would moderate the honor of the other.[2]

In old age, he faced the realization that his hopes had been unrealistic. The key to Arnulf's failures lay within his goals. Holiness and lordly magnificence were both reasonable goals for a medieval bishop, but in many ways they were incompatible. Holiness is a subjective and introspective virtue. Others may observe the outward manifestations of holiness, but its depth and sincerity can be judged only by the individual conscience and by God. Arnulf had derived his own definition of holiness at least in part from his contacts with

St. Bernard. He admired the patience, humility, and poverty of Cistercian monks who removed themselves from the distractions of the world and sought divine understanding through holy conversation and inner contemplation. As early as 1155, he had recognized the dangers of a life within the court of Henry II and had frequently sought release from his temporal duties so that he could more diligently pursue his own spiritual growth. Yet he was not permitted to cast aside his episcopal responsibilities, and he seems never to have been able to quiet his doubts that a bishop who remained active in the secular world could achieve true holiness.

Magnificence, on the other hand, is a very public virtue. It derives from an individual's worldly condition and embodies the characteristics most often associated with medieval nobility—wealth, power, and courage. In the twelfth century, these traits had begun to take on a particularly Christian connotation.[3] Wealth provided the opportunity for generosity and good works. Power became a tool for the protection of the weak and the defense of the innocent, especially in a judicial sense. Courage, once a purely military virtue, manifested itself in "fighting the good fight," whether the battle was against the infidel in the Holy Land or those who threatened the peace of Christendom from within. Such noble characteristics were part of a bishop's stock in trade; concomitant with the office were temporal land holdings and episcopal tithes, judicial responsibility, and opportunities for active participation in the most important affairs of the day. For "new men" such as Arnulf, who did not come from a particularly aristocratic family, these ecclesiastical benefits provided the only avenues to magnificence. Arnulf recognized the advantages that accrued to his office. What he seemed not to understand was that these privileges had been bestowed by human hands and could be taken away by their bestowers.

One of the weaknesses of Arnulf's personal philosophy was that it took little notice of the individual. Unlike some of his contemporaries, who were becoming acutely aware of their own motivations and failings, Arnulf seldom explored his own feelings or those of others. His writings demonstrate none of the introspection of an Abelard or a Guibert of Nogent. Arnulf's correspondence was primarily directed toward the affairs of his diocese. It is almost impossible to tell from the contents whether the recipients of his letters were close friends or simply clerical associates. Even when writing of purely personal interests, he often seemed cold and matter-of-fact. The death of his brother John of Sées appeared in the letters only as a matter of inconvenience that kept him from visiting the new pope.[4] A letter addressed to a young woman who had been betrothed to another of his brothers before his death offered little more consolation than the hope that she would find more happiness in becoming a nun.[5] The overall impression left by Arnulf's correspondence is that he was a man uncomfortable with personal emotion.

That indication is confirmed by Arnulf's dealings with his associates. He seems to have conducted himself in terms of Platonic ideals: he was Bishop, serving Church and Monarchy, not the individual Arnulf with sometimes conflicting personal loyalties to those who wore the mitres and crowns. Even at his most perceptive, when he so accurately sketched for Becket the personality of King Henry, he did not advocate acting on that understanding. Rather, he urged that Becket concentrate on principles and generalities, leaving individual interests and personal feelings aside. One study of the growth of self-conscious individualism in the twelfth century has suggested that "greater awareness of the self precedes and permits greater awareness of the individuality, the special characteristics, and indeed the motives of others."[6] If this is so, perhaps Arnulf, locked as he was into the ideals of a former, less personalized age, could not be expected to appreciate the motivations of those with whom he came in contact. But that failure to adapt to changing attitudes and values led Arnulf increasingly into conflict with his contemporaries.

Despite his understanding of Henry's character, Arnulf experienced his most resounding failure in his relationship with the king. A more perceptive observer of human nature might have recognized in Henry's behavior after the Becket crisis the symptoms of embarrassment over past events and the desire to begin afresh with a new crop of curial bishops more willing to do the king's bidding. Arnulf, however, made no adjustment to the changing atmosphere of the court. He continued to play out the role he had set for himself from the beginning of his episcopacy, advising the king of his religious responsibilities, supporting the king's efforts whenever they seemed likely to benefit the church, and acting independently in matters of moral or ecclesiastical import.

A crucial breach in the relationship between Henry II and Arnulf occurred in the spring of 1175, just after the rebellion of the king's sons. Arnulf had planned to accompany Henry back to England and to join him in a pilgrimage to Canterbury. Shortly after his arrival at court, however, an unspecified argument disrupted those plans. Arnulf himself said only that he was dismissed by the king and that, frightened by the degree of the king's bitterness, he saw no solution but to flee at once from the face of the king's indignation.[7] After his initial panic had subsided, the bishop realized that his flight had been motivated less by fear than by pride, and he determined to rejoin the king and apologize.[8] On the journey from his manor of Nonant to the embarkation point at Barfleur, however, he fell ill and was forced to take refuge at the monastery of Cerisy-la-Forêt. A letter pleading for forgiveness elicited no response from the king.[9] When he recovered his health, Arnulf followed the royal party to England, but there, too, he was rebuffed. He wrote three more letters to the king during this period, defending his actions and reminding him of his former services. None seems to have been answered. The king traveled on to York and ignored a request that Arnulf be granted an audience.[10]

There is no specific explanation of what Arnulf had done to anger the king. The spring of 1175 was generally a period of reconciliation. The war between Henry and his sons was over. Henry had made peace with the Young King and had granted forgiveness to those who had participated in the rebellion.[11] Court records give no indication that any charges stemming from the rebellion

were made against the aging bishop of Lisieux. Arnulf himself admitted only
to the possibility that he might have done something "less than prudent
through ignorance or innocence."[12] And he insisted that there was "absolutely
no proof of my neglect of duty or deception."[13] Because of the coincidence of
time, however, several modern historians have assumed that Arnulf must
have been involved in the conspiracy of the king's sons.[14] Certainly the king's
anger with Arnulf seems to have erupted just at the end of the crisis, but the
evidence for the bishop's active involvement is circumstantial and, for the
most part, inconsistent with his character.

The most incriminating piece of evidence lies in a letter written by Arnulf
to Sevinus, abbot of Cour-Dieu, in December 1172. In it appeared the following
paragraph:

> As to the rest, concerning the business which is going on at present, there is
> nothing to be done until the Young King returns to Normandy from Anjou for
> Christmas. We will assist you then, along with others who have the same matter
> at heart, and we hope for useful assistance from the intervention of the king of
> France. In the meantime I have lodged [your messenger] and his brother who
> is with him in a certain monastery of your order [Val-Richer] that is near us,
> where nothing will exist to distract them from their rule or their observation of
> the hour.[15]

This cryptic message, sent to a man known to have been a recipient of the
French king's patronage, appears all the more suspicious because Arnulf
carefully excised it from the published edition of his letters. It did not appear
in the Migne or Giles collections of Arnulf's correspondence and was included
only in a Vatican manuscript compiled from unedited copies of the letters.[16]

The assumption that Arnulf was involved in the rebellion is also supported
by chroniclers. One manuscript of Benedict of Peterborough's *Gesta Regis
Henrici Secundi* contains a list of those who remained loyal to Henry II. It
includes the archbishops and bishops of England, the archbishop of Rouen,
and all the bishops of Normandy except Arnulf, who, it was said, had opened
his doors to the supporters of the Young King.[17] Later in the chronicle,
Benedict made the charge more specific by stating that the animosity of the
king existed because "during the time of war that had occurred between him
and his sons, [Arnulf] received friends and relatives from the household of his
sons."[18] The messengers from Sevinus of Cour-Dieu may have been intimately
connected with the coming rebellion, and word of their stay at Le Val-Richer
could have easily reached Henry's ears. There are, however, other bits of
evidence that contradict the impression that Arnulf sided with the Young King
in his campaign to discomfit his father. Arnulf continued to serve Henry II
during the fray. He, along with Rotrou, archbishop of Rouen, and Peter of
Blois, formed the delegation Henry sent to the king of France in the summer
of 1173 to urge him not to support the rebels.[19] He attended the royal
Christmas court at Caen in 1173, witnessing several charters for the king.[20]
And he continued to support the king's candidates for vacant bishoprics. In

fact, one of his letters to the pope during this period spoke quite critically of the Young King and those who supported him:

> The son, who was consecrated to the succession of the throne prematurely because of his father's affection, has begun to resist such a great favor, encouraged by the advice of those who have been able to draw him away from his father's side, and to pervert the simplicity of his youth more to his own loss than to his father's. Their desire is always therefore to pit him against his father, so that hatreds, which they themselves have seeded, spring up between them over all matters, and lest he, having experienced a change of heart for some reason, begin to recognize his debt of natural gratitude and to return to the paternal embrace.[21]

These are not the words of someone involved in the attempt to overthrow the father through the son.

Arnulf had almost no contact with those who actually participated in the rebellion. Benedict of Peterborough gave the names of eighty-eight partisans of the Young King on the Continent.[22] Only three of them—William Patrick, Geoffrey de Rancon, and Saher de Quincy—can be linked in any way to the wide circle of Arnulf's acquaintances.[23] William Patrick and Geoffrey de Rancon witnessed royal charters with Arnulf in the early 1150s; there is no evidence of any later association.[24] A certain Saher de Quincy was a frequent co-witness with Arnulf.[25] It was his son, however, who played a minor role in the [26] On the Continent, the Young King drew his support from the French throne, the houses of Blois, Brittany, and Maine, and the great barons of Poitiers and Angoulême. Anjou and almost all of central Normandy remained loyal to Henry II.[27] Despite Arnulf's ties to the French throne, it is difficult to imagine him at the center of any organized opposition to the English king.

In England, the only prelate who betrayed his loyalty to the king was Hugh de Puiset, bishop of Durham. Because of their episcopal rank, Hugh and Arnulf are often linked in discussions of the rebellion.[28] Records, however, reveal only two meetings between them—one at Fontevrault in 1154 and the other at the peace settlement between Henry and the king of France in 1160.[29] Further, Hugh's role in the rebellion was one of opportunism and indecision, motivated more by proximity to the king of Scotland than by opposition to Henry II.[30] Hugh was never an active participant in the war, and there is no reason to assume a conspiracy, or even the link of influence, between the two bishops.

Arnulf was associated throughout the rebellion with magnates who fervently supported Henry II. Besides his loyal episcopal colleagues in Normandy and his own metropolitan, Rotrou of Rouen, Arnulf was in contact with several leaders of the royal party at court. These included Richard de Humeto, the king's constable; William de Mandeville, who commanded his army; and such supporters as Robert de Stuteville and Hugh de Lacy.[31] The names of two other loyal members of the king's party stand out among Arnulf's contacts:

Richard Barre and Walter of Coutances. Immediately before the rebellion, both were members of the household of the Young King; Richard Barre was the keeper of his seal and Walter was his chaplain. In 1173 both men left his service, preferring to cast their lot and hopes of future preferment with Henry II.[32] Arnulf's first known contact with Richard Barre had occurred at the end of the Becket crisis, when they traveled together to Sens on the king's behalf. Richard was rewarded for his service with an archdeaconry in the diocese of Lisieux. Walter of Coutances later caused Arnulf much trouble, but in 1175 the two men were close enough that Arnulf wrote to Walter asking for his intercession in his difficulties with the king.[33] Thus any attempt to prove guilt by association would have to place Arnulf firmly on the side of the king.

Arnulf's role in the rebellion must remain conjectural. It seems clear, however, that whatever he did during this time of crisis was enough to turn Henry permanently against him. Kate Norgate may have come close to the mark when she accused him of using "his diplomatic gifts in temporizing between the two parties, instead of seeking to make peace between them or to keep his straying flock in the path of loyalty as a true pastor should."[34] Temporization in the hope of achieving a compromise is exactly what one would expect from Arnulf. For Henry, however, another compromise would have been unacceptable. Coming from the aging advisor who had forced the king's humbling at Avranches, the suggestion would have been particularly annoying.

Henry had more than one reason for wishing to replace the bishop of Lisieux. Arnulf was by now in his seventies, and ill health had sometimes prohibited him from traveling in the king's service. The king preferred to surround himself with people whose energy could match his own, and in his court were several young men just waiting for the opportunity to serve. By 1175, Henry had filled several English bishoprics with loyal courtiers, but the supply of dioceses was limited. Normandy offered an unusual opportunity to reward faithful service, for Henry had continued the policy of his Anglo-Norman predecessors in regard to the church.[35] From the time of William the Conqueror, the dukes of Normandy had jealously preserved their right to nominate to vacant bishoprics. Henry had judiciously but subtly influenced episcopal elections in Normandy throughout his reign, so much so that only once was there any opposition to the free election of the king's choice. This occurred in 1159, when Henry successfully opposed the election of Achard to the see of Sées and intruded his own almoner, Froger, despite Arnulf's protests.[36] The diocese of Lisieux was a rich plum ready to be dropped into the hands of a deserving curial official, if only Arnulf did not stand in the way.

Henry had learned, however, that there was no easy way to rid himself of an irritating priest. Bishops occupied an almost unassailable position in the church hierarchy. Even those who were clearly royal appointees gained, along with their consecration, an enviable immunity from royal displeasure. A bishop held his diocese for life, unless he was translated to a higher office, was removed by the pope for grievous heresy, or willingly resigned. And voluntary resignations were not usually accepted, as Arnulf had discovered during his early attempts to take up a monastic career. Canon law forbade a bishop to abandon his flock, even if he were threatened by invasion or persecuted by wicked men.[37] Because Henry had no way of forcing Arnulf from his office of bishop, he approached him from his more vulnerable position as an English baron.

The attempt to remove Arnulf began with an attack on his most valuable temporal possession. Henry's gift of the chapelry of Bosham in Sussex had provided the financial edge that made it possible for Arnulf to begin construction of his new cathedral. For over twenty years Arnulf had relied on its revenues and on the position within the English baronage to which it entitled him. In 1177, Henry took Bosham away from Arnulf and returned it to the bishop of Exeter. The exchange was done in such a way that Arnulf felt the full force of the king's displeasure while being unable to complain of any injustice.

Benedict of Peterborough gave the date of the formal exchange as July 12, 1177. According to Benedict, Arnulf had come to realize that he had held the chapelry of Bosham unjustly and against his own conscience. Therefore Arnulf promised Bartholomew of Exeter that if Bartholomew were able to obtain the permission of the king, he would yield those rights that he claimed in Bosham. As soon as the king saw Arnulf's open letter, he complied with the request and confirmed the exchange.[38]

Arnulf's version of the event was somewhat different. He was shocked by this sudden blow to his financial status and took his complaint directly to Henry when the king arrived in Normandy in August.[39] In a bitter letter to Bartholomew, dated in the fall of 1177, Arnulf recorded the king's disingenuous response. Henry explained "that he would not have taken it away, but the testimony of my letter [to Bartholomew], which he produced, urged him to support what I wanted to be done, because in this case he did not want to oppose my wishes in any way."[40] Arnulf protested to Bartholomew that his intentions had been misinterpreted:

> You ought to remember that you asked me a long time ago not to stand in the way of your success if you were able in any way to get your wish from the king, saving to me through your hand all the revenues of the chapel so long as I lived; and I under that express condition granted to you what you wanted, provided that the king himself recognized it. Nor did I wish to require any other guarantees from you because it seemed to me that the faithful word of a priest and bishop should suffice.[41]

Apparently, Arnulf had been tricked into putting into writing his willingness to see Bosham revert to the diocese of Exeter, while accepting in return only a verbal promise that his revenues would not be affected. It is not difficult to see behind these events a deliberate and well-executed plot to strip Arnulf of his major English holding; it must have been masterminded by Henry and Bartholomew, who were together at Winchester immediately before and after the transfer of Bosham.[42]

If Henry hoped thereby to drive the bishop of Lisieux into retirement, he had underestimated his opponent. Financial difficulties only strengthened the bishop's resolve to remain at his post until his debts could be honorably discharged. With the help of Peter of Pavia, an old friend who had recently been appointed as cardinal-priest of St. Chrysogonus, Arnulf struck a bargain with Henry when the three were together at Rouen at the end of 1177.[43] As the bishop later reminded the king and all others who would listen to him, Henry agreed "to aid me freely out of royal generosity, so that I might retire from that position in which I am no longer able to remain without danger to my health and so that I might retire to a more peaceful and more apostolic life."[44] As was often the case with Henry, the promise came more easily than its fulfillment.

Henry resumed his travels through his continental possessions without making any payment to Arnulf but leaving his new seneschal, William fitz Ralph, and his vice-chancellor, Walter of Coutances, to handle his affairs in Normandy.[45] These two descended upon Lisieux, determined to bring the matter of a recalcitrant bishop to a swift close. Walter's goal was to obtain the bishopric for himself; William was the enforcer who could make it happen. Between them they charted a course of harassment, coercion, and blackmail designed to drive Arnulf from his see. Their first attempt was little more than a bribe based on the king's promise of financial assistance. Walter offered to hand over the cash immediately, provided that Arnulf make a public declaration in support of Walter's candidacy and that he urge the canons of Lisieux to elect Walter when Arnulf died or retired. Arnulf described his indignation in a letter to Peter of Pavia: "I have answered him plainly that this is simony, and that I will take nothing from him in this cause."[46]

A fair assessment of the role of Walter of Coutances in the attempt to drive Arnulf from his see is difficult, for the only record of his activities exists in the somewhat hysterical accounts of the beseiged bishop. Walter had long been a friend to Arnulf. Certainly he was a faithful servant of the king, as he proved during the rebellion of the king's sons and in his role as acting chancellor. He succeeded to the bishopric of Lincoln in 1183 and was translated to Rouen in 1184, a position he held until his death in 1207. In later years his episcopal service proved him to be a dedicated prelate.[47] But in this attempt to succeed to the bishopric of Lisieux, Walter seems to have allowed his personal ambition to overcome his finer instincts. Walter's career at court was precariously bound to the longevity of Henry II. He realized that the Young King regarded him as a traitor because of his role in the rebellion. It was vitally important that he achieve an unassailable position such as a bishopric before the death of the father raised the son to a position from which he could exact vengeance. The opportunity offered by the valuable bishopric of Lisieux was too great to be ignored.[48]

Walter evidently did not take an active role in Arnulf's harassment after the initial attempts to purchase support for his candidacy, although Arnulf later accused him of misusing the king's seal on false charges against him.[49] By

Arnulf's own admission, Walter returned to England with the king in July 1178, leaving others to secure his nomination.[50] Within the cathedral chapter of canons, Walter had recruited a certain Hubert who served as his campaign manager. Hubert held a position of some importance in the chapter, for he witnessed a charter for the king's chancellor in 1175.[51] By 1184 he was an archdeacon and an envoy to the pope.[52] Arnulf said that Hubert "daily procured for him [Walter] as many canons as he could and bound others by oath in a sacrilegious faction, so that when I die or retire, they will agree to the election of the king's choice."[53] Among the important personages who pleaded with Arnulf to accede to the king's wishes were the bishop of Bayeux and the archbishop of Rouen.[54] But the greatest pressure came from William fitz Ralph, Henry's seneschal for Normandy.

In the late summer of 1178, William conceived and executed an attack on Arnulf that neatly stripped him of all authority. Once again the details appear only in Arnulf's convoluted account:

> William fitz Ralph not long ago deprived me of all my revenues, both from the city and from the diocese, on that occasion when I was not able to produce in court a certain poor knight whom he summoned to the curia on an ecclesiastical charge and for whom he alleged that I had stood surety. Simply because he was my nephew, he threatened to bind him with fetters and shut him up in prison, if by chance he fell into his hands; imputing to him without any truth, that he had rescued from the hands of his captors a certain deacon, who, from my table and the episcopal palace, was being dragged to prison by his officials.[55]

None of the charges can be verified. This appears to be a case in which an illegal arrest of a deacon on church property was made deliberately to stir up a protest from Arnulf's household. Threats of what would happen to the nephew if he appeared in court were strong enough to ensure his nonappearance. And Arnulf's reputation as a patient and long-suffering supporter of his nephews, no matter how vexing their behavior, would have lent credence to the allegation that the bishop had pledged his bond.

Even had all the charges been valid, the punishment William fitz Ralph inflicted on Arnulf far exceeded the dictates of justice. He began by confiscating into the royal treasury all the revenues of the diocese: tithes, prebends, oblations, churches, altars, and even the free alms that Arnulf had granted. He forbade all administration of ecclesiastical justice. Then he forced the bishop to leave the city of Lisieux, while ordering him not to leave Normandy. To ensure that Arnulf would not find shelter and sympathy within his own diocese, he issued an edict that ordered the clergy to provide nothing to their bishop, under penalty of confiscation of their own goods.[56]

After being forced to wander for ten days, relying on the generosity of strangers for food and shelter, Arnulf took refuge at the monastery of St. Victor in Paris. There he described himself as "in good health but so debilitated by old age that I am not able to take seven steps in a row, or mount a horse, or dismount, without assistance."[57] Still he refused to resign his bishopric while his reputation lay in tatters and while the assets of his diocese remained in the hands of the king. In a letter to the pope, he explained the conditions under which he wanted to retire:

> The day of my departure and retirement must be left to my discretion, lest treacherous evil be able to make a mockery of me and insult me, and rejoice in my simplicity, because it will appear to be a trick. For if I agree under any condition to resign my bishopric, having been a party to the confiscation of all the goods of the church, I will have allowed the subsequent abuse, the power and greed of the secular hand will take possession, and my creditors will in no way be satisfied, . . . and I will be found accused before God by a betrayal of faith and condemned before men by a deserved reputation of public infamy.[58]

When it thus became apparent that Arnulf would not willingly resign, the canons of his cathedral chapter took overt action against their bishop.[59] By 1179 even his loyal archdeacons, Hugh de Nonant and Gilbert de Glanville, joined the chorus of those who demanded his resignation. Gilbert once again pressed Arnulf to declare in favor of the succession of Walter of Coutances, and Arnulf responded with a lecture on the evils of simony.[60] The canons then took their case to the pope, accusing Arnulf of having misused the funds of the church. In one sense their accusations had validity, for the confiscations imposed by William fitz Ralph had included the income of the chapter as well as that of the bishop, and it was that loss of revenue that Arnulf wanted to recoup before he retired. If Arnulf's protest to the pope is to be believed, however, the canons dredged up grievances ranging all the way back to the entry fee he had paid for his temporalities and his expenses during the Second Crusade.[61]

Arnulf found to his despair that not even the pope was willing to defend him any longer: "You heard them, and rather than coming to my aid, you listened favorably; for even though I was innocent and absent, and condemned by no edict, I was punished, and suspended from the power of episcopal rank. . . ."[62] Alexander's ruling granted Arnulf permission to retire, but it also assigned the settlement of the canons' claims to a panel of judges-delegate that included Richard, bishop of Avranches; Osbern, abbot of Bec; and Simon, abbot of Savigny. All, according to Arnulf, were known to be opposed to him and to be allied with Walter of Coutances and the king himself.[63] Their verdict was predictable: Arnulf was guilty of financial mismanagement. The judges ordered him to pay one hundred pounds to the canons to replace funds that they had spent on the needs of the church. Further, they confiscated even the liturgical garments that Arnulf had been planning to take with him into retirement. As Arnulf described his fate, "They sent me out deprived of money and sacred vestments."[64] It should be noted, however, that these confiscations were later rescinded by the pope at Arnulf's request. His chasuble, dalmatic, and tunic formed part of Arnulf's legacy to the canons of St. Victor.[65]

Arnulf's career ended, as it had begun, on a note of compromise. He had taken up permanent residence at St. Victor in Paris, but his retirement from the bishopric could not become official until he had formally surrendered his secular position into the hands of the king. The two men met for the last time at Gisors in July 1181.[66] There they seem to have reached some sort of reconciliation, for Arnulf later wrote to Henry in gratitude: "It will be all the more pleasing to me, if I am seen to have gone to sleep dying in the arms of my king, if your favor accompanies me in death into the presence of a higher lord."[67] Arnulf once again declared his innocence, and the king granted him a retirement settlement of two hundred pounds. The amount was recorded in a later letter complaining that once again William fitz Ralph had failed to make payment on the king's promise.[68] The subsequent nomination of Ralph de Varneville, the king's chancellor, to the see of Lisieux may indicate a further royal concession to Arnulf's wishes.[69] There was no further mention of the candidacy of Walter of Coutances once Arnulf had made his peace with the king.

In the few remaining years of his life, the longtime bishop found a home as "brother Arnulf, canon of Saint Victor of Paris." In a final letter written to Richard of Ilchester, he expressed his newly discovered peace of mind:

> You know how long I have intended to retire to a religious life, in the example of our Lord, but the business of the world held me back and burdened me with many obstacles. Now at last I have conquered all through the grace of God, and I have entered the church of St. Victor of Paris, leaving behind all those things that seemed to hinder my progress and advancement. I, poor and naked, have followed the poor and naked Christ, having been led by him and desiring to be shaped in every desire to his humility and poverty, so far as it will be granted to me and commanded by his pity. I have lived up to this point caring more for my body than for the salvation of my soul, yet proposing and desiring to consecrate myself at last to the Lord, which intention divine pity has always preserved to the proper time, and guided me, debilitated by old age but healthy in body and in all my limbs and whole in spirit.[70]

It had been Arnulf's misfortune that he had entered into his episcopate with a preconceived and perhaps already outdated idea of the proper role of a bishop. Like a scientific paradigm that guides researchers to fill in the blanks in human understanding of the physical world, so Arnulf's world view led him to seek the solutions to all his dilemmas within a pattern of ecclesiastical and secular interaction that had taken shape in the late eleventh century. His goals were modeled on those prelates who had preceded him in that less complicated era. For forty years he had endeavored to emulate their dual functions as bishop and baron. He sought both holiness and magnificence, hoping that those virtues would temper and enhance each other. He advocated ecclesiastical cooperation with the secular authorities, arguing that church and monarchy must work together or risk their own salvation. And he justified all duplicity and compromise by the greater needs of a united Christendom.

In the end, his paradigm collapsed. The model on which he had based his decisions proved unadaptable to the changing conditions of the late twelfth century. New ideas conflicted fundamentally with old ideals. Strong national monarchies, buttressed by increasingly efficient bureaucracies, called less frequently upon the guidance of bishops. The papacy extended its jurisdiction and thereby challenged the very monarchs on whom it had once been forced to rely. Even the interpretation of the apostolic life underwent a transformation toward a more inward-looking spirituality.

Arnulf had witnessed these changes and approved of many of them, but he had been unwilling to alter his paradigm to accommodate them. He angered his clergy by forcing them to conform to his own standards of morality without satisfying their spiritual needs. He alienated his fellow bishops by not taking a strong enough stand in defense of ecclesiastical freedom. He irritated his superiors within the church hierarchy by his continued support of the king. Similarly, he enraged his king by his failure to understand the royal need for independence from ecclesiastical control. At the end of his career he stood alone, overtaken by a new world that had little patience with a vacillating, backward-looking bishop. By seeking both holiness and magnificence he had achieved neither. Eventually he realized that the search for secular magnificence had been the barrier that prevented him from achieving true holiness. He chose holiness, but the choice came too late to alter his reputation as a man who could not be trusted. Perhaps only his brother canons at St. Victor understood the full significance of the change that had overtaken Arnulf's last days. Several years after his death they recorded his new attitude above his tomb:

> You who were wealthy and a powerful bishop,
> Why did you exchange your state for that of a pauper?
> Yea, I became a pauper from a great estate.
> I was rich in the world; it was greater to be rich in God.[71]

Epilogue

When Arnulf died on August 31, 1184, the world took little note of his passing. No major chronicler mentioned him after his official resignation. The canons of St. Victor published his obituary, buried him in their church near the altar dedicated to St. Dionysius, and celebrated a solemn mass on each anniversary of his death. He had bequeathed to them the remnants of his estate: his ecclesiastical vestments and ornaments to adorn their altar, money to pay their debts and supplement their income, two silver vases, and his personal library. To the rest of the world, Arnulf left two additional legacies: one inscribed on parchment, the other carved in stone.

The collected writings of Arnulf of Lisieux constitute a valuable but almost untapped source of information about the late twelfth century. Modern historians have tended to ignore the evidence of his correspondence and other literary efforts, both because of his reputation for untrustworthiness and because the letters themselves contain few historical details. But Arnulf functioned as a critic of his times, not as a chronicler. He alternately admonished, cajoled, censured, and advised his associates. He spoke of the changes he witnessed and the goals he advocated. He warned of trends that disturbed him and sought to disrupt developments that seemed to him to be going in the wrong direction. In short, he spoke as an old-fashioned bishop. His letters were meant not to describe his age but to delineate its faults and to suggest a need for correction.

The cathedral of St.-Pierre-de-Lisieux, too, has been largely overlooked, particularly by art historians who are disturbed by its inconsistencies in style and period. Few have understood that it represents Arnulf's ideal solution to the problems of his world. Solid Romanesque foundations support the innovations of soaring Gothic arch and penetrating light. Cistercian simplicity of design focuses the attention of worshipers on spiritual concerns rather than mundane riches. Images of a king and his family serve as structural supports for the central arch of the cathedral, illustrating Arnulf's belief that monarchy must support the Christian church. And a patient and bemused bishop oversees the whole from his unobtrusive niche in the north aisle. The medium of stone allowed Arnulf to express in his cathedral the solutions he could not impose upon the real world.

Together these two legacies provide an instructive counterpoint to the widely accepted view of the twelfth century as a period of dynamic growth and untrammeled enthusiasm. Arnulf's message does not contradict Haskins's picture of a twelfth-century renaissance. In many ways his words confirm the growth of knowledge, the spread of law, and a renewed interest in literary elegance that characterized this period. But Arnulf's discontents also reveal a palimpsest beneath the surface of Haskins's thesis: the ideals that were obscured when new institutions supplanted the old. Arnulf mourned the passing of a simpler age and sought to preserve the traditions of the past within the innovations of the future. He failed. But within his failure lies the key to a clearer understanding of the dilemmas that confronted twelfth-century bishops.

Itinerary of Arnulf of Lisieux

This itinerary does not claim to be complete. Documentation of the movements of Arnulf has been taken from the internal evidence of his correspondence and from contemporary chronicles, as well as from charters that can be dated to within a specific year. Letter references are cited by the number Frank Barlow assigned to each letter in his Latin edition, *The Letters of Arnulf of Lisieux*. Manuscript references appear only for those charters that I have been able to view in person or in photographs. Other charters are designated by the printed collections in which they appear (see Abbreviations and Bibliography for full citations).

YEAR	LOCATION	ACTIVITIES	DOCUMENTATION
1105	Near Sées	Arnulf was born sometime between this year and 1109.	Barlow, in *Letters*, p. xi.
1122	Sées	His formal education had begun by this year.	Hermant, *Histoire du diocèse de Bayeux* (Caen, 1703).
1131	Rouen	He attended meeting between Henry I and Innocent II.	*Cal. Doc. Fr.*, p. 508.
1133	Summer, in Italy	Arnulf was in Bologna to study Roman law. It was here that he wrote the *Invectiva*.	MGH, *Libelli de lite*, 3:84.
1137	Before April, at Westminster	Arnulf was attending Stephen's court.	*Regesta*, vol. 3., p. 189.
1139	Rome	Arnulf defended Stephen's claims at a papal court.	John of Salisbury, *Memoirs of the Papal Court*, p. 83.
1141	After March in Normandy	Arnulf was elected bishop of Lisieux.	*The Letters of Peter the Venerable*, 1:261–62.

YEAR	LOCATION	ACTIVITIES	DOCUMENTATION
1142	Rouen	Although he had not been recognized by Geoffrey of Anjou, Arnulf was conducting diocesan business.	Round, *Cal. Doc. Fr.*, no. 909.
1143	Lisieux	Arnulf claimed the temporalities of his see after paying a considerable fine to Geoffrey. He began temporary repairs to the cathedral.	Letters 2 and 137.
1144	Sées	John of Sées died, and Arnulf traveled to Sées, arriving too late to control the election of John's successor.	HF 15:696.
1146	Rome Easter (March 31) at Vézelay	Arnulf did much traveling during this year. He went to Rome to protest the election of Gerard to the see of Sées and to request permission to enter a monastery. He was also present to hear St. Bernard preach the Second Crusade.	HF 15:603. Letter 118.
1147	Neubourg Saumur June 11, from Paris to the Holy Land	Entrusting his diocese to Bishop Rotrou of Evreux, Arnulf left on crusade. He was appointed as legate with authority over the Anglo-Norman troops.	Caen, ADC, H.1809 (copy). Paris, BN, MS Nouv. Acq. Lat. 2097, p. 9. Evreux, ADE, H.73.

YEAR	LOCATION	ACTIVITIES	DOCUMENTATION
1148	May, at Acre Paris	Arnulf was present at the council that discussed the taking of Acre but returned to France shortly thereafter.	William of Tyre, PL 201:673.
1149	Paris Angevin court	Arnulf was sent by Abbot Suger to the court of Geoffrey and Matilda to try to avert war between them and the French. His support of the Angevins dated from this meeting.	Letters 4 and 6.
1150	Rouen	By this time, Arnulf was an active member of Henry's entourage.	Paris, BN, MS Lat. 18369.
1151	Rouen Argentan Lisieux Tours	Charters indicate that he was traveling with Henry as he extended his control over Normandy.	Rouen, BM, MS 2192, p. 101.
1152	Summer, in Lisieux	Since Henry held a meeting of his chief supporters at Lisieux shortly after his marriage to Eleanor, it can be assumed that Arnulf was also present.	Robert of Torigni, RS 82, 4:162–164.

YEAR	LOCATION	ACTIVITIES	DOCUMENTATION
1153	Rouen Tours Argentan Le Mans Lisieux	Between 1151 and 1153, Arnulf received the rights of fairs at Touques and Nonant and witnessed many of the charters issued by Henry. An order signed by Henry at Lisieux during this period is particularly important because it appoints Arnulf as one of Henry's chief justiciars.	Chartres, ADEL, Tiron Cart., fol. 49d. Chartres, ADEL, G.2984 Paris, BN, MS Lat. 5480, t. I, p. 258. Paris, BN, MS Nouv. Acq. Lat. 2097, p. 12. Paris, BN, MS Lat. 18369, fol. 53.
1154	Le Mans Perigueux Fontevrault Rouen Torigni December, from Lisieux to England. December 19 at Westminster	Arnulf accompanied Henry to England for his coronation. At the end of this year he was rewarded with the valuable chapelry of Bosham, which provided him a handsome income for the next twenty-two years.	Chartres, ADEL, H.1374, fol. 49^{v}. Paris, AN, L.1018. Caen, ADC, G (Évêché de Bayeux). Bayeux, Cathedral Archives, Livre Noir, fol. 5. Bayeux, Cathedral Archives, Cart., no. 40.

YEAR	LOCATION	ACTIVITIES	DOCUMENTATION
1155	February, at York March 27, at Westminster Domfront October 9, to Rome	Arnulf accompanied Henry on his early progresses through England and attended the Great Council held at Westminster. Then he returned to Normandy to serve with Robert de Neubourg as Henry's chief justiciar. In the fall, he joined a mission sent by Henry to gain papal permission for the invasion of Ireland. While in Rome he again requested permission to retire to a monastery.	Eyton, *Itinerary*, pp. 7–8. Caen, ADC, Cart. Austin Canons, Bayeux, I.17. Rouen, ADSM, Y.44. Paris, BN, MS Lat. 10077, fol. 91. Rouen, BM, Cart. de Fécamp, MS 1207, fol. 4. Rouen, ADSM, G.4047. Avranches, BM, Mont St. Michel Cart., n. 210. Letter 118.
1156	February 1 to Rouen Easter (April 15) at Lisieux December 13, at La Suave-Majeure	Arnulf rejoined the royal court at the beginning of February, and it was probably at this point that he earned the enmity of John of Salisbury by reporting to Henry what had occurred in Rome. A letter indicated that he intended to return to his episcopal duties by spring, but he rejoined Henry's court in time for Christmas.	Eyton, *Itinerary*, p. 17. Delisle-Berger, no. 25.

YEAR	LOCATION	ACTIVITIES	DOCUMENTATION
1157	January at Caen, Bayeux, Falaise, and Rouen Before April 8, to Domfront and Barfleur	Arnulf presided as justiciar at the Assize held in Caen, then traveled through Normandy with the royal court until Henry left for England. By the end of the year, however, he had been replaced by Rotrou as justiciar. He began to plan for the rebuilding of his cathedral.	Paris, BN, MS Lat. 18369, fol. 27. Avranches, BM, Mont St. Michel Cart., fol. 115. Caen, ADC, H.1835. Caen, ADC, H.4034. Paris, AN, L.967.
1158		There are no exact records for Arnulf during this year. However, Henry made a progress through Normandy, ending at Cherbourg in time for Christmas, and it is likely that Arnulf rejoined the court at that time.	Eyton, *Itinerary*, pp. 41–42.
1159	Tours	Arnulf was at court at the beginning of the year. At some point he resumed his duties as justiciar at Tours. Most of the year was spent on personal correspondence and diocesan business. In the fall he became involved with the disputed election of Pope Alexander III.	Paris, BN, MS Lat. 5419A, fol. 103. Letters 23 and 24.

YEAR	LOCATION	ACTIVITIES	DOCUMENTATION
1160	Argentan	Arnulf was with the court at least until June and was present at the signing of the peace treaty between Henry and France. His major concern was to make sure that Henry and the bishops of England did not waver in their support of Alexander III.	Eyton, *Itinerary*, p. 49. Alençon, ADO, H.1863. Paris, BN, MS Lat. 17049, fol. 85. Evreux, ADE, G.122, fol. 40. Letters 27, 28, and 29.
1161	Lisieux	Although Henry remained on the Continent, there is no evidence that Arnulf attended the court. His personal correspondence was limited to his disputes with his nephews and with the bishop of Sées.	Letters 33, 34, and 35.
1162	Domfront	Arnulf attended Henry's court at least once.	St. Lô, ADM, Savigny Cart., II, p. 532.
1163	May 19–21, at Tours October, in England October–January, at Sens	Arnulf delivered one of the opening sermons at the Council of Tours. In the fall, he traveled to England to offer suggestions to Henry on how to handle Becket. During the next three months, he and Richard of Poitiers made six trips to the papal court at Sens, trying to win support for Henry's position.	Paris, BN, MS Lat. 14763. Mansi 21:1167–1175. Herbert of Bosham, *Materials* 3:273–274. Ralph de Diceto, RS 68, 1:312.

YEAR	LOCATION	ACTIVITIES	DOCUMENTATION
1164	Nonant Lisieux October at Sens	Henry had not been pleased with the results of his delegations to the pope, and Arnulf returned to his manor at Nonant. After Becket fled England, however, Arnulf again consulted the pope at Sens.	Nicholas of Rouen, *Materials* 5:147. Alexander III, *Materials* 5:85.
1165	Lisieux	Arnulf remained in his diocese and occupied himself writing admonishing letters to all concerned in the Becket crisis. He also became involved with the correction of the monasteries of Grestain and St. Evroult.	Letters 42, 43, 46, 47, 48, 49, and 89.
1166	June 1, at Chinon Pontigny November, at Rouen	Arnulf attended the Council of Chinon, then traveled to Pontigny to carry a message from Henry to Becket. In November, Arnulf was again at court, seeking money and permission to retire. Henry later presented him with sixty marks.	*Cal. Doc. Fr.*, no. 737. Herbert of Bosham, *Materials* 3:393–94. Anon., *Materials* 6:72–73. Letter 53.

YEAR	LOCATION	ACTIVITIES	DOCUMENTATION
1167	Lisieux August and September, at Rouen October, at Valognes November, at Argentan	During the first half of the year, Arnulf was occupied with publishing the first edition of his letters, but by August he was back at the court of the king. He attended the funeral of Matilda and wrote some poems in her honor. His plans for retirement at Mortemer seem to have fallen through, and he was once again witnessing charters for Henry.	Eyton, *Itinerary*, pp. 107–111. Paris, BN, MS Lat. 10086. Letter 1.
1168	Lisieux	There are no records for Arnulf, but he may have been heavily engaged with work on the cathedral.	
1169	January, at Argentan September, at Bur	Arnulf was with Henry at Argentan when he concluded a treaty with France and held an abortive meeting with Becket. He rejoined Henry in late August and attended the meeting between Henry and the two papal legates. During the same time, construction was proceeding on the cathedral.	Caen, ADC, Cart. Austin Canons, II, 849. Letter 55.

YEAR	LOCATION	ACTIVITIES	DOCUMENTATION
1170	July 22, at Freteval Lisieux Christmas at Bur	Arnulf attended the reconciliation between Henry and Becket, but he was also quite busy with diocesan affairs, particularly his disputes with the abbess of Montivilliers and the abbey of St. Evroult. During December he wrote a series of letters condemning Becket's actions in England. He appears to have been with Henry for Christmas and was still with him when the news of Becket's murder arrived.	Paris, BN, MS Nov. Acq. 1245. Letter 68.
1171	January, at Argentan February, in Sens Spring, in Lisieux June, in Rouen and Quevilly August, at Caen	Arnulf witnessed Henry's reaction to Becket's death and wrote an eloquent letter in his defense to the pope. During the summer, he was again with the royal court, witnessing charters in Normandy. His major activity during this period, however, seems to have been as a papal judge-delegate. This was also the spring the cathedral foundation gave way.	Rouen, ADSM, fonds du Mont-aux-Milades. Eyton, *Itinerary*, pp. 153–162. Delisle-Berger, nos. 433 and 522. Paris, BN, MS Lat. 10074, fol. 214 (copy). Letter 72. William of Canterbury, *Materials* 1:256–257.

YEAR	LOCATION	ACTIVITIES	DOCUMENTATION
1172	May, at Savigny and Avranches	Arnulf seems to have been instrumental in bringing about the settlement between the king and the legates at the Council of Avranches. There is, however, no charter evidence that he was an active member of the court. His letters indicate that he was doing a great deal of traveling during the summer and that royal affairs preoccupied him. He was also preparing a second edition of his letters.	Herbert of Bosham, *Materials* 7:513. Letters 82, 84, 85, 86, and 87.
1173	January, at Paris Christmas, at Caen	There is circumstantial evidence that Arnulf supported the Young King's rebellion. Nevertheless, he went to Paris to ask Louis VII to stay out of the civil war. By Christmas he was again at the royal court, witnessing documents for Henry.	Caen, ADC, H.669. Eyton, *Itinerary*, pp. 177–178. Letter 76. Peter of Blois, PL 207:446–447.

YEAR	LOCATION	ACTIVITIES	DOCUMENTATION
1174	Lisieux	Although the settlement of the civil war was attested by several charters and witnessed by most of the prominent barons and bishops of Normandy, Arnulf's name does not appear. His correspondence is limited to canonical issues.	Letters 98, 99, and 100.
1175	March, at Nonant April–May, at Cerisy-la-Forêt June, to London and York September, to Normandy	Arnulf and Henry quarreled openly. Arnulf fled to his manor of Nonant in the spring. Later, he resolved to rejoin Henry in England but fell ill at Cerisy-la-Forêt. By the time he recovered and crossed to England, he was unable to catch up with Henry. He returned home without having an audience.	Letters 105 and 106.
1176		There is no record of Arnulf's activities. Henry remained in England.	

YEAR	LOCATION	ACTIVITIES	DOCUMENTATION
1177	Lisieux Autumn, at Caen	On July 12, Henry reclaimed the income from Bosham and reassigned it to the bishop of Chichester. Sometime during September, Arnulf and Henry were reconciled at the court at Caen. Arnulf did not, however, get his money back.	Bayeux, Cathedral Archives Cart. Evreux, ADE, H.711. Benedict of Peterborough, *Gesta* 1:182. Eyton, *Itinerary*, p. 218. Letter 111.
1178	Lisieux Autumn, to Paris	Arnulf was trying to arrange for his retirement and fighting the accusations of Henry that would force him to leave the bishopric in disgrace. By autumn he had fled to St. Victor, Paris, hoping that the pope and his other friends would intercede on his behalf.	Letters 125 and 126.
1179	February–March, in Burgundy July 1, at Rouen	Arnulf had planned to attend the Lateran Council in March, but he fell ill in Burgundy and was forced to abandon the trip. By the time he returned to Normandy, his diocese had been stripped of its temporalities. Determined to carry out his episcopal duties until he had been granted an honorable retirement, he was present at Rouen to assist with a transfer of relics in July.	Rouen, ADSM, G.3666 (copy). Letters 128 and 137.

YEAR	LOCATION	ACTIVITIES	DOCUMENTATION
1180	Lisieux to Paris	Sometime in the early part of the year, the pope released Arnulf from his duties, and he began the move to St. Victor, still hoping to clear his name and make peace with Henry.	Letter 137.
1181	July, at Gisors	Arnulf had his final meeting with	Eyton, *Itinerary*, p. 240.
	Paris	Henry and formally resigned his office. The two were somewhat reconciled. He remained at St. Victor from then on.	Letters 139 and 149.
1184	August 31, at Paris	Arnulf died at the monastery of St. Victor.	HF, *Obituaires*, 1:580.

Abbreviations

ADC	Archives Départementales du Calvados (Caen)
ADE	Archives Départementales de l'Eure (Evreux)
ADEL	Archives Départementales de l'Eure-et-Loir (Chartres)
ADM	Archives Départementales de la Manche (St. Lô)
ADO	Archives Départementales de l'Orne (Alençon)
ADSM	Archives Départementales de la Seine-Maritime (Rouen)
AN	Archives Nationales (Paris)
BL	British Library (London)
BM	Bibliothèque Municipale
BN	Bibliothèque Nationale (Paris)
Bodl.	Bodleian Library (Oxford)
Cal. Doc. Fr.	*Calendar of Documents Preserved in France, Illustrative of the History of Great Britain and Ireland.* Vol. 1, A.D. 918–1206. Edited by John Horace Round. London: Eyre and Spottiswoode, 1899.
DB	*Domesday Book: A Survey of the Counties of England.* Edited by John Morris. 35 vols. Chichester: Phillimore, 1975–1985.
Delisle-Berger	Léopold Delisle. *Recueil des actes de Henri II, roi d'Angleterre et duc de Normandie, concernant les provinces françaises et les affaires de France.* Edited by Élie Berger. 4 vols. Paris, 1916.
HF	*Recueil des historiens des Gaules et de la France.* Edited by Martin Bouquet et al. Vols. 15 and 23. Paris: Aux dépens des libraires, 1739–1904.
HMSO	Her Majesty's Stationery Office
JL	*Regesta Pontificum Romanorum ad annum 1198.* Edited by Philippe Jaffé; 2d ed., edited by Samuel Löwenfeld. 2 vols. Liepzig: Veit et Comp.,1885–1888.
Letters	*The Letters of Arnulf of Lisieux.* Edited by Frank Barlow. Camden Society, Third Series. Vol. 61. London: Royal Historical Society, 1939.
Mansi	*Sacrorum conciliorum nova et amplissima collectio.* Edited by Johannes Dominicus Mansi. Vols. 21 and 22. Graz: Akademische Druck-U. Verlagsanstalt, 1961.
MGH	Monumenta Germaniae Historica. Hannover: Hahn, 1826–.
MGH SS	Monumenta Germaniae Historica. *Scriptores.*
Materials	*Materials for the History of Thomas Becket.* Edited by James Craigie Robertson and J. B. Sheppard. 7 vols. RS 67. London: HMSO, 1875–1885.
PL	*Patrologiae cursus completus: series Latina.* Edited by J.-P. Migne. Paris, 1844–1864.
Orderic	Orderic Vitalis. *The Ecclesiastical History.* Translated by Marjorie Chibnall. 6 vols. Oxford: Clarendon Press, 1975.
PR	*The Great Roll of the Pipe.* Edited by John Horace Round. London: Wyman and Sons, 1884; Kraus Reprint, 1966.
Red Book	*The Red Book of the Exchequer.* Edited by Hubert Hall. 3 vols. London: HMSO, 1896.
Regesta	*Regesta Regum Anglo-Normanorrum, 1066–1154.* 3 vols. Oxford: Clarendon Press, 1913–1968.

RS   [Rolls Series] *Rerum Britannicarum Medii Aevi Scriptores, or Chronicles and Memorials of Great Britain and Ireland during the Middle Ages.* London: HMSO, 1858– .

VCH   *Victoria County History.*

Notes

Introduction

1. Arnulf, *The Letters of Arnulf of Lisieux*, ed. Frank Barlow, Camden Society, Third Series, vol. 61 (London, 1939).

2. *The Cambridge Medieval History*, vol. 5: *Contest of Empire and Papacy*, ed. J. R. Tanner, C. W. Previte Orton, and Z. N. Brooke (London, 1964), p. 557; David C. Douglas, in *English Historical Documents*, vol. 2: *1042–1189*, 2d ed. (London, 1981), p. 791, note 1; W. L. Warren, *Henry II* (Berkeley, 1973), p. 123; Mary G. Cheney, *Roger, Bishop of Worcester: 1164–1179* (Oxford, 1980), p. 47.

3. MGH, *Libelli de lite*, 3:81–108, and MGH SS 12:707–720.

4. PL 201:173–194.

5. *Letters*, p. 31.

6. See, for example, *Sacrorum conciliorum nova et amplissima collectio*, ed. Joannes Dominicus Mansi, vol. 21 (Graz, 1961), cols. 1167–1175.

7. *Calendar of Documents Preserved in France, Illustrative of the History of Great Britain and Ireland*, vol. 1: *A.D. 918–1206*, ed. John Horace Round (London, 1899).

8. *Regesta Regum Anglo-Normannorum, 1066–1154*, vol. 3: *Regesta Regis Stephani ac Mathildis Imperatricis ac Gaufridi et Henrici Ducum Normannorum, 1135–1154*, ed. H. A. Cronne and R. H. C. Davis (Oxford, 1968).

9. Robert W. Eyton, *Court, Household, and Itinerary of King Henry II* (London, 1878).

10. *Recueil des actes de Henri II*, ed. Léopold Delisle, rev. Élie Berger, vols. 1 and 2 (Paris, 1920).

11. Caen, ADC, H.7774.

12. *Cal. Doc. Fr.*, pp. xviii–xxii.

13. Delisle-Berger, nos. 44, 58, 66, 67, and 76.

14. *Cal. Doc. Fr.*, no. 734.

15. Eyton, *Itinerary*, p. 17.

16. *Letters*, pp. 17–18.

17. Eyton, *Itinerary*, p. 21.

18. Charles V. Langlois, "Formulaires de lettres du XIIe, du XIIIe et du XIVe siècle," *Notices et extraits des manuscrits de la Bibliothèque Nationale* 34 (1891):1.

19. William Stubbs, *Seventeen Lectures on the Study of Medieval and Modern History and Kindred Subjects* (Oxford, 1886; repr., New York, 1967), pp. 146–147.

20. Peter the Venerable, *The Letters of Peter the Venerable*, ed. Giles Constable, vol. 2 (Cambridge, Mass., 1967), pp. 6–12.

21. Arnulf, *Letters*, p. 1.

22. Charles H. Haskins, *Studies in Mediaeval Culture* (New York, 1929), pp. 190–192.

23. Quoted by James J. Murphy, *Rhetoric in The Middle Ages: A History of Rhetorical Theory from Saint Augustine to the Renaissance* (Berkeley, 1974), p. 216.

24. *Letters*, p. 145.

25. *Letters*, p. 211.

26. *Letters*, p. 137.

27. *Letters*, p. 85.

28. Murphy, *Rhetoric*, pp. 211–212, and Charles S. Baldwin, *Medieval Rhetoric and Poetic (to 1400): Interpreted from Representative Works* (Gloucester, Mass., 1959), p. 207, note 2.

29. Giles Constable, *Letters and Letter Collections* (Turnhout, 1976), pp. 56–57.

30. *Letters*, p. 1.
31. *Letters*, p. 2.
32. *Letters*, p. lxii.
33. *Letters*, p. 136.
34. *Letters*, p. 136.
35. Lisieux, BM, Norm. 5G5.
36. *Letters*, pp. 69–78.
37. *Letters*, pp. 153–158.
38. *Letters*, pp. 143–144 and 166–168.
39. *Letters*, p. lxxxv.
40. Arnulf, "Arnulfi Lexoviensis episcopi Epistolae," ed. J.A. Giles (Oxford, 1844), pp. xi–xii.
41. *Letters*, pp. 63–64 and 79–80.
42. *Letters*, pp. 122–123.
43. *Letters*, pp. 208–210.
44. Giles, in "Epistolae," p. vii.
45. *Letters*, p. lxxxvii.
46. *Letters*, p. lxxxvii.
47. In light of these findings, I intend to bring out a translation of the Arnulf correspondence, restoring the original manuscript order of the letters and reflecting the purpose for which they were originally compiled.
48. *Letters*, nos. 42 and 76.
49. Mary G. Cheney, "The Recognition of Pope Alexander III: Some Neglected Evidence," *English Historical Review* 84 (July 1969):486–487, note 1.
50. The most satisfactory discussion of this matter is Giles Constable, "The Alleged Disgrace of John of Salisbury in 1159," *English Historical Review* 69 (January 1954):67–76.
51. *The Letters of John of Salisbury*, vol. 1: *The Early Letters (1153–1161)*, ed. W. J. Millor and H. E. Butler, rev. C. N. L. Brooke (London, 1955), p. 30.
52. *The Early Letters*, p. 195.
53. John of Salisbury, *Memoirs of the Papal Court*, trans. Marjorie Chibnall (London, 1956), p. 55.
54. *Materials for the History of Thomas Becket*, ed. J. C. Robertson, RS 67 (London, 1885), 5:105.
55. John of Salisbury, *Memoirs of the Papal Court*, p. xxxvii, note 2.
56. These poems may be found in several manuscripts of the Arnulf letters and have been included in PL 201:199, nos. 11 and 12.
57. Cf. Cheney, *Roger, Bishop of Worcester*, p. 229, and Sarell Everett Gleason, *An Ecclesiastical Barony of the Middle Ages: The Bishopric of Bayeux, 1066–1204* (Cambridge, Mass., 1936).
58. Thomas S. Kuhn, *The Structure of Scientific Revolutions*, 2d ed. (Chicago, 1970), p. 175.
59. See, for example, Richard J. Bernstein, *The Restructuring of Social and Political Theory* (Philadelphia, 1976), pp. 88–93.
60. John B. Morrall, *Political Thought in Medieval Times* (Toronto, 1980), p. 45.
61. Kuhn, *Scientific Revolutions*, p. 19.

I. The Construction of a Paradigm

1. John H. Round, "Bernard, the King's Scribe," *English Historical Review* 14 (July 1899):427, and Orderic Vitalis, *The Ecclesiastical History*, trans. Marjorie Chibnall (Oxford, 1975), 6:142–143.
2. David S. Spear, *The Norman Episcopate under Henry I, King of England and Duke of Normandy (1106–1135)* (Ann Arbor, 1982), pp. 42–45.
3. Orderic 6:143–145.

4. See *Regesta Regum Anglo-Normannorum, 1066–1154*, vol. 2: *Regesta Henrici Primi*, ed. Charles Johnson and H. A. Cronne (Oxford, 1956), nos. 626, 675, 807, and 808.

5. The document most frequently cited is *Regesta* 2, no. 1584, tentatively dated in 1129 at Rouen. It is discussed by Round, "Bernard, the King's Scribe," p. 426, and Charles H. Haskins, *Norman Institutions* (Cambridge, Mass., 1918), pp. 88–89 and note 18. Other cases which came before John of Lisieux may be found in *Regesta* 2, nos. 819, 951, 1002, 1183, 1184, 1337, 1352, 1422, 1589, 1593, 1672, 1689, 1690, 1902, and 1907.

6. Orderic 6:144–145.

7. Orderic 6:340–341.

8. See Arnulf, *The Letters of Arnulf of Lisieux*, ed. Frank Barlow, Camden Society, Third Series, vol. 61 (London, 1939), pp. xi–xii, note 3, and Marcel Pacaut, *Louis VII et les élections épiscopales dans le royaume de France* (Paris, 1957), p. 124.

9. See *Regesta* 2, no. 1364.

10. Orderic, 6:340–341.

11. *Letters*, pp. 55–56.

12. Noël Deshays, *Mémoires pour servir à l'histoire des évêques de Lisieux* (1754), repr. in H. de Formeville, *Histoire de l'ancien évêché-comté de Lisieux* (Lisieux, 1873), 2:47.

13. Arnulf, *Invectiva in Girardum Engolismensem Episcopum*, ed. J. Dieterich, MGH, *Libelli de lite* 3:85.

14. Deshays, *Mémoires*, p. 47.

15. *Libelli de lite* 3:83.

16. Barlow, in *Letters*, pp. xv–xvi.

17. Deshays, *Mémoires*, p. 47. The source of his information, Abbé Hermant, *Histoire du diocèse de Bayeux* (Caen, 1703), is obscure.

18. Heinrich Böhmer, *Kirche und Staat in England und in der Normandie im XI. und XII. Jahrhundert: Eine historische Studie* (Leipzig, 1899; repr., 1968), pp. 142–146, and Spear, *The Norman Episcopate*, p. 81.

19. Thomas S. Kuhn, *The Structure of Scientific Revol.utions*, 2d ed. (Chicago, 1970), p. 90.

20. The emergence of these parties is discussed in detail by Stanley Chodorow, *Christian Political Theory and Church Politics in the Mid–Twelfth Century: The Ecclesiology of the Gratian's Decretum* (Berkeley, 1972), pp. 27–46, and Franz-Josef Schmale, *Studien zum Schisma des Jahres 1130* (Graz, 1961). Their conclusions are, however, disputed by Johannes Haller, *Das Papsttum: Idee und Wirklichkeit*, vol. 2, part 2 (Esslingen am Neckar, 1962), passim, and Mary Stroll, *The Jewish Pope: Ideology and Politics in the Papal Schism of 1130* (Leiden, 1987), pp. xvi–xvii.

21. Herbert Bloch, "The Schism of Anacletus II and the Glanfeuil Forgeries of Peter the Deacon of Monte Cassino," *Traditio* 8 (1952):164, and Chodorow, *Christian Political Theory*, p. 34. The exact count, however, is somewhat in doubt; see P. F. Palumbo, "Nuova Studi (1942–1962) sullo scisma di Anacleto II," *Bollettino dell' Istituto storico italiano per il medio evo e Archivio Muratoriano* 75 (1963):100, note 1.

22. Hans-Walter Klewitz, "Das Ende des Reformpapsttums," *Deutsches Archiv für Geschichte des Mittelalters* 3 (1939):372–373.

23. Richard Zöpffel, *Die Doppelwohl des Jahres 1130* (Göttingen, 1872), pp. 328 and 341.

24. Klewitz, "Das Ende des Reformpapsttums," p. 373.

25. Their identities can be determined from the signatures attached to papal documents given by Philippe Jaffé, *Regesta Pontificum Romanorum ad annum 1198*, 2d ed., vol. 1 (Leipzig, 1888), pp. 840–841 and 911–912. Much the same lists appear in William of Malmesbury, PL 179:49–52 and 689–690. The full prosopographic evidence concerning the two sides may be found in Klewitz, "Das Ende des Reformpapsttums," pp. 371–387.

26. Ivo of Chartres, *Panormia* III.c.2, in PL 161:1127–1130.

27. Chodorow, *Christian Political Theory*, p. 20.

28. Bishop Eberhard of Bamberg in a letter to Eberhard, Archbishop of Salzburg, after the 1160 Council of Pavia; included in Otto of Freising, *Gesta Friderici I*, ed. Roger Wilmans, MGH SS 20:487.

29. Abbot Suger, *Vita Ludovici*, PL 186:1330.

30. Ernald, *Vita Prima*, PL 185:271.

31. Bernard, *Epistolae*, PL 182:269.

32. *Libelli de lite* 3:84.

33. *Libelli de lite* 3:104.

34. *Libelli de lite* 3:85.

35. *Libelli de lite* 3:81, note 7.

36. Wilhelm Janssen, *Die päpstlichen Legaten in Frankreich: Vom Schisma Anaklets II bis zum Tode Coelestina III (1130–1198)* (Cologne, 1961), p. 5.

37. *Gerard, évêque d'Angoulême, légat du saint siège* (Bull. de la Soc. Archéol. et Hist. de la Charente, 1864).

38. *Libelli de lite* 3:86.

39. *Libelli de lite* 3:87.

40. *Libelli de lite* 3:87.

41. *Libelli de lite* 3:87.

42. *Libelli de lite* 3:89.

43. *Libelli de lite* 3:89, note 3.

44. *Libelli de lite* 3:90.

45. *Libelli de lite* 3:92–93.

46. See Chodorow, *Christian Political Theory*, pp. 28–29, and Reginald Lane Poole, *Studies in Chronology and History*, ed. Austin Lane Poole (Oxford, 1934), p. 208.

47. Engelbert Mühlbacher, *Die streitige Papstwahl des Jahres 1130* (Innsbruck, 1876; repr., 1966), p. 54.

48. *Libelli de lite* 3:95.

49. *Libelli de lite* 3:95.

50. "Quousque igitur abutere patientia Dei?" *Libelli de lite* 3:86. Cf. Cicero's demand in his "First Oration against Cataline": "Quo usque tandem abutere, Catalina, patientia nostra." *Orations of Cicero: With a Selection from His Letters*, ed. Frank Garner Moore (Boston, 1925), p. 3.

51. *Libelli de lite* 3:88.

52. "Non attendabatur honestas, sed manus honustas [onustas] potius expectabas." *Libelli de lite* 3:89.

53. For example, see the accounts of the Jewish massacre at York, which followed the coronation of King Richard in 1189, in Kate Norgate, *Richard the Lion Heart* (London, 1924; repr., New York, 1969), p. 98, and John Gillingham, *Richard the Lionheart* (New York, 1978), pp. 130–131.

54. For a discussion of French and Norman attitudes toward Jews, see Lester K. Little, *Religious Poverty and the Profit Economy in Medieval Europe* (Ithaca, N.Y., 1978), pp. 42–57, and, more recent, Norman Golb, *Les juifs de Rouen au moyen âge: Portrait d'une culture oubliée* (Rouen, 1985).

55. See, for example, *Sacrorum conciliorum nova et amplissima collectio*, ed. Joannus Dominicus Mansi, vol. 21 (Graz, 1961), particularly "Laternensis I," canon 3, col. 302, and "Laternensis II," canons 6 and 7, col. 527.

56. Georges Duby, *The Knight, the Lady, and the Priest: The Making of Modern Marriage in Medieval France*, trans. Barbara Bray (New York, 1983), pp. 116–120.

57. Böhmer, *Kirche und Staat*, pp. 276–283.

58. See, for example, Janssen, *Die päpstlichen Legaten in Frankreich*, p. 20, and Dieterich, *Libelli de lite* 3:83.

59. Henri Pellerin, "Saint Bernard et le pays lexovien: Ses rapports avec Arnoul, évêque de Lisieux," *Le Pays d'Auge* (April 1965):8.

60. *Letters*, pp. xvi–xvii; for his evidence, see Peter the Venerable, *The Letters of Peter the Venerable*, ed. Giles Constable, vol. 1 (Cambridge, Mass., 1967), p. 154.

61. Letter of Innocent II, dated May 20, 1131, in *Calendar of Documents Preserved in France, Illustrative of the History of Great Britain and Ireland*, vol. 1: *A.D. 918–1206*, ed. J. H. Round (London, 1899), p. 508; Mansi 21:407; *Regesta* 2:248; and Paris, BN, MS Lat. 5458.

62. Bloch, "The Schism of Anacletus II," pp. 166–167.

63. Bernard, *Epistolae*, PL 182:294.

64. Stroll, *The Jewish Pope*, pp. 160–168.

65. *Libelli de lite* 3:85–86. Cf. Bernard's justification of Innocent's election, previously discussed.

66. Pellerin, "Saint Bernard et le pays lexovien," p. 13.

67. *Libelli de lite* 3:103.

II. The Search for Political Allegiance

1. Martin Brett, *The English Church under Henry I* (Oxford, 1975), pp. 204–211.

2. *The Letters of John of Salisbury*, vol. 2: *The Later Letters (1163–1180)*, ed. W. J. Millor and C. N. L. Brooke (Oxford, 1979), p. 24.

3. David Walker, "Crown and Episcopacy under the Normans and Angevins," in *Anglo-Norman Studies V: Proceedings of the Battle Conference, 1982*, ed. R. Allen Brown (Woodbridge, 1983), p. 220.

4. David S. Spear, *The Norman Episcopate under Henry I, King of England and Duke of Normandy (1106–1135)* (Ann Arbor, 1982), p. 49.

5. See Andrew W. Lewis, "Anticipatory Association of the Heir in Early Capetian France," *American Historical Review* 83 (1978):927.

6. See Achille Luchaire, *Histoire des institutions monarchiques de la France sous les premiers Capétiens, 987–1180*, 2d ed., vol. 1 (Paris, 1891), pp. 60–87; Robert Fawtier, *The Capetian Kings of France: Monarchy and Nation, 987–1328*, trans. Lionel Butler and R. J. Adam (London, 1964), pp. 48–58; and Ferdinand Lot and Robert Fawtier, eds., *Histoire des institutions françaises au Moyen Âge*, vol. 2: *Institutions royales* (Paris, 1958), pp. 12–16.

7. The best general discussion of the history of the Norman dukes is David Bates, *Normandy before 1066* (London, 1982). Chronicle sources for specific dukes include Dudo of Saint-Quentin, *De moribus et actis primorum Normanniae ducum*, ed. Jules Lair (Caen, 1865), and William of Jumièges, *Gesta Normannorum ducum*, ed. Jean Marx (Rouen, 1911).

8. The relative merits of the candidates are discussed by David C. Douglas in *The Norman Conquest: Its Setting and Impact* (New York, 1966), pp. 58–60.

9. Orderic Vitalis, *The Ecclesiastical History*, trans. Marjorie Chibnall (Oxford, 1975), 4:82–84.

10. See, for example, David C. Douglas, *The Norman Fate: 1100–1154* (Berkeley, 1976), pp. 15–17, and C. Warren Hollister and Thomas K. Keefe, "The Making of the Angevin Empire," *Journal of British Studies* 12 (1973):1–3.

11. Orderic, 6:518; Robert of Torigni, *Chronica*, ed. Richard Howlett, RS 82, 4:111; *The Anglo-Saxon Chronicle*, ed. Dorothy Whitelock et al. (London, 1961), pp. 192–193; *Gesta Stephani*, trans. K. R. Potter (Oxford, 1976), p. 10.

12. William of Malmesbury, *Historiae Novellae*, ed. William Stubbs, RS 90, 2:528.

13. Malmesbury, RS 90, 2:529–530.

14. See, for example, *The Anglo-Saxon Chronicle*, pp. 192–193, and *Gesta Stephani*, p. 10.

15. See *Regesta Regum Anglo-Normannorum, 1066–1154*, vol. 2, *Regesta Henrici Primi*, ed. Charles Johnson and Henry A. Cronne (Oxford, 1956), nos. 1450, 1466, and 1474.

16. Malmesbury, RS 90, 2:530.

17. Robert of Torigni, RS 82, 4:128–129.

18. R. H. C. Davis, *King Stephen, 1135–1154* (Berkeley, 1967), p. 22. Also see John H. Round, *Geoffrey de Mandeville: A Study of the Anarchy* (New York, 1892; repr., 1972), pp. 16–20.

19. *Regesta Regum Anglo-Normannorum, 1066–1154*, vol. 3: *Regesta Regis Stephani ac Mathildis Imperatricis ac Gaufridi et Henrici Ducum Normannorum, 1135–1154*, ed. H. A. Cronne and R. H. C. Davis (Oxford, 1968), nos. 48 and 944.

20. For the documents which prove his continued service, see *Regesta* 3, nos. 298, 327, 608, and 843. Also see the comment of Davis, *King Stephen*, p. 22, note 21.

21. Orderic 6:551.

22. Spear, *The Norman Episcopate*, p. 41.

23. See *Regesta* 3, nos. 594 and 681.

24. Orderic 6:471.

25. Henri Pellerin discusses the political repercussions of the schism in "Saint Bernard et le pays lexovien: Ses rapports avec Arnoul, évêque de Lisieux," *Le Pays d'Auge* (April 1965):3–19.

26. *Libelli de lite* 3:107.

27. *The Letters of Peter the Venerable*, ed. Giles Constable, vol. 1 (Cambridge, Mass., 1967), p. 262.

28. *Recueil des historiens des Gaules et de la France*, ed. Martin Bouquet et al. (Paris, 1878), 15:582.

29. *Regesta* 3, no. 506.

30. *Sacrorum conciliorum nova et amplissima collectio*, vol. 21, ed. J. D. Mansi (Graz, 1961), and Raymonde Foreville, *Latran I, II, III, et Latran IV* (Paris, 1965). For the various arguments concerning the date, see Kate Norgate, *England under the Angevin Kings*, vol. 1 (London, 1887), p. 370; Round, *Geoffrey de Mandeville*, pp. 250–261; Ioannis Saresberiensis, *Historiae pontificalis quae supersunt*, ed. Reginald L. Poole (Oxford, 1927), pp. 107–113; Dom Adrian Morey and C. N. L. Brooke, *Gilbert Foliot and His Letters* (Cambridge, 1965), pp. 105–123; and *The Letters of Peter the Venerable*, 2:252–256.

31. Gilbert Foliot in a letter to Brian fitz Count, in Gilbert Foliot, *The Letters and Charters of Gilbert Foliot*, ed. Dom Adrian Morey and C. N. L. Brooke (Cambridge, 1967), p. 65. Cf. John of Salisbury, *Memoirs of the Papal Court*, trans. Marjorie Chibnall (London, 1956), p. 83.

32. John of Salisbury, *Memoirs*, pp. 84–85.

33. In her introduction to John of Salisbury's *Memoirs*, p. xliii, Marjorie Chibnall concedes that Salisbury constructed this passage from arguments he heard on other occasions.

34. Eadmer, *Historia Novorum in Anglia*, ed. Martin Rule, RS 81, pp. 121–126.

35. A charter of King Stephen, given in full by Richard of Hexham, *De gestis Regis Stephani*, RS 82, 3:148, contains the following declaration: "Ego Stephanus Dei gratia assensu cleri et populi in regem Angliae electus, et a Willelmo Cantuariensi archiepiscopo et sanctae Romanae ecclesiae legato consecratus, et *ab Innocentio sanctae Romanae sedis pontifice confirmatus* [italics mine], respectu et amore Dei sanctam ecclesiam liberam esse concedo, et debitam reverentiam illi confirmo."

36. Robert of Torigni, RS 82, 4:131.

37. Robert of Torigni, RS 82, 4:142.

38. Orderic 6:551.

39. HF 15:582–583.

40. *The Letters of Peter the Venerable*, 1:261–262.

41. Arnulf, *The Letters of Arnulf of Lisieux*, ed. Frank Barlow (London, 1939), p. 209.

42. *Letters*, p. 4.

43. Davis, *King Stephen*, p. 145.

44. *Calender of Documents Preserved in France, Illustrative of the History of Great Britain and Ireland*, vol. 1: *A.D. 918–1206*, ed. J. H. Round (London, 1899), no. 909. Charles H.

Haskins, *Norman Institutions* (Cambridge, Mass., 1918), p. 130, note 23, cites two additional charters for this period, but their existence can no longer be verified.

45. *Letters*, p. 209.
46. Heinrich Böhmer, *Kirche und Staat in England und in der Normandie im XI. und XII. Jahrhundert: Eine historische Studie* (Leipzig, 1899; repr., 1968), pp. 315–316.
47. *Letters*, p. 4.
48. *Letters*, p. 5.
49. HF 15:603.
50. HF 15:604.
51. See the letter Arnulf wrote to Pope Alexander III after the death of Gerard in 1157, in *Letters*, p. 57.
52. *Letters*, p. 181.
53. Mansi 21:692.
54. The chronicle of the monastery of Ste.-Barbe-en-Auge, printed in HF 14:502. For a slightly different version, see William of Tyre, *Historia rerum in partibus Transmarinsi gestarum*, in *Recueil des historiens des croisades: Historiens occidentaux*, vol. 1, part 2 (Paris, 1844; repr., Farnborough, 1969), p. 759.
55. John of Salisbury, *Memoirs*, pp. 54–55.
56. *Letters*, p. 210.
57. Odo of Deuil, *De profectione Ludovici VII in orientem*, trans. Virginia Gingerick Berry (New York, 1948), p. 77.
58. HF 15:500.
59. Odo of Deuil, *De profectione*, p. 71.
60. William of Tyre, *Recueil des croisades*, 1:759.
61. See John of Salisbury, *Memoirs*, pp. 57–58.
62. *Letters*, p. 9.
63. HF 15:521.
64. *Regesta* 3, no. 635.
65. *Regesta* 3, no. 304.
66. *Regesta* 3, nos. 704 and 735.
67. *Letters*, p. 7.
68. Haskins, *Norman Institutions*, p. 130, note 26; Hollister and Keefe, "The Making of the Angevin Empire," p. 18; and W. L. Warren, *Henry II* (Berkeley, 1973), p. 38.
69. *Letters*, pp. xxvii–xxviii, note 7.
70. See *Cal. Doc. Fr.*, nos. 109, 127, 1000, 1406, 1407, and 1441; *Regesta* 3, nos. 64, 65, 71, 72, 325, 332, 462, 600, 729, 783, and 900; and *Recueil des actes de Henri II*, vol. 1, ed. Léopold Delisle, rev. Élie Berger (Paris, 1920), nos. 11, 14, 35–37, 42, 44, 68, 72, 74–76, 78, and 80.
71. Robert of Torigni, RS 82, 4:162–164.
72. Robert of Torigni, RS 82, 4:182.
73. Richard I confirmed this gift from his father in a charter dated June 20, 1189. Notification of the charter was included in the now-lost cartulary of the bishopric of Lisieux, fol. 203. A somewhat defective listing of it appears in H. de Formeville, *Histoire l'ancien évêché-comté de Lisieux* (Lisieux, 1873), 2:339.
74. Delisle-Berger, no. 80; *Cal. Doc. Fr.*, no. 1441; and *Antiquus cartularius ecclesiae Baiocensis (Livre Noir)*, ed. V. Bourrienne (Rouen, 1902), no. 7.

III. The Bishop as Baron

1. David Bates, *Normandy before 1066* (London, 1982), pp. 99–100, and "Notes sur l'aristocratie normande. I.-Hugues, évêque de Bayeux (1011 env.–1049)," *Annales de Normandie* 23 (1973):7–21.
2. For the lines of descent, see David C. Douglas, *William the Conqueror: The Norman Impact upon England* (Berkeley, 1964), tables 5 and 6, pp. 422–423, and "Table IV: The

Dukes of Normandy," in M. Jackson Crispin and Leonce Macary, eds., *The Falaise Roll: Recording Prominent Companions of William Duke of Normandy at the Conquest of England* (London, 1938; repr., Baltimore, 1985), pocket following p. 259.

3. Bates, *Normandy before 1066*, p. 202.

4. See H. de Formeville, *Histoire de l'ancien évêché-comté de Lisieux* (Lisieux, 1873), p. 425, and Louis Du Bois, *Histoire de Lisieux: Ville, diocèse et arrondissement* (Lisieux, 1845; repr., Brussels, 1977), p. 476.

5. This list appears in *Antiquus cartularius ecclesiae Baiocensis (Livre Noir)*, ed. V. Bourrienne (Rouen, 1902), no. 21. It is discussed by Sarell Everett Gleason, *An Ecclesiastical Barony of the Middle Ages: The Bishopric of Bayeux, 1066–1204* (Cambridge, Mass., 1936), pp. 40–52 and note 39.

6. *Recueil des historiens des Gaules et de la France*, ed. Martin Bouquet et al., vol. 23 (Paris, 1894), pp. 699–703.

7. HF 23:701. Marjorie Chibnall discusses these obligations in "Military Service in Normandy before 1066," in R. Allen Brown, ed., *Anglo-Norman Studies V: Proceedings of the Battle Conference, 1982* (Woodbridge, 1983), p. 75.

8. Orderic Vitalis, *The Ecclesiastical History*, trans. Marjorie Chibnall (Oxford, 1975), 3:17. His source was William of Poitiers; see William of Poitiers, *Gesta Guillelmi*, ed. Raymonde Foreville (Paris, 1952), pp. 138–142.

9. Orderic 3:21.

10. See, for example, Bates, *Normandy before 1066*, p. 173.

11. Orderic 5:323.

12. Ivo of Chartres, *Epistolae*, PL 162:154–163.

13. Orderic 5:323.

14. HF 23:693–694; *The Red Book of the Exchequer*, ed. Hubert Hall, vol. 2 (London, 1896), pp. 624–645.

15. *Red Book* 1:186–445. J. C. Holt discusses the significance and interpretation of the *Cartae Baronum* in "The Introduction of Knight Service in England," in R. Allen Brown, ed., *Anglo-Norman Studies VI: Proceedings of the Battle Conference, 1983* (Woodbridge, 1984), pp. 89–106.

16. HF 23:636–637.

17. Formeville, *Histoire de Lisieux*, 1:427–428.

18. Formeville, *Histoire de Lisieux*, 1:442–450.

19. Formeville, *Histoire de Lisieux*, 1:425–427.

20. Formeville, *Histoire de Lisieux*, 1:434–436.

21. Formeville, *Histoire de Lisieux*, 1:429–434.

22. Formeville, *Histoire de Lisieux*, 1:436–438.

23. Formeville, *Histoire de Lisieux*, 1:434–442.

24. Formeville, *Histoire de Lisieux*, 1:424.

25. Formeville, *Histoire de Lisieux*, 1:424–425.

26. *Magni Rotuli Scaccarii Normanniae sub regibus Angliae*, ed. Thomas Stapleton, vol. 1 (London, 1840), pp. 99 and cxxx.

27. Trigand, *Histoire de Normandie*, 4:524; quoted by Formeville, *Histoire de Lisieux*, 1:420.

28. Arnulf, *The Letters of Arnulf of Lisieux*, ed. Frank Barlow, Camden Third Series, vol. 61 (London, 1939), p. 181.

29. *The Great Roll of the Pipe for the Reign of King Henry the Second* (London, 1882–1925; repr., 1965–1966), 8 Henry II, p. 50.

30. *Calendar of Patent Rolls, Henry III, 1232–1247* (London, 1893), p. 455.

31. *Letters*, p. 174, note a. Also see *Liber Feodorum* 1:71.

32. *Red Book* 2:654.

33. *Red Book* 2:660.

34. See *Red Book* 2:696.
35. London, PRO, E 164/20 (Cartulary of Godstow), fol. 58r.
36. *Red Book* 1:340, 346, and 264.
37. See *Red Book* 2:816 and 822.
38. PR, 6 Henry II, p. 18.
39. PR, 8 Henry II, p. 50.
40. See VCH, *Hanteshire* 1:469.
41. PR, 6 Henry II, p. 48.
42. *Red Book* 2:816.
43. Charles R. Young, *The Royal Forests of Medieval England* (Philadelphia, 1979), pp. 34–36.
44. PR, 16 Henry II, p. 122. His exemption appears in *Red Book* 2:822.
45. *Regesta Regum Anglo-Normannorum, 1066–1154*, vol. 1: *Regesta Willelmi Conquestoris et Willelmi Rufi, 1066–1100*, ed. H. W. C. Davis (Oxford, 1913), nos. 140 and 145. These grants were confirmed by a charter included in vol. 2: *Regesta Henrici Primi*, ed. Charles Johnson and Henry Alfred Cronne (Oxford, 1956), no. 306.
46. *Domesday Book* (London, 1783), vol. 2, fol. 389.
47. See Donald Matthew, *The Norman Monasteries and Their English Possessions* (repr., Westport, Conn., 1979), pp. 33–34.
48. Matthew, *Norman Monasteries*, pp. 42–44.
49. Matthew, *Norman Monasteries*, pp. 151–152.
50. See *The Register of Eudes of Rouen*, trans. Sydney M. Brown (New York, 1964), pp. 66–72.
51. *Letters*, p. 175.
52. See R. W. Eyton, *Court, Household, and Itinerary of King Henry II* (London, 1878), pp. 2–6.
53. See *Regesta* 2, p. xxviii, and R. C. Van Caenegem, *Royal Writs in England from the Conquest to Glanville: Studies in the Early History of the Common Law* (London, 1959), p. 158.
54. Eyton, *Itinerary*, pp. 3 and 4.
55. *Letters*, p. 14.
56. See Charles H. Haskins, *Norman Institutions* (Cambridge, Mass., 1925), pp. 89–99.
57. Haskins, *Norman Institutions*, pp. 166–168.
58. Francis West, *The Justiciarship in England, 1066–1232* (Cambridge, 1966), pp. 27–30.
59. Jacques Boussard, *Le gouvernement d'Henri II Plantagenêt* (Paris, 1956), p. 370.
60. Haskins, *Norman Institutions*, p. 323. Note that Haskins calls Robert "seneschal and justiciar," but the text of the document he cites uses only the title "justiciar."
61. *Recueil des actes de Henri II*, ed. Léopold Delisle, rev. Élie Berger, vol. 1 (Paris, 1920), p. 286, no. 154.
62. *Cal. Doc. Fr.*, no. 734.
63. *Cal. Doc. Fr.*, no. 737; Eyton, *Itinerary*, p. 21.
64. Cartulary of Savigny, no. 273; printed by Haskins, *Norman Institutions*, p. 324.
65. *Cal. Doc. Fr.*, no. 299; Delisle-Berger, no. 98.
66. *Cal. Doc. Fr.*, no. 641; Delisle-Berger, no. 214.
67. *Cal. Doc. Fr.*, no. 1254; Delisle-Berger, no. 129.
68. *Cal. Doc. Fr.*, no. 482; Delisle-Berger, no. 309.
69. *Letters*, pp. 151–152.
70. Eyton, *Itinerary*, p. 49; Delisle-Berger, no. 141.
71. See Ralph de Diceto, *Opera Historica*, ed. William Stubbs, RS 68, 1:312.
72. *Letters*, p. 101.

IV. The Bishop in the Wider World of Christendom

1. See the lists in Pius Bonifacius Gams, *Series Episcoporum Ecclesiae Catholicae*, 2d ed. (Leipzig, 1931), pp. 180–201, 258–325, and 477–657.

2. The text of the agreement may be found in "Appendix II: Acta Sicula," MGH, *Legum*, sect. 4, pp. 588–590.

3. Freising, *Gesta Friderici*, MGH SS 20, part 4, sects. 8–9. Also see Marshall W. Baldwin, *Alexander III and the Twelfth Century* (Glen Rock, N.J., 1968), pp. 34–38.

4. Cardinal Boso, *Life of Alexander III*, trans. G. M. Ellis (London, 1973), p. 43. Cf. Gerhoh of Reichersberg, *De investigatione Antichristi Liber I*, ed. Ernest Sackur, MGH, *Libelli de lite* 3:360.

5. Boso, *Life of Alexander III*, p. 44, and Gerhoh, *Libelli de lite* 3:360–361. The best modern account is Lawrence F. Barmann, "The Papal Election of 1159," *American Ecclesiastical Review* 148 (January 1963):39–42.

6. Arnulf, *The Letters of Arnulf of Lisieux*, ed. Frank Barlow, Camden Third Series, vol. 61 (London, 1939), pp. 29–30.

7. *Letters*, p. 32.

8. *Letters*, pp. 32–33.

9. Wilhelm Janssen, *Die päpstlichen Legaten in Frankreich: Vom Schisma Anaklets II bis zum Tode Coelestina III (1130–1198)* (Cologne, 1961), pp. 61–62.

10. HF 15:760.

11. "Rescriptum generale a synodo," in *Gesta Friderici*, MGH SS 20:487.

12. R. W. Eyton, *Court, Household, and Itinerary of King Henry II* (London, 1878), p. 49, and *Recueil des actes de Henri II*, ed. Léopold Delisle, rev. Élie Berger, vol. 1 (Paris, 1920), nos. 98 and 148.

13. Delisle-Berger 1:251–253.

14. *The Letters of John of Salisbury*, vol. 1: *The Early Letters (1153–1161)*, ed. W. J. Millor and H. E. Butler, rev. C. N. L. Brooke (London, 1955), pp. 190–192.

15. *Letters*, p. 37.

16. *Letters*, pp. 40–41.

17. *Letters*, p. 42.

18. Mary G. Cheney, "The Recognition of Pope Alexander III: Some Neglected Evidence," *English Historical Review* 84 (July 1969):486–487, note 1, cites this as an example of Arnulf's use of *suggestio falsi*.

19. *The Letters of John of Salisbury*, 1:201–202. An editorial note, p. 201, identifies the "reliable sources" as the letter of Arnulf to the bishops.

20. *The Letters of John of Salisbury*, 1:226.

21. The exact location and date of this joint statement have been the subject of much discussion, since some contemporary accounts used Arnulf's misleading letter as proof of an early agreement. See Frank Barlow, "The English, Norman, and French Councils Called to Deal with the Papal Schism of 1159," *English Historical Review* 51 (April 1936):264–268. For the most recent synthesis of the evidence, see Cheney, "The Recognition of Alexander III," pp. 474–497.

22. Baldwin, *Alexander III and the Twelfth Century*, pp. 72–73.

23. Robert Somerville, *Pope Alexander III and the Council of Tours (1163): A Study of Ecclesiastical Politics and Institutions in the Twelfth Century* (Berkeley, 1977), pp. 4–8. Also see Brian Tierney, *Foundations of the Conciliar Theory: The Contribution of the Medieval Canonists from Gratian to the Great Schism* (Cambridge, 1968), pp. 75–77.

24. Boso, *Life of Alexander III*, p. 59. Somerville, *Pope Alexander III and the Council of Tours*, chap. 3, has attempted to identify the participants. See, particularly, his list of bishops, pp. 27–29.

25. Draco Normannicus [Stephen of Rouen], *Chronica*, ed. Richard Howlett, RS 82, 2:743.

26. See, for example, Charles-Joseph Hefele, *Histoire des Conciles: D'après les documents originaux*, ed. Dom H. Leclercq, vol. 5, part 2 (Paris, 1913), pp. 969–970.

27. Raymonde Foreville and Jean Rousset de Pina, *Du premier Concile du Latran à l'avènement d'Innocent III*, vol. 9, part 2, of *Histoire de l'église*, ed. Augustin Fliche and Victor Martin (Paris, 1953), pp. 72–73, note 4, note the impossibility of untangling the manuscript variations. Somerville, *Pope Alexander III and the Council of Tours*, pp. 15–16, also notes the problem but fails to solve it.

28. Draco Normannicus, RS 82, 2:744.

29. "Sermo ab Arnulpho Lexoviensi in concilio Turonsi habitus," in *Sacrorum conciliorum nova et amplissima collectio*, ed. Joannes Dominicus Mansi, vol. 21 (Graz, 1961), cols. 1167–1175. This text is based on Claude Mignault's 1585 edition, which was printed from Paris, BN, MS Lat. 14763.

30. The best example appears in Oxford, Bodl., Auct. F.I.8. This manuscript begins the second sermon at the clause *Porro fratres sumus ex codem patre Christo* (Mansi 21:1172). Its introduction reads, "In yesterday's sermon, merciful lords and fathers, I spoke with you about the unity and freedom of the church of God. . . ." [*Hesterno sermone, domini et patres misericordi, vobiscum de unitate ecclesiae Dei et libertate tractatum habuimus . . .*], fol. 123v. This version is also given in PL 201:157, with a slightly variant reading: *Hesterno sermone, domini et Patres charissimi, vobiscum ne unitate Ecclesiae Dei et libertate tractatum habuimus.*

31. Mansi 21:1172.

32. Mansi 21:1170.

33. Mansi 21:1173.

34. Draco Normannicus, RS 82, 2:751.

35. See *Letters*, pp. 115–116.

36. Caen, ADC, H.7774.

37. Caen, ADC, H.1846.

38. See Jane E. Sayers, *Papal Judges-Delegate in the Province of Canterbury, 1198–1254: A Study in Ecclesiastical Jurisdiction and Administration* (Oxford, 1971), chap. 1, and Mary G. Cheney, *Roger, Bishop of Worcester: 1164–1179* (Oxford, 1980), chap. 4.

39. *Letters*, pp. 22–23.

40. Stanley Chodorow, who is editing the French collections of decretals for publication, confirmed the following details in a letter to me on November 9, 1986. The decretal *In litteris*, dated 5 March 1177 at Viesti, contained eight separate clauses addressed to Arnulf. These appear in *Regesta Pontificum Romanorum ad annum 1198*, ed. Philippe Jaffé, 2d ed., vol. 2 (Leipzig, 1888), nos. 13915, 13921, and 14219. The full text of the rulings may be found in Mansi 22:253–254, 302, 361, 366, 380, and 409. One other decretal in the Jaffé collection, no. 13899, was also sent to Lisieux. It was dated 29 January 1177, at Siponto. *Papsturkunden in Frankreich*, vol. 2: *Normandie*, ed. Johannes Ramackers (Göttingen, 1937), attributes several decretals to Arnulf, but the only verifiable one is no. 157.

41. See my article, "The Decretal *In Litteris* and the Case of Henry the Counterfeiter," *Comitatus: A Journal of Medieval and Renaissance Studies* 19 (1988):46–57.

42. *Letters*, pp. 128–130.

43. *Letters*, pp. 130–131.

44. *Letters*, pp. 131–133.

V. The Bishop in His Diocese

1. Arnulf, *The Letters of Arnulf of Lisieux*, ed. Frank Barlow, Camden Third Series, vol. 61 (London, 1939), p. 18.

2. H. de Formeville, *Histoire de l'ancien évêché-comté de Lisieux* (Lisieux, 1873), "Pouillés," pp. 28–79, passim.

3. Formeville, *Histoire de Lisieux*, "Pouillés," pp. 28–79.

4. Formeville, *Histoire de Lisieux*, "Pouillés," pp. 24–99.

5. Orderic Vitalis, *The Ecclesiastical History*, trans. Marjorie Chibnall (Oxford, 1975), 3:27–35. Also see Charles H. Haskins, *Norman Institutions* (Cambridge, Mass., 1918), pp. 30–38.

6. Robert L. Benson, *The Bishop-Elect: A Study in Medieval Ecclesiastical Office* (Princeton, 1968), pp. 8–9.

7. *Decretum Magistri Gratiani*, ed. Aemilius Friedberg, in *Corpus Iuris Canonici*, vol. 1 (Graz, 1955), dist. 23, c.2.

8. Constance Brittain Bouchard, *Spirituality and Administration: The Role of the Bishop in Twelfth-Century Auxerre* (Cambridge, Mass., 1979).

9. *Letters*, p. 135.

10. See the letter to Bartholomew, bishop of Exeter, concerning a certain Jordan, who had been a student at Lisieux, in *Letters*, p. 137.

11. *Letters*, p. 29.

12. "Ad audientiam nostram," in *Acta pontificum romanorum*, ed. J. van Pflugk-Harttung (Tübingen, 1881–1888), 2:369. This letter is also catalogued in *Regesta Pontificum Romanorum ad annum 1198*, ed. Philippe Jaffé, 2d ed. (Leipzig, 1888), no. 10982.

13. *Letters*, p. 68.

14. *Letters*, pp. 177–178.

15. *Letters*, p. 178.

16. *Letters*, p. 162.

17. *Letters*, pp. 176–177, and Haskins, *Norman Institutions*, p. 171. Also see my article, "The Decretal *In Litteris* and the Case of Henry the Counterfeiter," *Comitatus: A Journal of Medieval and Renaissance Studies* 19 (1988):46–61.

18. *Letters*, p. 161.

19. "Sermo ab Arnulpho Luxoviensi in concilio Turonensi habitus," in *Sacrorum conciliorum nova et amplissima collectio*, ed. Joannes Dominicus Mansi, vol. 21 (Graz, 1961), col. 1170.

20. PL 145:490.

21. See M. D. Chenu, "Monks, Canons, and Laymen in Search of the Apostolic Life," *Nature, Man, and Society in the Twelfth Century: Essays on New Theological Perspectives in the Latin West*, trans. Jerome Taylor and Lester K. Little (Chicago, 1979), pp. 202–238.

22. R. W. Southern, *Western Society and the Church in the Middle Ages* (Harmondsworth, 1970), p. 244.

23. For a comment on the spiritual seductiveness of Bernard, see Gerhart B. Ladner, "Terms and Ideas of Renewal," in Robert L. Benson and Giles Constable, eds., *Renaissance and Renewal in the Twelfth Century* (Cambridge, Mass., 1982), p. 13.

24. Arnulf, *Invectiva in Girardum Engolismensem Episcopum*, ed. J. Dieterich, MGH, *Libelli de lite* 3:107.

25. *Letters*, p. 181.

26. *Letters*, p. 181.

27. John of Salisbury, *Metalogicon* 4.42, in PL 199:945.

28. See Robert of Torigni, *Chronica*, RS 82, 4:145, for the details of events at Sées and for the failed attempts of Arnulf's uncle to reform the chapter at Lisieux.

29. Louis Du Bois, *Histoire de Lisieux: Ville, diocèse et arrondissement* (Lisieux, 1845; repr., Brussels, 1977), 2:192.

30. François Neveux, "Lisieux au moyen âge," *Art de Basse-Normandie* 89–91 (1984–1985):34.

31. For many of my references here I am indebted to Prof. David S. Spear of Furman University, whose work on cathedral chapters has sometimes paralleled my own. He has been generous in sharing his unpublished materials and documentation. In those cases where his research has merely confirmed my findings, I have listed only the documents I have personally examined.

32. See Haskins, *Norman Institutions*, pp. 321–322; Caen, ADC, H.1809 and H.7774.

33. See Caen, ADC, H.1809 and H.7774; *Calendar of Documents Preserved in France, Illustrative of the History of Great Britain and Ireland*, ed. J. H. Round (London, 1899), no. 456.

34. Ralph V. Turner, "Richard Barre and Michael Belet: Two Angevin Civil Servants," *Medieval Prosopography* 6 (1985):25–48. Also see R. W. Eyton, *Court, Household, and Itinerary of King Henry II* (London, 1878), pp. 129, 153–154, and 172; *Papsturkunden in Frankreich*, vol. 2: *Normandie*, ed. Johannes Ramackers (Göttingen, 1937), nos. 228 and 234; and Caen, Université de Caen, MS 21420, no. 316.

35. See *Letters*, p. 90, and Haskins, *Norman Institutions*, p. 322, where his name is given as Robert de Altaribus. He later appears as a papal judge-delegate in *Antiquus Cartularius Ecclesiae Baiocensis (Livre Noir)*, ed. V. Bourrienne (Rouen, 1902) 1:138.

36. *Letters*, p. 211.

37. Caen, ADC, H.7771 and H.7061; Paris, BN, MS Lat. 11055, fol. 95r; *Letters*, pp. 141, 143, 195–196, and 203; and *Materials for the History of Thomas Becket*, ed. J. C. Robertson, RS 67, 3:525–526.

38. Caen, ADC, H.7061; Paris, BN, MS Lat. 11055, fol. 95r.

39. *Papsturkunden in Frankreich*, no. 211.

40. His activities as a canon are discussed in *Letters*, pp. 203–204. Also see *Cal. Doc. Fr.*, nos. 54–56, 58, 63, 111, 269, 308, 460, 535–536, 603, 1088, and 1253, and *Magni Rotuli Scaccarii Normanniae sub regibus Angliae*, ed. Thomas Stapleton, vol. 1 (London, 1840), pp. 237, 247, and 249.

41. See Achille Luchaire, *Manuel des institutions françaises, période des capétiens directs* (Paris, 1892), pp. 1–63.

42. See Caen, ADC, H.1809, and Evreux, ADE, H.76. The *Gallia Christiana* 11:809 shows Fulk in office as early as 1142. He is also mentioned by Haskins, *Norman Institutions*, p. 322, and in *Letters*, p. 212.

43. See Caen, ADC, H.7774, H.1846, and H.6548; Lisieux, BM, uncat.; and Caen, Université de Caen, MS 21420, no. 316. John's name also appears in the records of the Norman Exchequer for 1180 and 1184, where he was fined for his participation in a duel involving several members of the cathedral chapter. See *Magni Rotuli*, pp. cxxxii and 122. The latest reference appears in *Cartulaires de Saint Ymer-en-Auge et de Bricquebec*, ed. Charles Bréard (Rouen, 1908), no. 16, pp. 23–24.

44. Caen, ADC, H.6548. Also see *Letters*, p. 178, and *Magni Rotuli*, p. cxxxii.

45. See Caen, ADC, H.7061.

46. *Magni Rotuli*, pp. 122 and 261–262.

47. Paris, BN, MS. Lat. 11055, no. 185.

48. Caen, ADC, H.7061, H. 7775, and H.1846; Paris, BN, MS Lat. 11055, no. 185; *Letters*, pp. 203–204. No suggestions have been made as to the probable expansion of "Cust'," found only in Arnulf's letter.

49. Caen, ADC, H.6550.

50. Evreux, ADE, H.711, no. 38.

51. Caen, ADC, H.1846.

52. The earliest record of Sylvester's activities was published by R. N. Sauvage, "Fragments d'un cartulaire de Saint-Pierre-de-Lisieux," *Études Lexoviennes* 3 (1928):3–31. Other sources include Caen, ADC, H.1809, H.1846, and H.7061; a charter of Thomas Becket in *Cal. Doc. Fr.*, nos. 1337–1338; a charter of T.B. in *Regesta Decretalum Saec. XII*, ed. Stanley Chodorow and Charles Duggan (Vatican, 1982), no. 68; an exchequer fine in *Magni Rotuli*, p. cxxxii; and Arnulf's comments in *Letters*, pp. 54–55, 146, 199–201, and 203. A letter to Sylvester appears in *The Letters of John of Salisbury*, vol. 2: *The Later Letters (1163–1180)*, ed. W. J. Millor and C. N. L. Brooke (Oxford, 1979), no. 215.

53. See Caen, ADC, H.1809, H.6548, and H.7771.

54. Eyton, *Itinerary*, p. 252, and *Cal. Doc. Fr.*, no. 1224. Also see David Spear, "Les doyens du chapitre cathedral de Rouen durant la période ducale," *Annales de Normandie* 33 (June 1983):103–104.

55. Caen, ADC, H.1809, and Haskins, *Norman Institutions,* p. 322.
56. Caen, ADC, H.1809.
57. Caen, ADC, H.1809; *Letters,* p. 35; Haskins, *Norman Institutions,* p. 322.
58. Haskins, *Norman Institutions,* p. 322.
59. Haskins, *Norman Institutions,* p. 322.
60. Haskins, *Norman Institutions,* p. 322.
61. Haskins, *Norman Institutions,* p. 322; Caen, ADC, H.7774.
62. Caen, ADC, H.7061.
63. *Cal. Doc. Fr.,* no. 34; *Letters,* pp. 183 and 193. After 1184 he appears as an archdeacon in *Cal. Doc. Fr.,* no. 42.
64. Caen, ADC, H.7061 and H.7771; also see *Letters,* pp. 206–207,and *Magni Rotuli,* pp. 122 and 261–262.
65. Caen, ADC, H.7774; also see *Letters,* p. 144.
66. Evreux, ADE, H.711.
67. Rouen, ADSM, H.26.
68. St. Lô, ADM, H.1956.
69. St. Lô, ADM, H.1956; and *Magni Rotuli,* pp. 122 and 261–262.
70. *Magni Rotuli,* pp. 122 and 261–262.
71. *Magni Rotuli,* pp. 122 and 261–262.
72. Caen, ADC, H.7774.
73. *Magni Rotuli,* p. 122.
74. *Materials* 5:302–314.
75. *Magni Rotuli,* pp. 122 and 261–262.
76. David S. Spear, "Membership in the Norman Cathedral Chapters during the Ducal Period: Some Preliminary Findings," *Medieval Prosopography* 5 (Spring 1984):8.
77. Formeville, *Histoire de Lisieux,* "Pouillés," p. 24.
78. *Letters,* p. 198.
79. *Letters,* p. 199.
80. *Letters,* p. 199. The same conspiracy is described in an earlier letter, pp. 54–55.
81. See *Letters,* p. 201.
82. A list of its holdings in 1189 is given in a confirmation charter issued by Richard I and reprinted in William Dugdale, *Monasticon Anglicanum* (London, 1846), vol. 6, part 2, pp. 1090–1091.
83. The letter appears in *Letters,* pp. 81–82. The abbot was incorrectly identified as William Huband both by the editors of the *Gallia Christiana* and by Charles Bréard in his *L'abbaye de Notre-Dame de Grestain* (Rouen, 1904), p. 44. For the correction of the error, see Barlow's comments in *Letters,* p. 80, note b.
84. *Letters,* pp. 85–86.
85. *Letters,* p. 88.
86. *Letters,* p. 84.
87. *Letters,* p. 83.
88. *Letters,* p. 83.
89. *Letters,* pp. 84–85.
90. *Letters,* p. 89.
91. *Letters,* p. 88.
92. *Letters,* p. 89.
93. *Letters,* p. 90.
94. Bréard, *L'abbaye de Notre-Dame de Grestain,* p. 56.
95. See *Letters,* p. 176, and Robert of Torigni, 4:280.
96. The most complete study of this complex issue appears in Jean-François Lamarignier, *Étude sur les privilèges d'exemption et de juridiction ecclésiastique des abbayes Normandes depuis les origines jusqu'en 1140* (Paris, 1937).
97. See Giles Constable, *Monastic Tithes: From Their Origins to the Twelfth Century* (Cambridge, 1964), particularly pp. 145–166.

98. See Formeville, *Histoire de Lisieux*, pp. 6–7, and Lamarignier, *Privilèges d'exemption*, pp. 42 and 50–63.
99. *Letters*, p. 28.
100. See Lamarignier, *Privilèges d'exemption*, pp. 222–223, and *Recueil des actes de Henri II*, ed. Léopold Delisle, rev. Élie Berger (Paris, 1920), no. 763, 2:415–416. Other pertinent papal documents are catalogued in JL, nos. 15613, 15622, and 15624.
101. G. H. White, "Appendix D: Henry I's Illegitimate Children," in G. E. Cokayne, ed., *The Complete Peerage*, 11 (London, 1949):118–119.
102. A copy of this charter exists at Paris, BN, MS Nov. Acq. 1245, fols. 112 and 252. A critical edition appears in Lamarignier, *Privilèges d'exemption*, pp. 240–246.
103. *Letters*, p. 119.
104. See Barlow's comments on the situation in *Letters*, pp. xxxvi–xxxvii.
105. See Lamarignier, *Privilèges d'exemption*, p. 242.
106. A sixteenth-century copy of this bull is preserved at Rouen, ADSM, Series H, Fonds de Abbaye de Montivilliers, carton I.
107. See Edwin Hall and James Ross Sweeney, "An Unpublished Privilege of Innocent III in Favor of Montivilliers: New Documentation for a Great Norman Nunnery," *Speculum* 49 (October 1974):677.
108. *Letters*, p. 146.
109. Orderic 5:261–262.
110. Marjorie Chibnall, "Le privilège de libre élection dans les chartes de Saint-Evroult," *Annales de Normandie* 28 (December 1978):341–342.
111. *Letters*, pp. 23–25.
112. *Letters*, pp. 25–26.
113. *Letters*, p. 26.
114. *Letters*, pp. 145–146.
115. *Letters*, p. 145.
116. See the Canons of the Council of Rheims, in Mansi 21:844, and JL, no. 10139.
117. *Letters*, p. 146.
118. The clearest of these bulls appears in JL, no. 12553. The hermitage of Rupe was specifically cited in no. 12598.
119. *Letters*, p. 146.
120. See JL, no. 13895.

VI. The Bishop as Builder

1. The findings of these excavations are contained in an unpublished report in the Archives of the Commission des Monuments Historiques, Paris, dossier Calvados 236 (Lisieux, St. Pierre, 6, 1910–1930). Their significance is discussed by William W. Clark, *The Cathedral of Saint-Pierre at Lisieux and the Beginning of Norman Gothic Architecture* (Ann Arbor, 1970), pp. 35–40.
2. Orderic Vitalis, *The Ecclesiastical History*, trans. Marjorie Chibnall, 3 (Oxford, 1975):14–15.
3. Robert of Torigni, *Chronica*, ed. Richard Howlett, RS 82, 4:131.
4. Louis Du Bois, *Histoire de Lisieux: Ville, diocèse et arrondissement* (Lisieux, 1845; repr., Brussels, 1977), p. 107.
5. Georges Duby, *The Age of the Cathedrals: Art and Society, 980–1420*, trans. Eleanor Levieux and Barbara Thompson (Chicago, 1981), p. 111.
6. These are approximate figures, adapted from those given by V. Hardy, *La cathédrale Saint-Pierre de Lisieux* (Paris, 1918), pp. 18, 24, and plan following p. 77.
7. Mérimée, quoted by Georges Duval, "La cathédrale Saint-Pierre de Lisieux," *Art de Basse Normandie*, nos. 89, 90, and 91 (1984–1985):98.
8. This opinion was first expressed by Charles Vasseur, *Études historiques et archéologiques sur la cathédrale de Lisieux: Première partie, Histoire* (Caen, 1881); cited by

Georges Huard, "La cathédrale Saint-Pierre de Lisieux aux XIe et XIIe siècles," *Études Lexoviennes* 2 (1919):10. His dating was modified only slightly by Louis Serbat, *Guide du Congrès archéologique de France: LXXVe session tenue à Caen en 1908 par la Société Française d' Archéologie*, 1 (Caen, 1909), 301; cited by Huard, "La cathédrale," p. 11.

9. This interpretation was pressed by Louis Adolphe Régnier, *Bulletin des Sociétés savants de Caen* (1909–1910), pp. 123–129; cited by Huard, "La cathédrale," p. 11.

10. See Georges Duval, "La cathédrale Saint-Pierre de Lisieux," *Sanctuaires et Pèlerinages* 7 (1961):17–30. Also see Xavier Barral I Altet, "Sculptures gothiques inédites de la Cathédrale de Lisieux," *Bulletin Monumental* 139 (1981):7–16.

11. See Du Bois, *Histoire de Lisieux*, p. 111. More recently, William W. Clark, "The Nave of Saint Pierre at Lisieux: Romanesque Structure in a Gothic Guise," *Gesta* 16 (1977):31, has suggested a new set of dates—1160 to 1190.

12. Arnulf, *The Letters of Arnulf of Lisieux*, ed. Frank Barlow, Camden Third Series, vol. 61 (London, 1939), pp. 3–4.

13. See, for example, Louis Serbat, *Lisieux*, Petites monographies des grands édifices de la France (Paris, 1926), pp. 10–11.

14. See *Letters*, pp. 88, 114, 190, and 209.

15. Huard, "La cathédrale," p. 7.

16. Giles Constable, *Monastic Tithes: From Their Origins to the Twelfth Century* (Cambridge, 1964), pp. 47–56.

17. *Letters*, p. 114.

18. *Letters*, p. 114.

19. *Letters*, p. 88.

20. See John James, *Chartres: The Masons Who Built a Legend* (London, 1982), p. 136.

21. William of Canterbury, *Miracularum gloriosi martyris Thomae, Cantuariensis Archiepiscopi*, ed. James Craigie Robertson, RS 67: *Materials for the History of Thomas Becket*, 1:256–257.

22. See Barlow, in *Letters*, p. xlvi.

23. *Materials* 1:xxx.

24. See Barlow, in *Letters*, p. xlviii, note 6, and Clark, "The Nave of Saint Pierre," p. 30.

25. Clark, *The Cathedral of Saint-Pierre at Lisieux*, pp. 294–296.

26. Clark, *The Cathedral of Saint-Pierre at Lisieux*, p. 83.

27. Georges Duval, "Lisieux: La cathédrale Saint-Pierre," Ph.D. diss., Concours d'architecte des Monuments Historiques, 1956. I am grateful to Dr. William W. Clark for furnishing me with a typescript of this work.

28. Clark, *The Cathedral of Saint Pierre at Lisieux*, p. 110.

29. Clark, *The Cathedral of Saint-Pierre at Lisieux*, pp. 70–71.

30. Clark, *The Cathedral of Saint-Pierre at Lisieux*, p. 115.

31. *Letters*, p. xlvii.

32. *Letters*, p. 190.

33. *Letters*, p. 209.

34. See the account of Robert Clavel, master builder for Autun Cathedral, provided by Jean Gimpel, *The Cathedral Builders*, trans. Carl F. Barnes, Jr. (London, 1961), pp. 60–65.

35. Otto von Simson, *The Gothic Cathedral: Origins of Gothic Architecture and the Medieval Concept of Order* (Princeton, 1956), p. 97.

36. James, *Chartres*, pp. 65–70.

37. Robert Branner, *Gothic Architecture* (New York, 1961), pp. 17–18.

38. *Letters*, p. 134.

39. Bernard, "Apologia ad Guillelmum," PL 182:915.

40. Simson, *The Gothic Cathedral*, pp. 144–145.

41. Sumner McK. Crosby, *The Apostle Bas-Relief at Saint Denis* (New Haven, Conn., 1972), pp. 35–36; Jules Roussel, *La sculpture française: Époque romane*, vol. 1 (Paris, 1927),

plates 8, 41, 29, and 30; Otto Cartellieri, *Abt. Suger von Saint-Denis, 1081–1151* (Berlin, 1898).

42. Duval, "Lisieux: La cathédrale Saint-Pierre," pp. 42–44; Clark, *The Cathedral of Saint-Pierre at Lisieux*, pp. 142–148; and William W. Clark and Robert Mark, "The First Flying Buttresses: A New Reconstruction of the Nave of Notre-Dame de Paris," *Art Bulletin* 66 (March 1984):47–64.

43. See Branner, *Gothic Architecture*, p. 22.

44. A complete reconstruction has been proposed by William W. Clark, "The Central Portal of Saint-Pierre at Lisieux: A Lost Monument of Twelfth-Century Gothic Sculpture," *Gesta* 11 (1972):46–58.

45. G. Huard, "Quelques lettres de Bénédictins normands a Dom Bernard de Montfaucon," *Bulletin de la Société des Antiquaires de Normandie* 28 (1906):373.

46. Elizabeth Parker McLachlan, "The Pembroke College New Testament and a Group of Unusual English Evangelist-Symbols," *Gesta* 14 (1975):6.

47. See Adolf Katzenellenbogen, *The Sculptural Programs of Chartres Cathedral* (Baltimore, 1959), pp. 37–40 and plates 26 and 27.

48. Willibald Sauerländer, *Gothic Sculpture in France, 1140–1270*, trans. Janet Sondheimer (New York, 1972), pp. 27–28. Sauerländer's statements offer a strong argument against Clark's contention that the portal of St. Pierre was not constructed until after 1185. In a personal letter dated June 9, 1987, Clark conceded this point.

49. Casts of these two heads were made for the Trocadero Museum, and pictures of the casts have been published by Roussel, *La sculpture français*, 1, plate 34.

50. Hardy, *La cathédrale Saint-Pierre*, p. 41; Duval, "La cathédrale Saint-Pierre," *Sanctuaires*, p. 23.

51. See, for example, Gervase of Canterbury, *Chronica*, ed. William Stubbs, RS 73, 1:149.

52. Sauerländer, *Gothic Sculpture*, p. 18.

53. Robert Branner, "Keystones and Kings: Iconography and Topography in the Gothic Vaults of the Île-de-France," *Gazette des Beaux Arts*, ser. 6, 57 (January–June 1969):65–82, notes the existence of grotesque corbel heads at Saint-Germain-des-Prés and Noyon, but he concludes that they were exceptions to the general rule which confined figure sculptures to the keystones of Gothic vaults. Sauerländer, *Gothic Sculpture*, plate 257, illustrates a single occurrence of corbel heads, but such heads came from Rheims and were carved late in the thirteenth century. According to Clark's letter of June 9, 1987, another example exists at Le Mans.

54. Clark, *The Cathedral of Saint-Pierre at Lisieux*, p. 173, and "The Central Portal of Saint-Pierre at Lisieux," pp. 49–50.

55. Walter Cahn, "The Tympanum of the Portal of Saint-Anne," *Journal of the Warburg and Courtauld Institutes* 32 (1969):67–71.

56. See Katzenellenbogen, *Chartres Cathedral*, pp. 27–36.

57. Elizabeth A. R. Brown and Michael W. Cothren, "The Twelfth-Century Crusading Window of the Abbey of Saint-Denis," *Journal of the Warburg and Courtauld Institutes* 49 (1986):17.

58. Cahn, "The Tympanum of the Portal of Saint-Anne," pp. 58–59; and, more recently, Kathryn Horste, "'A Child Is Born': The Iconography of the Portail Ste.-Anne at Paris," *Art Bulletin* 69 (June 1987):207–208.

59. William M. Hinkle, "The King and the Pope on the Virgin Portal of Notre-Dame," *Art Bulletin* 48 (1966):2–3.

60. These sculptures may be seen at the Cloisters in New York City. The guidebook dates their carving to about 1160.

61. I am grateful to Professor Amy Vandersall of the Fine Arts Department of the University of Colorado at Boulder for suggesting this method. The king's head has been used as a basis for this discussion because it is well preserved and because it has more counterparts for comparison than do the other heads. The head of the queen and the

head of the workman are fairly rare subjects for sculpture in the twelfth century. The mitred head may be a sixteenth-century reproduction of the original, according to Clark, "The Central Portal of Saint-Pierre at Lisieux," note 31.

62. See Katzenellenbogen, *Chartres Cathedral*, pp. 42–44, and Sauerländer, *Gothic Sculpture*, plates 12 and 13.

63. This head was displayed in *The Renaissance of the Twelfth Century: An Exhibition Organized by Stephen K. Scher* (Providence, R.I., 1969), p. 159. Cahn, "The Tympanum of the Portal of Saint-Anne," p. 55, confirms that the sculpture of this portal was executed in the years immediately following 1163 and used by the thirteenth-century builders without major alterations.

64. These heads were also featured in *The Renaissance of the Twelfth Century* exhibition catalogue, pp. 149–159. Other archivolt heads from the west portals of St.-Denis appear in the Romanesque Room of the Department of Sculptures in the Louvre. See Sauerländer, *Gothic Sculpture*, plate 3.

65. See Katzenellenbogen, *Chartres Cathedral*, pp. 91–95. These heads are also illustrated in Sauerländer, *Gothic Sculpture*, plates 50 and 82–86.

66. *Letters*, p. 101.

67. Ivo of Chartres, *Epistolae*, PL 162:246, and Suger, *Epistolae*, PL 186:1386.

68. Branner, "Keystones and Kings," p. 76.

69. Erwin Panofsky, *Gothic Architecture and Scholasticism* (New York, 1957), p. 26; and Gimpel, *Cathedral Builders*, pp. 53–55.

70. Examples may be seen in John Harvey, *The Mediaeval Architect* (London, 1972), plates 16–28, following p. 160.

71. Gimpel, *Cathedral Builders*, p. 30.

72. Clark, "The Nave of Saint Pierre at Lisieux," pp. 29–38.

VII. The Pivotal Crisis: The Becket Controversy

1. See *Materials for the History of Thomas Becket*, ed. James Craigie Robertson, RS 67, 1:14, 2:377, and 4:29.

2. *Recueil des actes de Henri II*, ed. Léopold Delisle, rev. Élie Berger (Paris, 1920), no. 225.

3. Arnulf, *The Letters of Arnulf of Lisieux*, ed. Frank Barlow, Camden Third Series, vol. 61 (London, 1939), p. xl.

4. Raymonde Foreville, *Thomas Becket dans la tradition historique et hagiographique* (London, 1981), no. 10, pp. 444–448.

5. *Materials* 4:12.

6. *Letters*, p. 13.

7. *Letters*, p. 14.

8. *Letters*, p. xliii.

9. *Letters*, p. 63.

10. *Letters*, p. 63.

11. In *Sacrorum conciliorum nova et amplissima collectio*, ed. J. Mansi (Graz, 1961), 21:1173.

12. Beryl Smalley, *The Becket Conflict and the Schools: A Study of Intellectuals in Politics* (London, 1973), pp. 236–239. Also see John W. Baldwin, *Masters, Princes and Merchants: The Social Views of Peter the Chanter and His Circle* (Princeton, 1970), pp. 175–179.

13. Herbert of Bosham, in *Materials* 3:273–274.

14. Anonymous I, in *Materials* 4:29. The story is confirmed by William of Canterbury, in *Materials* 1:14, and Edward Grim, in *Materials* 2:377.

15. For one such modern reaction, see David Knowles, *The Episcopal Colleagues of Archbishop Thomas Becket* (Cambridge, 1951), pp. 58–59.

16. Frank Barlow, *Thomas Becket* (Berkeley, 1986), p. 96.

17. *Materials* 1:14.

18. *Materials* 4:30 and 2:377.

19. Ralph de Diceto, *Opera Historica*, ed. William Stubbs, RS 68, 1:312. The failure of most of these missions is revealed in a letter from Alexander III to Thomas Becket, in *Materials* 5:85.

20. *Materials* 5:147.

21. *Letters*, pp. 69–70.

22. *Letters*, pp. 72–73.

23. *Letters*, p. 76.

24. Smalley, *The Becket Controversy and the Schools*, p. 167.

25. *Letters*, p. 77.

26. Herbert of Bosham, in *Materials* 3:525–526; *Calendar of Documents Preserved in France*, ed. J. H. Round (London, 1899), nos. 1337 and 1338.

27. Herbert of Bosham, in *Materials* 3:393–394.

28. *Letters*, pp. 95–96.

29. *Materials* 6:72–73.

30. *Letters*, p. 96.

31. *Materials* 6:74.

32. *Letters*, pp. 100–101.

33. *Letters*, p. 101.

34. *Letters*, pp. 104–105.

35. *Letters*, p. 106.

36. A recent citation occurs in an editorial essay, "The Devilish Doctrine of Deniability," *Time*, December 15, 1986.

37. *Letters*, pp. 122–123.

38. *Letters*, p. 123.

39. *Materials* 7:438.

40. R. W. Eyton, *Court, Household, and Itinerary of King Henry II* (London, 1878), pp. 153–155.

41. See *Letters*, pp. 125–127.

42. *Materials* 7:513 and 521.

43. *Letters*, p. 142.

44. Z. N. Brooke, "The Effect of Becket's Murder on Papal Authority in England," *Cambridge Historical Journal* 2 (1928):213–228; Mary Cheney, "The Compromise of Avranches of 1172 and the Spread of Canon Law in England," *English Historical Review* 56(April 1941):177–197; and H. Mayr-Harting, "Henry II and the Papacy, 1170–1189," *Journal of Ecclesiastical History* 16 (1965):39–53.

45. See Herbert of Bosham, in *Materials* 3:524–526.

46. Herbert of Bosham, in *Materials* 3:546, and Geraldus Cambrensis, RS 21, 4:76; also see Mary Cheney, "The Compromise of Avranches," p. 196.

47. Ralph de Diceto, RS 68, 1:410.

48. Charles Duggan, *Twelfth-Century Decretal Collections and Their Importance in English History* (London, 1963).

49. *Materials* 5:105.

50. For an entertaining look at the origins of this image, see Robert K. Merton, *On the Shoulders of Giants: A Shandean Postscript* (New York, 1965), p. 193.

VIII. The Breakdown of a Paradigm

1. Arnulf, *The Letters of Arnulf of Lisieux*, ed. Frank Barlow, Camden Third Series, vol. 61 (London, 1939), p. 183.

2. *Letters*, pp. 180–181.

3. Alexander Murray, *Reason and Society in the Middle Ages* (Oxford, 1978), pp. 355–362.

4. *Letters*, p. 4.

5. *Letters*, pp. 7–9.

6. John F. Benson, "Consciousness of Self and Perceptions of Individuality," in Robert L. Benson and Giles Constable, eds., *Renaissance and Renewal in the Twelfth Century* (Cambridge, Mass., 1982), p. 269.

7. *Letters*, p. 165.

8. *Letters*, p. 165.

9. *Letters*, pp. 166–168.

10. *Letters*, pp. 170–173.

11. See Robert W. Eyton, *Court, Household, and Itinerary of King Henry II* (London, 1878), pp. 185–189, and Benedict of Peterborough, *Gesta Regis Henrici Secundi*, RS 49, 1:77–79.

12. *Letters*, p. 166.

13. *Letters*, p. 185.

14. Kate Norgate, *England under the Angevin Kings*, vol. 2 (London, 1887; repr., New York, 1969) pp. 140–141; A. L. Poole, *From Domesday Book to Magna Carta: 1087–1216*, 2d ed. (Oxford, 1955), p. 334, note 2; W. L. Warren, *Henry II* (Berkeley, 1973), p. 123; Eyton, *Itinerary*, p. 171; and Barlow, in *Letters*, pp. l–lii.

15. *Letters*, p. 127.

16. Vat. Lat. MS 6024. This manuscript has been described by Barlow in *Letters*, pp. lxxiii and lxxxii. He cites *Neues Archiv* 3 (1878):150–151; M. Poupardin, "Dix-huit lettres inédites," *Bibl. de l'École des Chartes* 63 (1902); and Z. N. Brooke, "The Register of Mr. David," in *Essays on History Presented to R. Lane Poole* (Oxford, 1927).

17. Benedict of Peterborough, *Gesta*, RS 49, 1:51, note 4. Many scholars now believe that this manuscript was an early draft of the work of Roger of Hoveden.

18. Benedict of Peterborough, *Gesta*, RS 49, 1:278.

19. Peter of Blois, PL 207:446–447.

20. Caen, ADC, H.669, and Eyton, *Itinerary*, pp. 177–178.

21. *Letters*, p. 155.

22. Benedict of Peterborough, *Gesta*, RS 49, 1:45–47; Roger of Hoveden, *Chronica*, RS 51, 2:52–53.

23. My own prosopographic study of Arnulf's contacts has identified by name some 370 people with whom he was associated during his career: his correspondents, the members of his cathedral chapter, his fellow witnesses to royal and episcopal charters, and all those mentioned by name in his letters or diplomatic sources.

24. Caen, ADC, H.4034; Eyton, *Itinerary*, p. 21; *Regesta Regum Anglo-Normannorum, 1066–1154*, vol. 3., ed. H. A. Cronne and R. H. C. Davis (Oxford, 1968), p. 332.

25. Eyton, *Itinerary*, p. 157. Other examples appear in *Calendar of Documents Preserved in France*, ed. J. H. Round (London, 1899), nos. 110 and 482.

26. See Eyton, *Itinerary*, pp. 171, 174, and 186–187.

27. Jacques Boussard, *Le gouvernement d'Henri II Plantagenêt* (Paris, 1956), pp. 477–479.

28. See Norgate, *England under the Angevin Kings*, p. 141.

29. *Recueil des actes de Henri II*, ed. Léopold Delisle, rev. Élie Berger (Paris, 1920), nos. 78 and 141.

30. G. V. Scammell, *Hugh du Puiset, Bishop of Durham* (Cambridge, 1956), pp. 35–43.

31. Eyton, *Itinerary*, 177–178, and *Cal. Doc. Fr.*, no. 530.

32. Benedict of Peterborough, *Gesta*, RS 49, 1:43, and Peter A. Poggioli, *From Politician to Prelate: The Career of Walter of Coutances, Archbishop of Rouen, 1184–1207* (Ann Arbor, 1984), pp. 20–21.

33. See *Letters*, pp. 164–165.

34. Norgate, *England under the Angevin Kings*, pp. 140–141.

35. I. P. Shaw, "The Ecclesiastical Policy of Henry II on the Continent, 1154–1189," *Church Quarterly Review* 151 (October 1950–March 1951):137–155.

36. *Letters*, pp. 57–58 and 61–62.

37. *Decretum Magistri Gratiani*, ed. A. Friedberg, in *Corpus Iuris Canonici*, vol. 1 (Graz, 1955), C.7, q.1. Also see Edward M. Peters, "The Archbishop and the Hedgehog," in Kenneth Pennington and Robert Somerville, eds., *Law, Church, and Society* (Philadelphia, 1977), pp. 174–178.

38. Benedict of Peterborough, *Gesta*, RS 49, 1:182.

39. Eyton, *Itinerary*, p. 218.

40. *Letters*, p. 174.

41. *Letters*, p. 174.

42. Eyton, *Itinerary*, pp. 217–218.

43. *Cal. Doc. Fr.*, no. 351, and Delisle-Berger, no. 486.

44. *Letters*, p. 186. Also see pp. 183, 189, 191, and 193.

45. Eyton, *Itinerary*, p. 222.

46. *Letters*, p. 191.

47. His career has been described in detail in Poggioli, *From Politician to Prelate*. Also see Sidney R. Packard, "King John and the Norman Church," *Harvard Theological Review* 15 (1922):27–30.

48. Poggioli, *From Politician to Prelate*, pp. 25–30.

49. *Letters*, p. 209.

50. *Letters*, p. 193.

51. *Cal. Doc. Fr.*, no. 34.

52. *Cal. Doc. Fr.*, no. 42.

53. *Letters*, p. 193.

54. *Letters*, pp. 183 and 187.

55. *Letters*, p. 192.

56. *Letters*, pp. 192–193.

57. *Letters*, p. 192.

58. *Letters*, p. 190.

59. See *Letters*, pp. 200–201.

60. *Letters*, p. 195.

61. *Letters*, pp. 209–210.

62. *Letters*, p. 208.

63. *Letters*, p. 209.

64. *Letters*, p. 210.

65. *Gallia Christiana* 11:778; *Recueil des historiens de la France: Obituaires de la Province de Sens*, vol. 1: *Diocèses de Sens et de Paris*, ed. Auguste Molinier (Paris, 1902), p. 580.

66. Eyton, *Itinerary*, p. 240; *Letters*, pp. 214–216.

67. *Letters*, pp. 214–215.

68. *Letters*, pp. 215–216.

69. *Gallia Christiana* 11:779.

70. *Letters*, p. 217.

71. "Tu qui dives eras, et magnus episcopus, ob quid
Sortem mutasti pauperiore statu?
Imo pauperiem mutavi fornore magno,
Mundo dives eram, plus fuit esse Deo."
Gallia Christiana 11:778.

Bibliography

Sources

Manuscripts

Arnulfus Lexoviensis. *Epistolae*. Cambridge, Corpus Christi College, no. 273, fols. 198–227v.

_____ . *Epistolae*. Lisieux, BM, Norm. 5G5.

_____ . *Epistolae*. Oxford, Bodl., Auct. F.I.8, fols. 100–120v.

_____ . *Epistolae*. Oxford, Bodl., Digby, 209.

_____ . *Epistolae*. Oxford, St. John's College, MS 126, fols. 51–67v.

_____ . *Epistolae*. Paris, BN, MS Lat. 491, fols. 99–160.

_____ . *Epistolae*. Paris, BN, MS Lat. 2595, fols. 1–40.

_____ . *Epistolae*. Paris, BN, MS Lat. 2596.

_____ . *Epistolae*. Paris, BN, MS Lat. 13219, fols. 28–87.

_____ . *Epistolae*. Paris, BN, MS Lat. 14148, fols. 44–64.

_____ . *Epistolae*. Paris, BN, MS Lat. 14763.

_____ . *Epistolae*. Paris, BN, MS Lat. 15166, fols. 1–30.

_____ . *Epistolae*. Paris, BN, MS Lat. 17468, fols. 106–131.

_____ . *Sermones*. Paris, BN, MS Lat. 2594.

Alençon, ADO, H.1956.

Avranches, BM, Mont St. Michel Cartulary, fols. 115, 210.

Caen, ADC, Cartulary of Plessis Grimould, 1:30–31; 2:849–850.

Caen, ADC, G. (Évêché de Bayeux).

Caen, ADC, H.668.

Caen, ADC, H.1809.

Caen, ADC, H.1846.

Caen, ADC, H.6510, fol. 18.

Caen, ADC, H.6548.

Caen, ADC, H.6550.

Caen, ADC, H.7061.

Caen, ADC, H.7771.

Caen, ADC, H.7774.

Caen, Université de Caen, MS 21420.

Chartres, ADEL, Cartulary of Tiron, fols. 49d–50.

Chartres, ADEL, G.122, fols. 40–41d.

Chartres, ADEL, G.2984.

Chartres, ADEL, H.73.

Chartres, ADEL, H.711.

Chartres, ADEL, H.1374, fol.49v.

Evreux, ADE, H.711.

Lisieux, BM, uncatalogued.

London, BL, Cotton Vitellius E.xiii, fols. 204–288.

London, BL, Royal 10.B.iv, fols. 42v–57v.

London, BL, Royal 10.C.iv, fols. 137r–155.

London, PRO, E 164/20, Cartulary of Godstow, fol. 58r.

Oxford, Bodl., Dodsworth MS 110, fols. 22 and 43v.

Paris, Archives of the Commission des Monuments Historiques, dossier Calvados 236 (Lisieux, St.-Pierre, 6, 1910–1930).

Paris, BN, MS Lat. 3922 A, fols. 148r–167; 245.
Paris, BN, MS Lat. 5419 A, fol. 103.
Paris, BN, MS Lat. 5458, no. 98.
Paris, BN, MS Lat. 10074, fol. 214.
Paris, BN, MS Lat. 10086.
Paris, BN, MS Lat. 11055, fols. 21d–27d.
Paris, BN, MS Lat. 12678.
Paris, BN, MS Lat. 14193, no. 16.
Paris, BN, MS Lat. 16992, fols. 76–78.
Paris, BN, MS Lat. 17049, fol. 85.
Paris, BN, MS Lat. 18369, fol. 27.
Paris, BN, MS Nouv. Acq. Lat. 1428, fol. 16.
Paris, BN, MS Nouv. Acq. Lat. 2097, fols. 9–12.
Rouen, ADSM, G.3666.
Rouen, ADSM, G.4047.
Rouen, ADSM, H, Fonds de Abbaye de Montivilliers, carton I.
Rouen, ADSM, H.1
Rouen, ADSM, H.26.
Rouen, ADSM, Y.44.
Rouen, BM, MS 1207 (Y.51), fol. 4.
Rouen, BM, MS 2192 (Y.17), fol. 101.
Rouen, BM, MS S.3, fol. 168.

Printed Sources

Acta pontificum romanorum. Edited by Julius van Pflugk-Harttung. 2 vols. Tübingen: F. Fues, 1881–1888.
Alexander III. *Opera Omnia.* Edited by J. P. Migne. PL 200. Paris: Garnier Fratres, 1855.
Ancient Charters Royal and Private prior to A.D. 1200. Edited by John Horace Round. PR 10. London: Wyman and Sons, 1888; Kraus Reprint, 1966.
The Anglo-Saxon Chronicle. Edited by Dorothy Whitelock, David C. Douglas, and Susie I. Tucker. London: Eyre and Spottiswoode, 1961.
Antiquus cartularius ecclesiae Baiocensis (Livre Noir), ed. V. Bourrienne. Rouen: A. Lestringant, 1902.
Arnulf. *Invectiva in Girardum Engolismensem Episcopum,* MGH, *Libelli de lite.* Vol. 3. Edited by J. Dieterich. Munich, 1897.
———. *Arnulfi Archidiaconi in Girardum Engolismensem Invectiva.* MGH SS. Vol. 12. Hannover: Hahn, 1856; Kraus Reprint, 1963.
———. "Arnulfi Lexoviensis episcopi Epistolae." Edited by John Allen Giles. In *Patres Ecclesiae Anglicanae.* Oxford: J. H. Parker, 1844.
———. *The Letters of Arnulf of Lisieux.* Edited by Frank Barlow. Camden Society, Third Series, vol. 61. London: Royal Historical Society, 1939.
———. *Opera Omnia.* Edited by J. P. Migne. PL 201. Paris: Garnier Fratres, 1903.
Benedict of Peterborough. *Gesta Regis Henrici Secundi.* Vol. 1. Edited by William Stubbs. RS 49. London: HMSO, 1867; Kraus Reprint, 1965.
Bernard of Clairvaux. *Epistolae.* Edited by J. P. Migne. PL 182. Paris: Garnier Fratres, 1893.
Boso, Cardinal. *Life of Alexander III.* Edited by Peter Munz. Translated by G. M. Ellis. London: Basil Blackwell, 1973.
Calendar of Documents Preserved in France, Illustrative of the History of Great Britain and Ireland. Vol. 1, *A.D. 918-1206.* Edited by John Horace Round. London: Eyre and Spottiswoode, 1899.
Calendar of Patent Rolls, Henry III, 1232–1247. Vol. 3. London: HMSO, 1893.
Cartulaires de Saint-Ymer-en-Auge et de Bricquebec. Edited by Charles Bréard. Rouen: A. Lestringant, 1908.

Chronica Monasterii Casinensis. Edited by Wilhelm Wattenbach. MGH SS. Vol. 7. Hannover: Hahn, 1846; Kraus Reprint, 1963.

Constitutiones et acta publica imperatorum et regum. Vol. 1. Edited by Ludwig Weiland. MGH, *Legum,* section 4. Hannover, 1893; Kraus Reprint, 1963.

Les décrétales et les collections de décrétales. Edited by Gérard Fransen. Typologie des sources du Moyen Âge occidental. Turnhout: Brepols, 1972.

Decretales ineditae saeculi XII. Edited by Stanley Chodorow and Charles Duggan. Monumenta Iuris Canonici, Series B: Corpus Collectionum, vol. 4. Vatican: Biblioteca apostolica vaticana, 1982.

Decretum Magistri Gratiani. Edited by Aemilius Friedberg. Vol. 1 of *Corpus Iuris Canonici.* Graz: Akademische Druck-U. Verlagsanstalt, 1955.

Documents de L'Histoire de la Normandie. Edited by Michel De Boüard. Toulouse, 1972.

Domesday Book. London, 1783.

Domesday Book: A Survey of the Counties of England. 35 vols. Edited by John Morris. Chichester: Phillimore, 1975–1985.

Draco Normannicus [Stephen of Rouen]. *Chronica.* Edited by Richard Howlett. RS 82: *Chronicles of the Reigns of Stephen, Henry II, and Richard I.* Vol. 2. London: Eyre and Spottiswoode, 1889.

Dudo of Saint-Quentin. *De moribus et actis primorum Normanniae ducum.* Edited by Jules Lair. Memoirs de la Société des Antiquaries de Normandie, 3d ser., 3.2, Caen, 1865.

Eadmer. *Historia Novorum in Anglia.* Edited by Martin Rule. RS 81. London: Longman, 1884.

English Historical Documents. Vol. 2, *1042–1189.* Edited by David C. Douglas and George W. Greenaway. New York: Oxford University Press, 1953; 2d ed., London, 1981.

Epistolae pontificum romanorum ineditae. Edited by Samuel Löwenfeld. Leipzig: Veit et comp., 1885.

Ernald. *Vita Prima.* Edited by J. P. Migne. PL 185. Paris: Garnier Fratres, 1893.

Gallia Christiana. Vols. 9 and 10. Rouen. B.M. MS mm 30.

Geraldus Cambrensis. *Opera.* Edited by J. S. Brewer. RS 21, vol. 4. London: Longman, 1873.

Gerhoh of Reichersberg. *De investigatione Antichristi Liber I.* Edited by Ernest Sackur. MGH, *Libelli de lite,* vol. 3. Hannover: Hahn, 1897.

Gervase of Canterbury. *Chronica.* Edited by William Stubbs. RS 73. Vol. 1. London: HMSO, 1879; Kraus Reprint, 1965.

Gesta Abbatum Monasterii Sancti Albani. Edited by Henry Thomas Riley. Vol. 1, *A.D. 793–1290.* RS 28. Vol. 4. London: Longmans, Green, Reader, and Dyer, 1867.

Gesta Stephani. Translated by K. R. Potter. Oxford: Clarendon Press, 1976.

Gilbert Foliot. *Epistolae.* Edited by J. P. Migne. PL 190. Paris: Garnier Fratres, 1893.

_____ . *The Letters and Charters of Gilbert Foliot.* Edited by Dom Adrian Morey and C. N. L. Brooke. Cambridge: Cambridge University Press, 1967.

The Great Roll of the Pipe for the Reign of King Henry the Second. PR 1–2, 4–13, 15–16, 18–19, 21–22, 25–34, 36–38. Introduced by J. Horace Round. London: Wyman and Sons, 1882–1925; Kraus Reprint, 1965–1966.

Guillaume de Poitiers. *Gesta Willelmi Conquestoris.* Edited by J. P. Migne. PL 149. Paris: Garnier Fratres, 1882.

Handbook of British Chronology. Edited by F. Maurice Powicke and E. B. Fryde. 2d ed. London: Royal Historical Society, 1961.

Historia Pontificalis. MGH SS, 20: 534–535. Hannover: Hahn, 1868; Kraus Reprint, 1963.

Ioannis Saresberiensis. *Historia pontificalis quae supersunt.* Edited by Reginald L. Poole. Oxford: Clarendon Press, 1927.

Ivo of Chartres. *Opera Omnia.* Edited by J. P. Migne. PL 162. Paris: Garnier Fratres, 1889.

John of Salisbury. *Memoirs of the Papal Court.* Translated by Marjorie Chibnall. London: Thomas Nelson, 1956.

_____ . *Policraticus*. In Oxford, Bodl., Auct. F.I.8.

_____ . *Opera Omnia*. Edited by J. P. Migne. PL 199. Paris: Garnier Fratres, 1900.

The Letters of John of Salisbury. Vol. 1, *The Early Letters (1153–1161)*. Edited by W. J. Millor and H. E. Butler; revised by C. N. L. Brooke. London: Thomas Nelson, 1955.

The Letters of John of Salisbury. Vol. 2, *The Later Letters (1163–1180)*. Edited by W. J. Millor and C. N. L. Brooke. Oxford: Clarendon Press, 1979.

Liber Feodorum [The Book of Fees or Testa de Neville]. 2 vols. London: HMSO, 1920.

Magni Rotuli Scaccarii Normanniae sub regibus Angliae. Edited by Thomas Stapleton. 2 vols. London: Society Antiq. London, 1840.

Magnum Rotulum Scaccarii [31 Henry I]. Edited by Joseph Hunter. London: Eyre and Spottiswoode, 1844.

Materials for the History of Thomas Becket. 7 vols. RS 67. Edited by James Craigie Robertson. London: HMSO, 1875–1885.

The "Metalogicon" of John of Salisbury: A Twelfth-Century Defense of the Verbal and Logical Arts of the Trivium. Translated by Daniel D. McGarry. Berkeley: University of California Press, 1962.

Mignault, Claude (Minos). *Epistolae Arnulphi Episcopi Lexoviensis nunquam antehac in lucem editae, ex bibliotheca Odonis Turnebi Hadriani F*. Paris, 1585.

Miscellaneous Records of the Norman Exchequer, 1199–1204. Edited by Sidney Raymond Packard. Smith College Studies in History, vol. 12. Northampton, Mass., 1927.

Odo of Deuil. *De Ludovici VII Francorum Regis*. Edited by J. P. Migne. PL 185, part 2 (1205–1246). Paris: Migne, 1854.

_____ . *De profectione Ludovici VII in orientem*. Translated by Virginia Gingerick Berry. New York: W. W. Norton, 1948.

Orderic Vitalis. *The Ecclesiastical History*. Edited and translated by Marjorie Chibnall. 6 vols. Oxford: Clarendon Press, 1975.

Otto of Freising. *Gesta Friderici I*. Edited by Roger Wilmans. MGH SS. Vol. 20. Hannover: Hahn, 1868; Kraus Reprint, 1963.

Papsturkunden in England. Edited by Walther Holtzmann. Vol. 25 of *Abhandlungen der Gesellschaft der Wissenschaften zu Göttingen*. Berlin, 1930.

Papsturkunden in Frankreich. Vol. 2, *Normandie*. Edited by Johannes Ramackers. Vol. 21 of *Abhandlungen der Gesellschaft der Wissenschaften zu Göttingen*. Third series. Göttingen: Vandenhoeck und Ruprecht, 1937.

Peter of Blois. *Opera Omnia*. Edited by J. P. Migne. PL 207. Paris: Migne, 1855.

Peter of Celle. *Opera Omnia*. Edited by J. P. Migne. PL 202. Paris: Migne, 1855.

Peter Damian. *Opera Omnia*. Edited by J. P. Migne. PL 145. Paris, Migne, 1867.

Peter the Venerable. *The Letters of Peter the Venerable*. 2 vols. Edited by Giles Constable. Cambridge, Mass.: Harvard University Press, 1967.

_____ . *Opera Omnia*. Edited by J. P. Migne. PL 189. Paris: Garnier Fratres, 1890.

Ralph de Diceto. *Opera Historica*. Vol. 1. Edited by William Stubbs. RS 68. London: Longmans, 1876.

Recueil des actes de Henri II. Edited by Léopold Delisle. Revised by Élie Berger. Vols. 1 and 2. Paris: Imprimerie Nationale, 1920.

Recueil des historiens des croisades: Historiens occidentaux. Vol.1, part 2. Paris: Imprimerie Royale, 1844; reprinted, Farnesborough: Gregg, 1969.

Recueil des historiens de la France: Obituaires de la Province de Sens. Vol. 1, *Diocèses de Sens et de Paris*. Edited by Auguste Molinier. Paris: Imprimerie Nationale, 1902.

Recueil des historiens de la France: Pouillés. Vol. 2, *Pouillés de la Province de Rouen*. Edited by Auguste Longnon. Paris: Imprimerie Nationale, 1903.

Recueil des historiens des Gaules et de la France. Vols. 15 and 23. Edited by Martin Bouquet et al. Paris: Aux dépens des libraires, 1738–1904.

The Red Book of the Exchequer. 3 vols. Edited by Hubert Hall. London: HMSO, 1896.

Regesta Decretalium Saec. XII. Edited by Stanley Chodorow and Charles Duggan,

Monumenta Iuris Canonici, Series B: Corpus Collectionum. Vatican: Biblioteca Apostolica Vaticana, 1982.

Regesta pontificum Romanorum ad annum 1198. Edited by Philippe Jaffé. 2d ed., edited by Samuel Löwenfeld. 2 vols. Leipzig: Viet et Comp., 1885–1888.

Regesta pontificum Romanorum, inde ab anno post Christum natum 1198 ad annum 1304. Edited by August Potthast. 2 vols. Berlin, 1874–1875; repr., Graz: Akademische Druck-U. Verlagsanstalt, 1957.

Regesta Regum Anglo-Normannorum, 1066–1154. Vol. 1, *Regesta Willelmi Conquestoris et Willelmi Rufi, 1066–1100.* Edited by H. W. C. Davis. Oxford: Clarendon Press, 1913.

Regesta Regum Anglo-Normannorum, 1066–1154. Vol. 2, *Regesta Henrici Primi.* Edited by Charles Johnson and Henry Alfred Cronne. Oxford: Clarendon Press, 1956.

Regesta Regum Anglo-Normannorum, 1066–1154. Vol. 3, *Regesta Regis Stephani ac Mathildis Imperatricis ac Gaufridi et Henrici Ducum Normannorum, 1135–1154.* Edited by Henry Alfred Cronne and Ralph H. C. Davis. Oxford: Clarendon Press, 1968.

The Register of Eudes of Rouen. Translated by Sydney M. Brown. Edited by Jeremiah F. O'Sullivan. New York: Columbia University Press, 1964.

Repertorium der Kanonistik: Prodomus corporis glossarum I, 1140–1234. Edited by Stephan Kuttner. Studi e Testi, vol. 71. Vatican: Biblioteca Apostolica Vaticana, 1937.

Richard Fitz Nigel. *Dialogus de Scaccario [The Course of the Exchequer].* Translated by Charles Johnson. Edited by F. E. L. Carter and D. E. Greenway. Oxford: Clarendon Press, 1983.

Richard of Hexham. *De gestis Regis Stephani.* Edited by Richard Howlett. RS 82, vol. 3. London: Longman, 1886.

Robert of Torigni. *Chronica.* Edited by Richard Howlett. RS 82: *Chronicles of the Reigns of Stephen, Henry II, and Richard I.* Vol. 4. London: Eyre and Spottiswoode, 1889.

Roger of Hovedon. *Chronica.* 4 vols. Edited by William Stubbs. RS 51. London: HMSO, 1868; Kraus Reprint, 1964.

Rymer, Thomas. *Foedera, conventiones, litterae.* Edited by A. Clarke. 3 vols. in 6. London: Commissioners on the Public Records, 1816–30.

Sacrorum conciliorum nova et amplissima collectio. Vols. 21–22. Edited by Joannes Dominicus Mansi. Graz: Akademische Druck-U. Verlagsanstalt, 1961.

Select Charters and Other Illustrations of English Constitutional History: From the Earliest Times to the Reign of Edward the First. Edited by William Stubbs. 9th ed. Oxford: Clarendon Press, 1960.

Self and Society in Medieval France: The Memoirs of Abbot Guibert of Nogent, 1064–1125. Edited by John F. Benton. New York: Harper Torchbooks, 1970.

Sources of English Constitutional History: A Selection of Documents from A.D. 600 to the Present. Edited and translated by Carl Stephenson and Frederick George Marcham. New York: Harper and Row, 1937.

Studies in the Collections of Twelfth-Century Decretals: From the Papers of the Late Walther Holtzmann. Edited by C. R. Cheney and Mary G. Cheney. Monumenta Iuris Canonici, Series B: Corpus Collectionum, 3. Vatican: Biblioteca Apostolica Vaticana, 1979.

Suger. *Abbot Suger on the Abbey Church of St.-Denis and Its Art Treasures.* Edited by Erwin Panofsky. 2d ed., edited by Gerda Panofsky-Soergel. Princeton, N.J.: Princeton University Press, 1979.

_____. *Vita Ludovici.* Edited by J. P. Migne. PL 186. Paris: Garnier Fratres, 1893.

Summa Magistri Rolandi [Pope Alexander III]. Edited by Friedrich Thaner. Innsbruck: Scientia Verlag Aalen, 1962.

Thomas of Canterbury. *Opera Omnia.* Edited by J. P. Migne. PL 190. Paris: Garnier Fratres, 1893.

Ungedruckte Anglo-Normanische Geschichtsquellen. Edited by Felix Liebermann. Strassburg: Karl J. Trübner, 1879.

VCH. *A History of the County of Berkshire.* Vol. 3. Edited by P. H. Ditchfield and William Page. London: St. Catherine Press, 1923; repr., Dawsons of Pall Mall, 1972.

_____. *A History of the County of Buckingham.* Vols. 3–4. Edited by William Page. London: St. Catherine Press, 1925; repr., Dawsons of Pall Mall, 1969.

_____. *A History of the County of Dorset.* Vol. 3. Edited by R. B. Pugh. Oxford: University Press, 1968.

_____. *A History of the County of Gloucester.* Vol. 11. Edited by N. M. Herbert. London: Oxford University Press, 1976.

_____. *A History of the County of Hertford.* Vol. 2. Edited by William Page. London: Archibald Constable, 1908; repr., Dawsons of Pall Mall, 1971.

_____. *A History of the County of Kent.* Vol. 3. Edited by William Page. London: St. Catherine Press, 1932.

_____. *A History of the County of Northampton.* Vol. 4. Edited by L. F. Salzman. London: Oxford University Press, 1937.

_____. *A History of the County of Oxford.* Vol. 11: *Wootton Hundred.* Edited by Alan Crossley. Oxford: University Press, 1983.

_____. *A History of the County of Surrey.* Vol. 4. Edited by H. E. Malden. London: Constable and Co., 1912; repr., Dawsons of Pall Mall, 1967.

William of Canterbury. *Miracularum gloriosi martyris Thomae, Cantuariensis Archiepiscopi.* Edited by James Craigie Robertson. RS 67: *Materials for the History of Thomas Becket.* Vol. 1. London: HMSO, 1875; Kraus Reprint, 1965.

William of Jumièges. *Gesta Normannorum ducum.* Edited by Jean Marx. Rouen, 1911.

William of Malmesbury. *Historiae Novellae.* 2 vols. Edited by William Stubbs. RS 90. London, HMSO, 1887–1889; Kraus Reprint, 1964.

_____. *Opera Omnia.* Edited by J. P. Migne. PL 179. Paris: Garnier Fratres, 1893.

William of Poitiers. *Gesta Guillelmi.* Edited by Raymonde Foreville. Paris, 1952.

William of Tyre. *Historia rerum in partibus Transmarinis gestarum.* Edited by J. P. Migne. PL 201. Paris: Garnier Fratres, 1903.

_____. *Recueil des historiens des croisades: Historiens occidentaux.* Vol. 1, part 2. Paris, 1844; repr., Farnborough, 1969.

Secondary Works

Books

Allen, Kate, ed. *Domesday: 900 Years of England's Norman Heritage.* London: Millbank Publications, 1986.

Appleby, John T. *The Troubled Reign of King Stephen.* New York: Barnes and Noble, 1970.

Aubert, Marcel. *Cathédrales et trésors gothiques de France.* Paris: B. Arthaud, 1971.

Baker, Timothy. *The Normans.* London: Cassell, 1966.

Baldwin, Charles Sears. *Medieval Rhetoric and Poetic (to 1400): Interpreted from Representative Works.* Gloucester, Mass.: Peter Smith, 1959.

Baldwin, John W. *Masters, Princes and Merchants: The Social Views of Peter the Chanter and His Circle.* 2 vols. Princeton, N.J.: Princeton University Press, 1970.

Baldwin, Marshall W. *Alexander III and the Twelfth Century.* Vol. 3 of *The Popes through History.* Edited by Raymond H. Schmandt. Glen Rock, N.J.: Newman Press, 1968.

_____. *The First Hundred Years.* Vol. 1 of *A History of the Crusades,* ed. Kenneth M. Selton. Madison: University of Wisconsin Press, 1969.

_____. *The Medieval Church.* Ithaca, N.Y.: Cornell University Press, 1953.

Barlow, Frank. *The Feudal Kingdom of England, 1042–1216.* 2d ed. New York: David McKay, 1961.

_____. *Thomas Becket.* Berkeley: University of California Press, 1986.

Barraclough, Geoffrey. *The Medieval Papacy.* New York: W. W. Norton, 1979.

Barrow, G. W. S. *Feudal Britain: The Completion of the Medieval Kingdoms, 1066–1314.* London: E. Arnold, 1956.

Bates, David. *Normandy before 1066*. London: Longman, 1982.

Benson, Robert L. *The Bishop-Elect: A Study in Medieval Ecclesiastical Office*. Princeton, N.J.: Princeton University Press, 1968.

_____, and Constable, Giles, eds. *Renaissance and Renewal in the Twelfth Century*. Cambridge, Mass.: Harvard University Press, 1982.

Bernstein, Richard J. *Beyond Objectivism and Relativism: Science, Hermeneutics, and Praxis*. Philadelphia: University of Pennsylvania Press, 1985.

_____. *The Restructuring of Social and Political Theory*. Philadelphia: University of Pennsylvania Press, 1976.

Besse, Jean Martial Léon. *Abbeyes et prieurés de l'ancienne France*. Vol. 7. Archives de la France monastique. Paris: C. Poussielgue, 1914.

Böhmer, Heinrich. *Kirche und Staat in England und in der Normandie im XI. und XII. Jahrhundert: Eine historische Studie*. Leipzig: Dieterich, 1899; repr., 1968.

Bony, Jean. *French Gothic Architecture of the 12th and 13th Centuries*. Berkeley: University of California Press, 1983.

Boüard, Michel de. *Histoire de la Normandie*. Toulouse: Edouard Privat, 1970.

Bouchard, Constance Brittain. *Spirituality and Administration: The Role of the Bishop in Twelfth-Century Auxerre*. Speculum Anniversary Monographs, 5. Cambridge, Mass.: Medieval Academy of America, 1979.

_____. *Sword, Miter, and Cloister: Nobility and the Church in Burgundy, 980–1198*. Ithaca, N.Y.: Cornell University Press, 1987.

Boussard, Jacques. *Le comté d'Anjou sous Henri Plantagenêt et ses fils, 1151–1204*. Paris: H. Champion, 1938.

_____. *Le gouvernement d'Henri II Plantagenêt*. Paris: Librairie d'Argences, 1956.

Branner, Robert. *Gothic Architecture*. New York: George Braziller, 1965.

Bréard, Charles. *L'abbaye de Notre-Dame de Grestain: De l'ordre de Saint-Benoit à l'ancien diocèse de Lisieux*. Rouen: A. Lestringant, 1904.

Brett, Martin. *The English Church under Henry I*. Oxford: Oxford University Press, 1975.

Brooke, Christopher. *From Alfred to Henry III, 871–1272*. Vol. 2 of *A History of England*. Edited by Christopher Brooke and Denis Mack Smith. Edinburgh: Thomas Nelson and Sons, 1961.

Brooke, C. N. L., et al., eds. *Church and Government in the Middle Ages: Essays Presented to C. R. Cheney*. London: Cambridge University Press, 1976.

Brown, R. Allen. *The Normans and the Norman Conquest*. New York: Thomas Y. Crowell, 1968.

_____. *Origins of English Feudalism*. London: George Allen & Unwin, 1973.

_____, ed. *Proceedings of the Battle Conference on Anglo-Norman Studies*. 6 vols. Woodbridge, Suffolk: The Boydell Press, 1979–1984.

Burke, John Bernard. *The Roll of Battle Abbey, Annotated*. Originally published, 1848. Baltimore: Genealogical Publishing Company, 1985.

Cartellieri, Otto. *Abt. Suger von Saint-Denis, 1081–1151*. Berlin: Ebering, 1898.

Catalogue des Archives de la Société Historique de Lisieux: Manuscrits et Imprimés. 2 vols. Lisieux, 1885–1889.

Chalendard, Marie. *Saint Thomas de Cantorbery: Thomas Becket, 1118–1170*. Paris: Editions du Cèdre, n.d.

Cheney, Mary G. *Roger, Bishop of Worcester: 1164–1179*. Oxford: Clarendon Press, 1980.

Chenu, Marie Dominique. *Nature, Man, and Society in the Twelfth Century: Essays on New Theological Perspectives in the Latin West*. Translated by Jerome Taylor and Lester K. Little. Chicago: University of Chicago Press, 1979.

Chevalier, Ulysse. *Répertoire des sources historiques du moyen âge: bio-bibliographie*. Vol. 1. Paris: Alphonse Picard et fils, 1905.

Chodorow, Stanley. *Christian Political Theory and Church Politics in the Mid–Twelfth Century: The Ecclesiology of the Gratian's Decretum*. Berkeley: University of California Press, 1972.

Clanchy, Michael T. *England and Its Rulers, 1066–1272.* Totowa, N.J.: Barnes and Noble, 1983.

Clark, Albert Curtis. *The Cursus in Mediaeval and Vulgar Latin.* Oxford: Clarendon Press, 1910.

Clark, William Watson. *The Cathedral of Saint-Pierre at Lisieux and the Beginning of Norman Gothic Architecture.* Ann Arbor: University Microfilms, 1970.

Cokayne, George E., ed. *The Complete Peerage of England, Scotland, Ireland, Great Britain, and the United Kingdom.* New York: St. Martin's Press, n.d.

Constable, Giles. *Letters and Letter Collections.* Turnhout: Éditions Brepols, 1976.

_____. *Monastic Tithes: From Their Origins to the Twelfth Century.* Cambridge Studies in Medieval Life and Thought, new series, vol. 10. Cambridge: Cambridge University Press, 1964.

Coville, Alfred. *Les états de Normandie: Leurs origines et leur développement au XIVe siècle.* Paris: Imprimerie Nationale, 1894.

Crispin, M. Jackson, and Macary, Leonce, eds. *The Falaise Roll: Recording Prominent Companions of William Duke of Normandy at the Conquest of England.* London, 1938; Baltimore: Genealogical Publishing Company, 1985.

Crosby, Sumner McK. *The Apostle Bas-Relief at Saint-Denis.* New Haven, Conn.: Yale University Press, 1972.

Crouch, David. *The Beaumont Twins: The Roots and Branches of Power in the Twelfth Century.* Cambridge: Cambridge University Press, 1986.

Darby, Henry C. *Domesday England.* Cambridge: Cambridge University Press, 1977.

_____, and Versey, G. R. *Domesday Gazetteer.* Cambridge: Cambridge University Press, 1975.

Davis, R. H. C. *King Stephen, 1135–1154.* Berkeley: University of California Press, 1967.

Denifle, Heinrich. *La désolation des églises, monastères et hôpitaux en France pendant la guerre de cent ans.* 2 vols. Paris: A. Picard, 1897–99.

Deshays, Noël. *Mémoires pour servir à l'histoire des évêques de Lisieux.* Lisieux: 1754; repr. in H. de Formeville, *Histoire de l'ancien évêché-comté de Lisieux,* vol. 2, Lisieux: Emile Piel, 1873.

Déterville, Philippe. *Lisieux.* Condé-sur-Noireau: Éditions Charles Corlet, 1981.

Douglas, David C. *The Norman Achievement: 1050–1100.* London: Eyre and Spottiswoode, 1969.

_____. *The Norman Fate: 1100–1154.* Berkeley: University of California Press, 1976.

_____. *William the Conqueror: The Norman Impact upon England.* Berkeley: University of California Press, 1964.

Du Bois, Louis Marie. *Histoire de Lisieux: Ville, diocèse et arrondissement.* Lisieux: Durand, 1845; repr., Bruxelles: Éditions Culture et Civilisation, 1977.

Duby, Georges. *The Age of the Cathedrals: Art and Society, 980–1420.* Translated by Eleanor Levieux and Barbara Thompson. Chicago: University of Chicago Press, 1981.

_____. *The Knight, the Lady, and the Priest: The Making of Modern Marriage in Medieval France.* Translated by Barbara Bray. New York: Pantheon Books, 1983.

_____. *Saint Bernard: L'Art Cistercien.* Paris: Flammarion, 1976.

_____. *The Three Orders: Feudal Society Imagined.* Translated by Arthur Goldhammer. Chicago: University of Chicago Press, 1980.

Duchesne, Louis. *Fastes épiscopaux de l'ancienne Gaule.* Vol. 2: *L'Aquitaine et les Lyonnaises.* 2d ed. rev. Paris: Fontemoing, 1910.

Dugdale, William. *Monasticon Anglicanum: A History of the Abbies and Other Monasteries, Hospitals, Frieries, and Cathedral and Collegiate Churches . . .* 6 vols. London: James Bohn, 1846.

Duggan, Anne. *Thomas Becket: A Textual History of His Letters.* Oxford: Clarendon Press, 1980.

Duggan, Charles. *Twelfth-Century Decretal Collections and Their Importance in English*

History. University of London Historical Studies 12. London: Athlone Press, 1963.

Duval, Georges. "Lisieux: La chathédrale Saint-Pierre." Ph.D. diss., Concours d'Architecte des Monuments Historiques, 1956.

Engelhardt, Charles. *Essay sur Lisieux pendant le Haut Moyen Âge*. Caen: Delesques, 1914.

Eyton, Robert William. *Court, Household, and Itinerary of King Henry II*. London: Taylor and Co., 1878.

Farolie, M. *Notes pour servir a l'histoire de l'ancienne cathédrale de Lisieux*. Lisieux: J. J. Pigeon, 1840.

Fawtier, Robert. *The Capetian Kings of France: Monarchy and Nation, 987–1328*. Translated by Lionel Butler and R. J. Adam. London: Macmillan, 1964.

Fisquet, Honorè. *La France pontificale [Gallia Christiana]*. 21 vols. Paris: Repos, 1864–1873.

Fliche, Augustin, and Martin, Victor, eds. *Histoire de l'église: Des puis les origines jusqu'à nos jours*. 26 vols. Paris: Bloud and Gay, 1934–.

Focillon, Henri. *The Art of the West in the Middle Ages*. Translated by Donald King. Vol. 2: *Gothic Art*. Greenwich, Conn.: Phaidon Publishers, 1963.

Foreville, Raymonde. *Latran I, II, III, et Latran IV*. Paris: Éditions de l'Orante, 1965.

———. *L'Église et la royauté en Angleterre sous Henri II Plantagenêt*. Translated by Thomas Jones. Paris: Bloud and Gay, 1943.

———. *Thomas Becket dans la tradition historique et hagiographique*. London: Variorum Reprints, 1981.

———, and de Pina, Jean Rousset. *Du premier Concile du Latran à l'avènement d'Innocent III*. Book 2: *La papauté et l'ordre temporel, de 1154 à 1198*. Vol. 9 of *Histoire de l'église*, edited by Augustin Fliche and Victor Martin. Paris: Bloud and Gay, 1953.

Formeville, H. de. *Histoire de l'ancien évêché-comté de Lisieux*. 2 vols. Lisieux: Emile Piel, 1873.

Gall, Ernst. *Die gotische Baukunst in Frankreich und Deutschland*. Part I: *Die Vorstufen in Nordfrankreich von der Mitte des elften bis gegen Ende des zwölften Jahrhunderts*. Leipzig: Klinkhardt and Biermann, 1925.

Gams, Pius Bonifacius. *Series Episcoporum Ecclesiae Catholicae*. 2d ed. Leipzig: Verlag Karl W. Hiersemann, 1931.

Génestal, Robert. *Le privilegium fori en France: Du décret de Gratien a la fin du XIVe siècle*. 2 vols. Paris: E. Leroux, 1924.

Gerard, évêque d'Angoulême, légat du saint siège. Bull. de la Soc. Archéol. et Hist. de la Charente, 1864.

Gillingham, John. *The Angevin Empire*. New York: Holmes and Meier, 1984.

———. *Richard the Lionheart*. New York: Times Books, 1978.

———, and Holt, H. C., eds. *War and Government in the Middle Ages: Essays in Honour of J. O. Prestwick*. Cambridge: Boydell Press, 1984.

Gimpel, Jean. *The Cathedral Builders*. Translated by Carl F. Barnes, Jr. London: Evergreen Books, 1961.

Gleason, Sarell Everett. *An Ecclesiastical Barony of the Middle Ages: The Bishopric of Bayeux, 1066–1204*. Cambridge, Mass.: Harvard University Press, 1936.

Goff, Jacques le. *Les intellectuels au moyen âge*. Le Temps que court, vol. 3. Paris: Éditions du Seuil, 1955.

Golb, Norman. *Les juifs de Rouen au moyen âge: Portrait d'une culture oubliée*. Publications de l'Université de Rouen, no. 66. Rouen: The University, 1985.

Haller, Johannes. *Das Papsttum: Idee und Wirklichkeit*. Esslingen am Neckar: Port Verlag, 1962.

Hardy, V. *La cathédrale Saint-Pierre de Lisieux*. Paris: Frazier Soye, 1918.

Harvey, John. *The Mediaeval Architect*. London: Wayland Publishers, 1972.

Haskins, Charles Homer. *The Normans in European History*. Cambridge, Mass.: Harvard University Press, 1927.

———. *Norman Institutions*. Cambridge, Mass.: Harvard University Press, 1918.

_____ . *The Renaissance of the 12th Century*. New York: Meridian Books, 1962.

_____ . *The Rise of Universities*. Ithaca, N.Y.: Cornell University Press. 1957.

_____ . *Studies in Mediaeval Culture*. New York: Frederick Ungar, 1929.

Hefele, Charles-Joseph. *Histoire des Conciles: D'après les documents originaux*. Edited by Dom H. Leclercq. Vol. 5, part 2. Paris: Letouzey et Anè, 1913.

Hientschel, Donald Edward. *The Medieval Concept of an Ecclesiastical Office: An Analytical Study of the Concept of an Ecclesiastical Office in the Major Sources and Printed Commentaries from 1140 to 1300*. Canon Law Studies No. 363. Washington, D.C.: Catholic University of America Press, 1956.

Hollister, C. Warren, ed. *The Impact of the Norman Conquest*. New York: John Wiley, 1969.

_____ . *The Making of England, 55 B.C. to 1399*. Lexington, Mass.: D. C. Heath, 1976.

Holmes, Urban Tigner, Jr. *Daily Living in the Twelfth Century: Based on the Observations of Alexander Neckam in London and Paris*. Madison: University of Wisconsin Press, 1952.

Holtzmann, Walther. *Studies in the Collections of Twelfth-Century Decretals*. Edited by C. R. Cheney and M. G. Cheney. Monumenta Iuris Canonici, Series B: Corpus Collectionum, vol. 3. Vatican: Biblioteca Apostolica Vaticana, 1979.

Howgrave-Graham, Robert Pickersgill. *The Cathedrals of France*. London: B. T. Batsford, 1959.

Hughes, Philip. *The Church in Crisis: A History of the General Councils, 325–1870*. Garden City, N.Y.: Hanover House, 1961.

Imbart de la Tour, Pierre. *Les élections épiscopale pendant la deuxième moitié du XIIe siècle*. Paris: Hachette, 1890.

Inman, A. H. *Domesday and Feudal Statistics*. 1900. Repr., Port Washington, N.Y.: Kennikat Press, 1971.

James, John. *Chartres: The Masons Who Built a Legend*. London: Routledge and Kegan Paul, 1982.

Janssen, Wilhelm. *Die Päpstlichen Legaten in Frankreich: Vom Schisma Anaklets II bis zum Tode Coelestina III (1130–1198)*. Cologne: Böhlau Verlag, 1961.

Jolliffe, J. E. A. *Angevin Kingship*. 2d ed. London: A. and C. Black, 1963.

_____ . *The Constitutional History of Medieval England: From the English Settlement to 1485*. New York: W. W. Norton, 1961.

Kantorowicz, Ernst H. *The King's Two Bodies: A Study in Medieval Political Theology*. Princeton, N.J.: Princeton University Press, 1957.

Katzenellenbogen, Adolf. *The Sculptural Programs of Chartres Cathedral: Christ, Mary, Ecclesia*. Baltimore: Johns Hopkins University Press, 1959.

Kealey, Edward J. *Roger of Salisbury: Viceroy of England*. Berkeley: University of California Press, 1972.

Kelly, Amy. *Eleanor of Aquitaine and the Four Kings*. Cambridge, Mass.: Harvard University Press, 1950.

Knowles, David. *Christian Monasticism*. New York: McGraw-Hill, 1969.

_____ . *The Episcopal Colleagues of Archbishop Thomas Becket*. Cambridge: Cambridge University Press, 1951.

_____ . *The Evolution of Medieval Thought*. New York: Vintage Books, 1962.

_____ . *Great Historical Enterprises: Problems in Monastic History*. London: Thomas Nelson and Sons, 1962.

_____ . *The Monastic Order in England, 940–1216: A History of Its Development from the Time of St. Dunstan to the Fourth Lateran Council, 940–1216*. 2d ed. Cambridge: Cambridge University Press, 1963.

_____ . *Thomas Becket*. Stanford: Stanford University Press, 1971.

_____ , and Hadcock, R. Neville. *Medieval Religious Houses: England and Wales*. New York: St. Martin's Press, 1971.

Kuhn, Thomas S. *The Structure of Scientific Revolutions*, 2d ed. Vol. 2, no. 2 of International Encyclopedia of Unified Science. Chicago: University of Chicago Press, 1970.

Lamarignier, Jean-François. *Étude sur les privilèges d'exemption et de juridiction ecclésiastique des abbayes Normandes depuis les origines jusqu'en 1140*. Paris: A. Picard, 1937.

Lasteyrie, Robert Charles de. *L'Architecture religieuse en France a l'époque gothique*. Paris: A. Picard, 1926.

Léonard, Émile-G. *Histoire de la Normandie*. Paris: Presses Universitaires, 1948.

Le Patourel, John. *Norman Barons*. Hastings and Bexhill Branch: The Historical Association, 1966.

_____ . *The Norman Empire*. Oxford: Clarendon Press, 1976.

Liess, Reinhard. *Der frühromanische Kirchenbau des 11. Jahrhunderts in der Normandie*. München: Wilhelm Fink Verlag, 1967.

Little, Lester K. *Religious Poverty and the Profit Economy in Medieval Europe*. Ithaca, N.Y.: Cornell University Press, 1978.

Lot, Ferdinand, and Fawtier, Robert, eds. *Histoire des institutions françaises au Moyen Âge*. 3 vols. Paris: Presses Universitaires de France, 1957–1962.

Loyd, Lewis W. *The Origins of Some Anglo-Norman Families*. Edited by C. T. Clay and D. C. Douglas. Leeds: Harleian Society, 1951.

Loyn, Henry Royston. *The Norman Conquest*. 3d ed. London: Hutchison Publishing, 1982.

Luchaire, Achille. *Histoire des institutions monarchiques de la France sous les premiers Capétiens, 987–1180*. 2d ed. Paris, 1891.

_____ . *Manuel des institutions françaises, période des Capétiens directs*. Paris, 1892.

_____ . *Social France at the Time of Philip Augustus*. Translated by Edward Benjamin Krehbiel. New York: Peter Smith, 1929.

Maitland, Frederic William. *The Constitutional History of England*. Edited by H. A. L. Fisher. Cambridge: Cambridge University Press, 1961.

Mâle, Emile. *The Gothic Image: Religious Art in France of the Thirteenth Century*. Translated by Dora Nussey. New York: Harper Torchbooks, 1958.

Matthew, Donald. *The Norman Monasteries and Their English Possessions*. Westport, Conn.: Greenwood Press, 1979.

Meade, Marion. *Eleanor of Aquitaine: A Biography*. New York: Hawthorn/Dutton, 1977.

Merton, Robert K. *On the Shoulders of Giants: A Shandean Postscript*. New York: Free Press, 1965.

Morey, Dom Adrian, and Brooke, C. N. L. *Gilbert Foliot and His Letters*. Cambridge: Cambridge University Press, 1965.

Morrall, John B. *Political Thought in Medieval Times*. Medieval Academy Reprints for Teaching, 7. Toronto: University of Toronto Press, 1980.

Mühlbacher, Engelbert. *Die streitige Papstwahl des Jahres 1130*. Innsbruck, 1876; repr., Scientia Verlag Aalen, 1966.

Murphy, James J. *Rhetoric in the Middle Ages: A History of Rhetorical Theory from Saint Augustine to the Renaissance*. Berkeley: University of California Press, 1974.

Murray, Alexander. *Reason and Society in the Middle Ages*. Oxford: Clarendon Press, 1978.

Musset, Lucien Emile. *Normandie Romane*. 2 vols. Saint-Léger-Vauban: Zodiaque, 1967.

Norgate, Kate. *England under the Angevin Kings*. 2 vols. London, 1887; repr., New York: Burt Franklin, 1969.

_____ . *Richard the Lion Heart*. London: MacMillan, 1924; repr., New York: Russell and Russell, 1969.

Ohnsorge, Werner. *Die Legaten Alexanders III (1159–1169): Im ersten jahrzehnt seines pontifikats*. Berlin: E. Ebering, 1928.

Pacaut, Marcel. *Louis VII et les élections épiscopales dans le royaume de France*. Paris: Librairie Philosophique J. Vrin, 1957.

Panofsky, Erwin. *Gothic Architecture and Scholasticism*. New York: Meridian Books, 1957.

Pennington, Kenneth. *Pope and Bishops: The Papal Monarchy in the Twelfth and Thirteenth Centuries*. Philadelphia: University of Pennsylvania Press, 1984.

_____ , and Somerville, Robert, eds. *Law, Church, and Society*. Philadelphia: University of Pennsylvania Press, 1977.

Pernoud, Regine. *Eleanor of Aquitaine*. Translated by Peter Wiles. New York: Coward-McCann, 1968.

Piel, Abbé. *Inventaire historiques de actes transmis dur insinuations ecclésiastiques de l'ancien diocèse de Lisieux*. 2 vols. Lisieux, 1873.

Poggioli, Peter A. *From Politician to Prelate: The Career of Walter of Coutances, Archbishop of Rouen, 1184–1207*. Ann Arbor, Mich.: University Microfilms, 1984.

Pollock, Frederick, and Maitland, Frederic William. *The History of English Law: Before the Time of Edward I*. 2 vols. 2d ed. Cambridge: Cambridge University Press, 1978.

Poole, Austin Lane. *From Domesday Book to Magna Carta: 1087–1216*. 2d ed. Oxford: Oxford University Press, 1955.

Poole, Reginald Lane. *The Exchequer in the Twelfth Century*. Oxford: Clarendon Press, 1912.

_____ . *Lectures on the History of the Papal Chancery: Down to the Time of Innocent III*. Cambridge: Cambridge University Press, 1915.

_____ . *Studies in Chronology and History*. Edited by Austin Lane Poole. Oxford: Clarendon Press, 1934.

Powicke, Frederick Maurice. *The Loss of Normandy, 1189–1204: Studies in the History of the Angevin Empire*. 2d ed. Manchester: Manchester University Press, 1961.

_____ . *Ways of Medieval Life and Thought: Essays and Addresses*. Edited by A. L. Rowse. New York: Thomas Y. Crowell, 1971.

Regnier, Louis Adolphe. *Bulletin des Sociétés savants de Caen*. Caen: 1909–1910.

The Renaissance of the Twelfth Century: An Exhibition Organized by Stephen K. Scher. Providence, R.I.: Museum of Art, Rhode Island School of Design, 1969.

Reuter, Timothy, ed. *The Medieval Nobility*. Amsterdam: Elsevier North-Holland, 1979.

Round, John Horace. *Geoffrey de Mandeville: A Study of the Anarchy*. New York, 1892; repr., Burt Franklin, 1972.

Roussel, Jules. *La sculpture française*. Vol. 1, *Époque romane*. Paris: A. Morancé, 1927.

Runciman, Steven. *A History of the Crusades*. Vol. 2: *The Kingdom of Jerusalem and the Frankish East, 1100–1187*. New York: Harper Torchbooks, 1964.

Salmon, Pierre. *The Abbot in Monastic Tradition*. Washington, D.C.: Cistercian Publications, 1972.

Sanders, Ivor John. *English Baronies: A Study of Their Origin and Descent, 1086–1327*. Oxford: Clarendon Press, 1960.

Sauerländer, Willibald. *Gothic Sculpture in France, 1140–1270*. Translated by Janet Sondheimer. New York, 1972.

Sayers, Jane E. *Papal Judges-Delegate in the Province of Canterbury, 1198–1254: A Study in Ecclesiastical Jurisdiction and Administration*. Oxford: Oxford University Press, 1971.

Scammell, G. V. *Hugh du Puiset, Bishop of Durham*. Cambridge: Cambridge University Press, 1956.

Schmale, Franz-Josef. *Studien zum Schisma des Jahres 1130*. Graz: Böhlau Verlag, 1961.

Schreiber, Georg. *Kurie und Kloster im 12 Jahrhundert*. Stuttgart: F. Enke, 1910.

Serbat, Louis. *Guide du Congrès archéologique de France: LXXVe session tenue à Caen en 1908 par la Société Française d' Archéologie*. Tome Ier. Caen: 1909.

_____ . *Lisieux*. Petites monographies des grands édifices de la France. Paris: 1926.

Simson, Otto von. *The Gothic Cathedral: Origins of Gothic Architecture and the Medieval Concept of Order*. Princeton, N.J.: Princeton University Press, 1962.

Smalley, Beryl. *The Becket Controversy and the Schools: A Study of Intellectuals in Politics.* London: Basil Blackwell, 1973.

Somerville, Robert. *Pope Alexander III and the Council of Tours (1163): A Study of Ecclesiastical Politics and Institutions in the Twelfth Century.* Berkeley: University of California Press, 1977.

Southern, Richard W. *Grosseteste: The Growth of an English Mind in Medieval Europe.* Oxford: Clarendon Press, 1986.

_____ . *The Making of the Middle Ages.* New Haven, Conn.: Yale University Press, 1953.

_____ . *Medieval Humanism.* New York: Harper Torchbooks, 1970.

_____ . *Western Society and the Church in the Middle Ages.* Harmondsworth: Penguin Books, 1970.

Spear, David Scott. *The Norman Episcopate under Henry I, King of England and Duke of Normandy (1106–1135).* Ann Arbor: University Microfilms, 1982.

Stenton, Frank. *The First Century of English Feudalism, 1066–1166.* 2d ed. Oxford: Clarendon Press, 1961.

Strayer, Joseph R. *On the Medieval Origins of the Modern State.* Princeton, N.J.: Princeton University Press, 1973.

Stroll, Mary. *The Jewish Pope: Ideology and Politics in the Papal Schism of 1130.* Leiden: E. J. Brill, 1987.

Stubbs, William. *The Constitutional History of England: Its Origin and Development.* 3 vols. Oxford: Clarendon Press, 1880.

_____ . *Seventeen Lectures on the Study of Medieval and Modern History and Kindred Subjects.* Oxford: Clarendon Press, 1886; repr., New York: H. Fertig, 1967.

Tellenbach, Gerd. *Church, State, and Christian Society at the Time of the Investiture Contest.* Translated by R. F. Bennett. Oxford: Basil Blackwell, 1966.

Thibout, Marc. *Églises gothiques en France.* Paris: Éditions Aimery Somogy, 1957.

Tierney, Brian. *The Crisis of Church and State, 1050–1300.* Englewood Cliffs, N.J.: Prentice-Hall, 1964.

_____ . *Foundations of the Conciliar Theory: The Contributions of the Medieval Canonists from Gratian to the Great Schism.* Cambridge: Cambridge University Press, 1968.

Tradition and Change: Essays in Honour of Marjorie Chibnall. Edited by Diana Greenway, Christopher Holdsworth, and Jane Sayers. Cambridge: Cambridge University Press, 1985.

Ullmann, Walter. *Growth of Papal Government in the Middle Ages: A Study in the Ideological Relation of Clerical to Lay Power.* 2d ed. London: Methuen, 1962.

_____ . *A History of Political Thought in the Middle Ages.* Harmondsworth: Penguin Books, 1965.

_____ . *Law and Politics in the Middle Ages: An Introduction to the Sources of Medieval Political Ideas.* Ithaca, N.Y.: Cornell University Press, 1975.

_____ . *A Short History of the Papacy in the Middle Ages.* London: Methuen, 1974.

Valin, Lucien. *Le duc de Normandie et sa cour (912–1204): Étude d'histoire juridique.* Paris: L. Larose, 1910.

Van Caenegem, R. C. *Royal Writs in England from the Conquest to Glanville: Studies in the Early History of the Common Law.* Publications of the Seldon Society, vol. 77. London: Bernard Quaritch, 1959.

Vasseur, Charles. *Études historiques et archéologiques sur la cathédrale de Lisieux: Première partie, Histoire* (Extrait du *Bull. de la Soc. des Ant. de Norm.*) Caen: 1881.

Warren, Wilfrid Lewis. *Henry II.* Berkeley: University of California Press, 1973.

West, Francis. *The Justiciarship in England, 1066–1232.* Cambridge: Cambridge University Press, 1966.

West, George Herbert. *Gothic Architecture in England and France.* London: G. Bell and Sons, 1911.

Whitelock, Dorothy, et al. *The Norman Conquest: Its Setting and Impact.* New York: Charles Scribner's Sons, 1966.

Winston, Richard. *Thomas Becket.* New York: Alfred A. Knopf, 1968.
Wulf, Walter. *Die Kapitellplastik des Sugerbaus von Saint-Denis.* Frankfurt am Main: Peter Lang, 1978.
Young, Charles R. *The Royal Forests of Medieval England.* Philadelphia: University of Pennsylvania Press, 1979.
Zöpffel, Richard. *Die Doppelwohl des Jahres 1130.* Göttingen: Vandenhoeck und Ruprecht's Verlag, 1872.

Articles

Alexander, James W. "The Becket Controversy in Recent Historiography." *Journal of British Studies* 9 (1970):1–26.
Barlow, Frank. "The English, Norman, and French Councils Called to Deal with the Papal Schism of 1159." *English Historical Review* 51 (April 1936):264–268.
Barmann, Lawrence F. "The Papal Election of 1159." *American Ecclesiastical Review* 148 (January 1963):37–43.
Barral I Altet, Xavier. "Sculptures gothiques inédites de la Cathédrale de Lisieux." *Bulletin Monumental* 139 (1981):7–16.
Bates, David. "Notes sur l'aristocratie normande. I.-Hugues, évêque de Bayeux (1011 env.–1049)." *Annales de Normandie* 23 (1973):7–21.
Beauchet, Ludovic. "Origine de la juridiction ecclésiastique et son développement en France jusqu'au XIIe siècle." *Nouvelle Revue Historique de Droit Français et Étranger* 7 (1883):387–477, 503–536.
Benjamin, Richard. "The Angevin Empire." *History Today* 36 (February 1986):17–22.
Berlow, Rosalind Kent. "Spiritual Immunity at Véselay, Ninth to Twelfth Century." *Catholic Historical Review* 62 (October 1976):573–588.
Bloch, Herbert. "The Schism of Anacletus II and the Glanfeuil Forgeries of Peter the Deacon of Monte Cassino." *Traditio* 8 (1952):159–264.
Branner, Robert. "Keystones and Kings: Iconography and Topography in the Gothic Vaults of the Île-de-France." *Gazette des Beaux Arts*, ser. 6, 57 (January–June 1969):65–82.
Brooke, Zachary N. "The Effect of Becket's Murder on Papal Authority in England." *Cambridge Historical Journal* 2 (1928):213–228.
Brown, Elizabeth A. R., and Cothren, Michael W. "The Twelfth-Century Crusading Window of the Abbey of Saint-Denis: *Praeteritorum enim recordatio futurorum est exhibitio.*" *Journal of the Warburg and Courtauld Institutes* 49 (1986):1–40.
Brown, R. Allen. "England in Europe, 1066–1453: The Norman Impact." *History Today* 36 (February 1986):8–16.
Cahn, Walter. "The Tympanum of the Portal of Saint-Anne at Notre Dame de Paris and the Iconography of the Division of Powers in the Early Middle Ages." *Journal of the Warburg and Courtauld Institutes* 32 (1969):55–72.
Cheney, Mary G. "The Compromise of Avranches of 1172 and the Spread of Canon Law in England." *English Historical Review* 56 (April 1941):177–197.
_____ . "The Recognition of Pope Alexander III: Some Neglected Evidence." *English Historical Review* 84 (July 1969):474–497.
Chibnall, Marjorie. "Le privilège de libre élection dans les chartes de Saint-Evroult." *Annales de Normandie* 28 (December 1978):341–342.
Clark, William W. "The Central Portal of Saint-Pierre at Lisieux: A Lost Monument of Twelfth-Century Gothic Sculpture." *Gesta* 11 (1972):46–58.
_____ . "The Nave of Saint Pierre at Lisieux: Romanesque Structure in a Gothic Guise." *Gesta* 16 (1977):29–38.
_____ , and Mark, Robert. "The First Flying Buttresses: A New Reconstruction of the Nave of Notre-Dame de Paris." *Art Bulletin* 66 (March 1984):47–64.
Constable, Giles. "The Alleged Disgrace of John of Salisbury in 1159." *English Historical Review* 69 (January 1954):67–76.

Crosby, Everett U. "The Organization of the English Episcopate under Henry I." *Studies in Medieval and Renaissance History* 4 (1967):1–88.

Davis, R. H. C. "What Happened in Stephen's Reign." *History* 49 (1964):1–12.

Duval, Georges. "La cathédrale Saint-Pierre de Lisieux." *Art de Basse-Normandie* 89–91 (Winter 1984–1985):98–110.

———. "La cathédrale Saint-Pierre de Lisieux." *Sanctuaires et Pèlerinages* 7 (1961):17–30.

Gillingham, John. "England in Europe, 1066–1453: The Fall of the Angevin Empire." *History Today* 36 (April 1986):30–35.

Hall, Edwin, and Sweeney, James Ross. "An Unpublished Privilege of Innocent III in Favor of Montivilliers: New Documentation for a Great Norman Nunnery" [with text]. *Speculum* 49 (October 1974):662–679.

Hinkle, William M. "The King and the Pope on the Virgin Portal of Notre-Dame." *Art Bulletin* 48 (1966):1–13.

Hollister, C. Warren. "The Misfortunes of the Mandevilles." *History* 58 (1973):18–28.

———. "Normandy, France, and the Anglo-Norman Regnum." *Speculum* 51 (April 1976):202–242.

———. "1066: The 'Feudal Revolution.'" *American Historical Review* 73 (1968):708–723.

———, and Baldwin, J. W. "The Rise of Administrative Kingship." *American Historical Review* 83 (1978):867–905.

———, and Keefe, Thomas K. "The Making of the Angevin Empire." *Journal of British Studies* 12 (1973):1–25.

Holt, J. C. "The Introduction of Knight Service in England." In *Anglo-Norman Studies VI: Proceedings of the Battle Conference, 1983*, 89–106. Edited by R. Allen Brown. Woodbridge: Bydell Press, 1984.

Holtzmann, Walther. "Politics and Property in Early Medieval England." *Past and Present* 57 (1972):13–52.

Horste, Kathryn. "'A Child Is Born': The Iconography of the Portail Ste.-Anne at Paris." *Art Bulletin* 69 (1987):187–210.

Huard, Georges. "La cathédrale Saint-Pierre de Lisieux aux XIe et XIIe siècles." *Études Lexoviennes* 2 (1919):1–36.

———. "Quelques lettres de Bénédictins normands à Dom Bernard de Montfaucon." *Bulletin de la Société des Antiquaires de Normandie* 28 (1906).

Keefe, Thomas K. "Geoffrey Plantagenet's Will and the Angevin Succession." *Albion* 6 (1974):266–274.

King, Edmund. "King Stephen and the Anglo-Norman Aristocracy." *History* 59 (June 1974):180–194.

Klewitz, Hans-Walter. "Das Ende des Reformpapsttums." *Deutsches Archiv für Geschichte des Mittelalters* 3 (1939):371–412.

Knowles, David, Duggan, Anne J., and Brooke, C. N. L. "Henry II's Supplement to the Constitutions of Clarendon." *English Historical Review* 87 (October 1972):757–771.

Kuttner, Stephan. "Cardinalis: The History of a Canonical Concept." *Traditio* 3 (1945):129–214.

———. "The Scientific Investigation of Mediaeval Canon Law: The Need and the Opportunity." *Speculum* 24 (1949):493–501.

———, and Rathbone, Eleanor. "Anglo-Norman Canonists of the Twelfth Century: An Introductory Study." *Traditio* 7 (1949–1951):279–358.

Lally, J. E. "Secular Patronage at the Court of Henry II." *Bulletin of the Institute of Historical Research* 49 (1976):159–184.

Langlois, Charles V. "Formulaires de lettres du XIIe, du XIIIe et du XIVe siècle." *Notices et extraits des manuscrits de la Bibliothèque Nationale* 34 (1891).

Leedom, J. W. "The English Settlement of 1153." *History* 65 (October 1980):347–364.

Lemaitre, Claude. "Lisieux dans l'antiquité." *Art de Basse-Normandie* 89–91 (Winter 1984–1985):12–29.

Le Patourel, John. "The Plantagenet Dominions." *History* 50 (1965):289–308.

_____ . "What Did Not Happen in Stephen's Reign." *History* 58 (1973):1–17.

Lewis, Andrew W. "Anticipatory Association of the Heir in Early Capetian France." *American Historical Review* 83 (1978):906–927.

Leyser, Karl. "England and the Empire in the Early Twelfth Century." *Transactions of the Royal Historical Society.* Series 5, vol. 10 (1960):61–83.

McGurk, J. J. N., "Saint Thomas Becket, 1170–1970: Upon the Eighth Centenary of His Martyrdom." *History Today* 20 (December 1970):833–839.

McLachlan, Elizabeth Parker. "The Pembroke College New Testament and a Group of Unusual English Evangelist-Symbols." *Gesta* 14 (1975):3–18.

Mayr-Harting, H. "Henry II and the Papacy, 1170–1189." *Journal of Ecclesiastical History* 16 (1965):39–53.

Neveux, François. "Lisieux au moyen âge." *Art de Basse-Normandie* 89–91 (Winter 1984–1985):32–47.

Palumbo, P.F. "Nuova Studi (1942–1962) sullo scisma di Anacleto II," *Bollettino dell' Istituto storico italiano per il medio evo e Archivio Muratoriano* 75 (1963).

Pellerin, Henri. "Saint Bernard et le pays lexovien: Ses rapports avec Arnoul, évêque de Lisieux." *Le Pays D'Auge*, April 1965, pp. 3–19.

Pontal, Odette. "Les Évêques Normands." *Cahiers de Civilisation Médiévale: X^e-XIIe Siècles* 29 (January–June 1986):129–137.

Poole, Austin Lane. "Outlawry as a Punishment of Criminous Clerks." In *Historical Essays in Honour of James Tait.* Edited by J. G. Edwards, V. H. Galbraith, and E. F. Jacob. Manchester, 1933.

Poole, Reginald Lane. "The English Bishops at the Lateran Council of 1139." *English Historical Review* 38 (1923):61–63.

_____ . "Notes and Documents: Henry II, Duke of Normandy." *English Historical Review* 42 (October 1927):569–572.

Round, John Horace. "Bernard, the King's Scribe." *English Historical Review* 14 (July 1899):419–430.

Salter, Herbert Edward. "A Dated Charter of Henry I." *English Historical Review* 26 (1911):487–491.

Sauvage, René Norbert. "Fragments d'un cartulaire de Saint-Pierre-de-Lisieux." *Études Lexoviennes* 3 (1928):3–31.

Schriber, Carolyn P. "The Decretal *In Letteris* and the Case of Henry the Counterfeiter." *Comitatus: A Journal of Medieval and Renaissance Studies* 19 (1988):46–61.

Shaw, I. P. "The Ecclesiastical Policy of Henry II on the Continent, 1154–1189." *Church Quarterly Review* 151 (1950–1951):137–155.

Spear, David S. "Les dignitaires de la cathédrale de Rouen pendant la période ducale." *Annales de Normandie* 37 (1987):121–147.

_____ . "Les doyens du chapitre cathedral de Rouen durant la période ducale." *Annales de Normandie* 33 (1983):91–119.

_____ . "Membership in the Norman Cathedral Chapters during the Ducal Period: Some Preliminary Findings." *Medieval Prosopography* 5 (1984):1–18.

_____ . "The Norman Empire and the Secular Clergy, 1066–1204." *Journal of British Studies* 21 (1982):1–10.

Turner, Ralph V. "Richard Barre and Michael Belet: Two Angevin Civil Servants." *Medieval Prosopography* 6 (1985):25–48.

Walker, David. "Crown and Episcopacy under the Normans and Angevins." In *Anglo-Norman Studies V: Proceedings of the Battle Conference, 1982*, 220–233. Edited by R. Allen Brown. Woodbridge: Bydell Press, 1983.

White, Hayden V. "The Gregorian Ideal and Saint Bernard of Clairvaux." *Journal of the History of Ideas* 21 (1960):321–348.

Index

CAROLYN POLING SCHRIBER is Assistant Professor of Pre-Modern History at Rhodes College in Memphis, Tennessee. She is the author of articles on the life of Arnulf of Lisieux and is working on a translated edition of his letters.